A FAIRER SLICE OF THE CAKE
the task ahead

A FAIRER SLICE OF THE CAKE
the task ahead

Lynda King Taylor

BUSINESS BOOKS
London

First published 1976

©LYNDA KING TAYLOR, 1976

ISBN 0 220 66284 3

This book has been set 11 on 12 point IBM Baskerville, prepared for press by The Ivory Head Press, 170 Murray Road, London W5, and printed in Great Britain by W & J Mackay Limited, Chatham by photo-litho for the publishers, Business Books Limited, 24 Highbury Crescent, London N5

Contents

BIBLIOGRAPHY

Foreword

by Jack Jones, MBE, FCIT
General Secretary, Transport and General Workers' Union

It is almost a matter of commonsense that people will take greater pride and pleasure in their work if they are allowed to participate in the shaping of policies and decisions which affect that work. There is overwhelming evidence that the deeper the involvement in work, the greater the satisfaction. Work can, and should be a major source of fulfilment and growth for each individual. Yet for many it is not. In many areas in industry the design, organisation and control of jobs allows little room for the development of the worker. A comprehensive democratic strategy which gave a much wider degree of participation and as I believe is necessary, joint determination in the formulation of policy at boardroom and workplace level, would go far towards giving industry a human face.

The average worker today is more educated and more confident than his like before the war. Better education has opened up new insights for people, they have higher expectations of what work should provide for them and they are certainly less willing to resign themselves to being told what to do. There is clearly less respect for bureaucracy today.

The undermining of managerial authority has profound economic implications. In many companies and industries it will not be possible to carry through the necessary investment and re-organisation programmes unless the workers themselves are fully involved. There is great expertise on the shopfloor and in the office. At present it is left largely untapped.

I think that the case studies presented here will show the benefits that can accrue to all from more participation. I certainly hope they will be read and used, both by management and by trade unionists. They are not intended as 'blueprints' of the correct approach—conditions will vary and it is for management and trade unions on the spot to sort out what system they want.

Let us not be afraid to make changes and to experiment. Unless we do, it will become increasingly difficult for modern industry to function effectively. It is no longer a question of whether workers ought to play a greater part in the running of their firms but how this is to be done. To involve the worker in the running of his industry is not a revolutionary change—simply a recognition of a human right. Change will help put an end to an industrial subservience that is intolerable to an educated, intelligent workforce.

Trade unionists will welcome the work of Lynda King Taylor and I very much hope that her efforts and those of the Work Research Unit will go some way to convincing people of the absolute need for more participation and democracy at work.

JACK JONES

Preface

'Until fairly recent times it has been accepted, without much questioning, that the scope of many jobs is bound to be determined by the demands of technology, processes and systems. Employees have been given little opportunity to become involved in the planning and organisation of work. The consequence is an ever-increasing range of occupations with uninspiring contours within which the employee is confined.

'There is now, however, a growing realisation throughout all sectors of industry and commerce that jobs restricted in this way are the source of problems. The people who do them find little to engage their interest or extend their capabilities; they become dissatisfied and, all too often, the extent of their feeling is reflected in poor attendance, high rates of leaving, low output and so on.

'What is emerging, in effect, is a strong case for ensuring that the nature of jobs takes more account of the needs of people. Experience is showing that one of the major practical implications is that employees should be involved to a much greater extent in planning and organising work. This booklet contains an outline of the problem and of ways of achieving the necessary changes. It has been produced by the Tripartite Steering Group on Job Satisfaction, whose members include representatives of Government, the TUC and the CBI.

'Since it was formed in 1973, the Steering Group has received a good deal of evidence from people concerned at the workplace with problems of job satisfaction. As part of a programme to bring about improvements, the Steering Group has initiated a series of research projects and, on its recommendation, the Department of Employment has set up a Work Research Unit. The Unit provides management and trade unions in all kinds of enterprises, and other organisations, with assistance in taking practical steps to improve the design of jobs and the way in which work is organised.'

The above is an extract from the preface to *Making Work More Satisfying*, published by the Department of Employment and written in 1975 by John Fraser, Joint Parliamentary Under Secretary for Employment and Chairman of the Tripartite Steering Group on Job Satisfaction.

The Steering Group's Work Research unit, to which the author is a senior associate, is able to assist companies that wish to evolve change through employee participation and involvement similar to that illustrated in the case studies in this book.

The case studies illustrate various ways in which the interest in work can be improved through employee participation and involvement. Each case should be treated on its own merits—a style suitable for one company is not necessarily appropriate to another. The case study contents in each case will substitute for judgement.

I hope that the information in this book will be helpful to managements and trade unions and encourage them to take joint action to increase the satisfaction people get from their jobs.

London   LYNDA KING TAYLOR
March 1976

Acknowledgements

It is always more than difficult to acknowledge those who have helped directly or indirectly with a book of this nature— unfortunately always too many to mention by name.

There are those whose organisations appear within the book and who spared me considerable time and effort to discuss specific points of view, activities and ambitions. I have included my indebtedness to them at the commencement of each study.

There are those who gave me much encouragement—and time—to follow my own interests. In particular I would like to single out the many colleagues I worked alongside in PA International Management Consultants between 1972 and 1975.

I would also like to thank Ted Jube in New York for his patience and Len Crawford in Sydney for providing information. Patrick Friesner and his friends in Long Island, New York, especially Jerry Stember and Paul Werschelles, provided me with peace and quiet and a haven for the book to be thought out plus a typewriter for it to be written. Coffee percolating and typewriting were splendidly undertaken by Christine Pinder and Kornelia Klinkenberg gave me immense help on the tremendous task of compiling reading lists. My thanks to Corinna Wedderburn for her slog on the final draft and for also being the only person who knows where the apostrophe goes.

Helpful editorial advice on certain case studies was given

xiv by John Wellens of *Industrial and Commercial Training*, Lyndon Jones of the South West London College and Betty Knightly. Finally, my sincere thanks to my editor, Alan Reid, for his diligence and perseverance with my manuscript plus his positive editorial advice. My acknowledgement also goes to Business Books for their patience in allowing the book to be delayed due to a three-day week and two changes of Government. These factors contributed greatly to our belief in the need for such a book to be written.

A great source of inspiration were the many men and women I have worked alongside, and although some may not agree with all the content of this book, their suggestions and criticisms like their inspiration have proved invaluable. Without them there would be no cake.

LYNDA KING TAYLOR

Note

Twenty-five minute case studies on video and film relating to the fields of job satisfaction and worker participation are obtainable from the Central Office of Information, Hercules Road, London SE1.

Introduction

*'Unless they are conscious and willing, any kind of work
that requires their participation will turn out to be a
mere formality—and will fail.'*

Who said that? A trade union leader, the manager of a successful small engineering company, a politician renowned for
pursuing free enterprise, a communist statesman, or a psycho-
logist? The sentiment loses none of its commonsense or its
awareness of human needs for having been penned by Mao
Tse Tung—it could have come from any of those 'types'. It is
certainly one saying that could profitably be chanted every
morning in the subconscious of everyone who employs
people.

When I wrote *Not for Bread Alone—an appreciation of job
enrichment,* I was motivated by the belief that work is more
efficient when it is more enjoyable (resulting in happy employers and employees), and that if people are not allowed to
broaden their horizons they become obsolete, a dissatisfied
liability to themselves and their environment. Constantly
repeated debates on the compelling need for the UK to produce more, and conflict less, emphasise how vital it is to
capitalise on our manpower; but in the three years since writing *Not for Bread Alone* my original beliefs have been repeat-
edly endorsed. Little of substance has changed beyond a
smoother delivery through constant practice, of calls for a
more equal distribution of the country's income, for growth,

growth and more growth, for greater 'social justice' and industrial democracy.

The traditional pattern for 'progress' is easy to follow, and people from all sectors of life follow it time and time again, and exclaim the same cries when the traditional steps bring them to the traditional end—usually a pace ahead, or behind, the starting point. It starts off soundly enough: poverty is an enemy of good family life and a cause of endless social misfortune; poverty can be alleviated or even removed through redistribution of the national cake, but this cannot happen unless the cake is first made appreciably bigger. It is about here that the well-worn path begins to lead back in a circle.

Increased productivity is fundamental to economic growth, and since the UK is a 'low productivity' nation there should be ample room for improvement. Added to this are further spurs to growth—developments in science and technology; new and potent sources of capital investment; radical, rejuvenating approaches to the running of institutions and systems. But all along, in the repeated attempts to achieve growth, to make a bigger national cake, the most vital ingredient—*people* and their *motivation*—is continually ignored.

That any thesis expounding continued economic growth must now take into account far more ramifications than previously envisaged, has been made perfectly clear by the proliferation of environmental problems—the hazards and unsightliness of vast amounts of waste material; the littered, oil-spattered beaches; polluted air, rivers, lakes and seas; dangerously congested roads, air and shipping lanes; the terrible anonymity of suburbia. Environmental effect has consequently become something which is (usually) automatically considered in any planning or philosophy.

Not so, however, with people. Which is why I again turn to the impact on individuals of the society that creates them—a society which places the productive system on a pedestal. Emphasis on growth alone as a goal for British policy can—and does—create and perpetuate an alienated society. Single-minded industrial policies, even with aims as separate as pure competitive capitalism and thorough nationalisation, alike produce organisations which grow larger, monolithic, manned by employees who lose their identities in a stultifying swamp of sluggish cogs and complexities.

The great god Growth dictates the consumer society's life style through its priests of advertising and salesmanship; yet the *quality* of life is increasingly scarred by suicide, divorce, drug addiction, alcoholism, and a vicious circle of the causes and results of tension and dissatisfaction, such as crime at all levels, terrorism, traffic accidents—and the innumerable stresses of 'keeping up with the Jones'. Scandinavia, South Africa, Japan, Germany and the USA can all bear witness to a deterioration in their socio-psychological well-being... and the UK is no longer in a position to be complacent.

Alienation also depicts itself through cataclysmic shifts in reasoning, morals, ethics and behaviour, until the lines between cause and effect become increasingly blurred, and symptoms manifest themselves ever faster. In a productive system little emphasis is placed on gaining 'psychological' income from work: yet psychological impoverishment breeds many of the ills that much of our industrial society suffers from:

Stress and irritability
Bloody mindedness
Apathy
Lack of interest
Carelessness
Bad timekeeping
Militancy
Disenchantment
Unjustified absenteeism
Etc., etc.

In a consumer-orientated society, and particularly in an inflationary one, everyone demands more of the cake, for there is heavy emphasis on man's 'physical' needs for survival—to have enough wages to obtain food, clothing and shelter. Rising prices threaten security, adding fuel to the constantly stoked fires of acquisition. And yet it has been proven many times, in numerous industries and with various work groups, that the major disruptors of industrial peace stem from the psychological symptoms listed above. *Money alone* is not the answer.

People also have very definite psychological needs, and demands for their satisfaction are being manifested in every industrialised nation. People need

Security and social order
Affection and love
Status and success
Dignity and self-respect

Equal opportunity to learn—achieve—advance
Consideration as 'responsible' and 'democratic' people
Challenge and self-esteem

Without the opportunity to satisfy these needs, there will always be an alienation within and between communities—in industry this erupts most clearly between those who manage and those who are managed. The chasms caused breed ignorance and contempt. Everything, surely, should be done to prevent these and subsequent destructive attitudes from developing within our society.

In our attempts to improve living standards and to give everyone a fairer slice of the country's cake, we must ensure that what we do is not to the detriment of the 'quality' of life. It is here that we must take a different path from the traditional, even though we too realise that in order to give everyone a fairer slice of the cake we must increase our productivity.

The case study approach that I used in *Not for Bread Alone* has been highly praised, and I have therefore followed the same approach with this book. Again my criterion applied is not 'Is it correct?' or 'Is it right?', but simply 'Can managers, trade unionists and educationalists *learn* from, and *use* this information?' Different conditions at the time of reading do not negate the 'message' in each case study. My various interests have not been excluded from the book. The work environment, its impact upon the worker as an individual and its effect upon his or her attitudes have also been discussed within the context of each case study.

This brings me back to my second paragraph, to *Not for Bread Alone*—and specifically to the case studies in this book; work is more efficient when it is enjoyable; it is usually more enjoyable when there are opportunities within the task place for 'psychological' income, an income that can be determined through discussion and co-operation.

Democracy—like alienation—breeds at the grass roots, and potentially as easily. The way ahead for British industry is to systematically build into people's work lives the opportunity for motivation; to deliberately construct its organisations in such a way that employees can, and will want to, contribute much more than they can at present. And, simultaneously to ensure that power at the grass roots has been delegated *with responsibility*, for power without the latter is anarchy.

Invariably, attitudes will have to be changed—attitudes of

management, trade union leaders and employees at all levels.
So much so, that changing people's attitudes and behaviour is a fundamental part of this book. We shall not make real progress without change—the organisations in these studies only began to reap rewards when they acknowledged the need for change.

Even more evident than change, however, is the co-operation and participation between management and trade unions. Without it, of course, there cannot be change, for change requires faith and trust between everyone concerned. There will always be managers and trade union leaders who are so steeped in history, fear and prejudice that they will never take a step to bridge the gap that separates them. But surely most people can see the elaborate network of cause and effect that links everyone? Recognise that, acknowledge that all people count, and trust and co-operation must follow. With trust and co-operation, there is a chance for change, for growth, for an improved quality of life and for a fairer slice of the cake.

CASE
STUDIES

Case Study One
Vosper Thornycroft Limited
Southampton

The old order changeth, yielding place to new.

The Passing of Arthur, Tennyson

We've got the ships, we've got the men and we've got the money too.

G.W. Hunt, Music Hall Song, 1878

I am grateful to both John Rix and John Wilde at Vosper Thornycroft in Southampton for allowing me every facility within the shipyard, and to Nick Mitchell, the supervisor of the assignment, who provided me with much background information. I would also like to thank my various colleagues in Sweden for discussions they have shared with me on project management.

For years the entire UK shipbuilding industry has always had sufficient men, seldom sufficient ships, and never enough money. Profits within the industry have declined more than in any other, and labour relations in some yards have at times deteriorated to such an extent that the business of building and repairing ships might just as well have been buried at sea.

Absenteeism in shipbuilding, according to the Department of Employment, stands at almost 15 per cent. Few other industries compare with this figure, exceptions being some other branches of heavy engineering and the motor industry. What should cause even more concern is that of this 15 per cent, almost 9 per cent is uncertified or voluntary absence.

4 Only 5.9 per cent of absenteeism is accounted for by 'certified absence', i.e. a medical certificate verifying incapacity to work.

With absenteeism running at this rate—and with the majority significantly commencing on a Monday morning—one can understand how some yards can still be working inefficiently despite modernisation. Interference to production schedules through the absence of people is as serious a disease as is the absence of sub-contractor's parts in the motor industry. Such disruptions are aggravated throughout the ship repair industry by the cost-plus method of payment for any work undertaken for customers. With such a system, albeit the only one at present considered to be feasible, it is not difficult to appreciate the lack of management and trades union interest in solving various indirect problems like absenteeism when considering methods of increasing productivity. But delayed delivery dates, whether they are due to an indirect cause like absent employees or to design and production difficulties (as occurred with the QE2), all add up to a bad press internationally and a lack of confidence in British shipyards with potential overseas customers—not to mention the impetus given to the nationalisation floor in the British Government.

It is pleasing therefore that amid all the bad news it is possible to come up with the good; '...and we've got the money too'... £300 million—300 million pounds worth of confidence through orders placed in one year with two shipyards alone, Swan Hunter and Harland & Wolff.

Many industries have yet to realise that *survival* demands *efficiency*—those who do are discovering the pay-off. To the shipbuilding and ship-repair industry surviving by seeking efficiency has meant an overhaul of traditional management thinking, a re-appraisal of wage-payment structures and an identification of areas where improvements should be achievable—for example in the attitudes between employers and employees. It has inevitably meant *change*—the essential ingredient for survival and yet the most natural cause of fear in the human being.

A great deal of my time is spent in environments that are so desperately in need of *change*. Employees I work alongside talk about it, union members think about it and often get emotional about it, and management pays lip service to it. The latter often send selected personnel to courses and

conferences as part of their sophisticated management development programmes supposedly leading to change, only to
find that the re-educated personnel are unable to change
anything when they return to their organisational mortuaries.
This is mainly due to the environment itself not having been
simultaneously subjected to change initiatives, for the un-
initiated are frequently not prepared to allow change or to
tolerate the commitments and disciplines that change necessitates if it is to be successful. The case studies in this book
should go some way in explaining how some companies have
attempted to overcome such obstacles.

In statistics produced by the EEF (Engineering Employers'
Federation) from a study of their member companies in an
inflationary environment, it is interesting to note which factors 1000 firms thought were most likely to cause serious
problems for their companies within the following 6-12
months.

Industrial disputes, lack of export orders and foreign competition came very low on the list; but almost twice as many
firms indicated that increases in labour costs would provide
them with the greatest headache. For example, only 38 per
cent thought foreign competition would prove a serious problem, while 80 per cent were seriously worried by rising labour
costs.

One company that is aware of all the factors which I have
mentioned and is involving itself in change is Vosper Thornycroft of Southampton. Their greatest cost factor is the 'men'
in Hunt's slogan.

Motivated employees are more difficult to manage than
robots, but motivated individuals bring an involvement and
commitment to the workplace that can contribute greatly
to the efficiency and services of the company. Vosper
Thornycroft are aware that it is lack of motivation that
brings absenteeism, carelessness, poor timekeeping and labour
turnover, and they have sought to bring about change
through the commitment and participation of their employees in the Company. Concepts like 'Project Management'
became an antidote for some of the serious problems that
confronted the company's yards.

Vosper Thornycroft are part of the David Brown Group
and have between 5 and 6000 employees. They are one of
Britain's three warship builders and they also have a large re-

6 pair division handling commercial shipping. In May 1970, following concern expressed by some ship-owners at the cost of quality and service in the ship-repair field, John Rix, Chairman and Managing Director, proposed that a working party, a project group, should be formed to investigate this problem.

Before discussing in more detail the Vosper Thornycroft assignment and the project team it is worth discussing the concept and operation of project management.

I have frequent discussions with my European colleagues about industrial democracy. They tell me that this is the social aspiration we should be aiming for within the UK. Whether one is discussing social partnership, industrial democracy, works councils or social responsibility audits it all boils down to participation. It is very difficult to achieve consistent employee involvement from country to country just as it will prove difficult to establish legislation for the entire European Economic Community (EEC). What works well in one country cannot be guaranteed to work at all in another. The theory behind speed limits, for instance, is the same the world over, but in practice imposition and enforcement vary from country to country, and this is the case with modern management studies and thinking. What we must do within the UK is get away from the so-called 'nitty-gritty' chatter. For example, should it be called job enrichment? Or involvement? Or rotation? Or OD? Or industrial democracy? Or job satisfaction? Or what-the-hell? We need more doers than talkers.

In the USA a bill has been debated in Senate called the Worker Alienation Bill which contains provision for the retraining of tens of thousands of industrial engineers who were brought up on the concepts of Frederick Taylor—in order that they should discover and improve those forms of work structure which are most conducive to both productivity and human values. Major allocations of Federal funds are being considered for projects to be undertaken in both the private and public sectors, and for stimulus grants to reward concerns who want to embark on parallel projects. Closer to the UK, works councils and employee involvement have become a way of life from Germany to Scandinavia. But in the UK many—too many—companies are still talking and/or experimenting. Job enrichment experiments in *change* have been and always will be doomed from the outset, for this

kind of employee participation must become a way of life,
must be married into the thinking, structure and philosophy
of a company, as all the case studies will prove. Change must
be a 'common sense' approach to life. To me it *is* only common
sense that if we have a new generation of employees
starting work with new aspirations, ideals and awareness of
their need for fulfilment, then we must create a new environment
and a new generation of jobs to suit those aspirations.

If we do not, the employee will sabotage the machine, or
the man who made it, with a great deal of success. This has
been discovered and proved in other societies, some considered
in advance of our own, like Scandinavia and in particular
Sweden, and project management has been seen as a
way to satisfy some of the needs of the individual at the
work place.

The concept of project management has enjoyed many
pay-offs within Scandinavia and it is particularly pleasing to
see traditional firms in the UK, like Vosper Thornycroft,
using such an approach as a way of change within their company.
They are not arguing over what they should call their
new way of thinking nor if and how they should experiment.
They are simply admitting the fact that they have had problems
and that the only way to solve them is through change.
Having admitted that, this company chose to bring about
change and worker participation through project management.

How project management works

The basic principle of project management is that change
should be tackled by setting up teams (project teams) each
with four or five members drawn from the company departments
most concerned. There is usually a consultant, or a
'catalyst', whose function, apart from neutrality, is an advisory
one, involving and gaining the commitment of the
project group members. One of the advantages of working
along these lines is that the teams work as groups and any
new procedures adopted are seen as having been devised by
the project teams themselves, and not as a jargonised system
being brought in from outside the company.

A project team is only as effective as its monitor and
within Vosper Thornycroft the monitor was its Chairman and

8 Managing Director, John Rix. Although he was not a member of the original working party the project group knew they had the support of the Board, who gave them both the responsibility and the accountability for any decisions and actions undertaken as a result of their conclusions. The accountability aspect is very important, people must be accountable for their responsibility... they must carry-the-can, otherwise there will be a diminishing of commitment. It is never enough to simply remind people that they are responsible.

Thus the Board can become the *Steering Group*, deciding what the problems are, bringing experience to bear upon various suggestions, and identifying major areas of responsibility. The system must also allow for rapid revision of the project problems to accommodate changes in circumstances, e.g. changes in:

1 Availability of finance.
2 Availability of manpower.
3 Priorities of projects.
4 Parameters of individual projects.
5 The programme of projects to be tackled.

Figure 1.1 indicates the effective management and control of a project and it will be seen that it requires a basic series of elements which are covered in a sequence and then continuously re-cycled.

For Vosper Thornycroft the problem was the concern at the cost and quality of service their customers were receiving

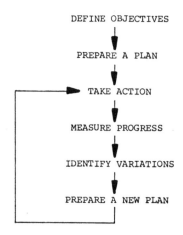

Figure 1.1 Elements of control in Project Management

in the repair field. It was decided that the Project Team should have the following terms of reference:

> *To examine all significant factors affecting the efficiency of the Ship Repair Division from the preparation of the original refit list and its costing to completion, invoicing and receipt of payment with the objects of:*
>
> 1 *Identifying, and where practicable, quantifying causes of variances and/or inefficiencies attributable both to Vosper Thornycroft and to the owners.*
> 2 *Identifying those areas where improvements should be achievable.*
> 3 *Preparing a plan to secure such improvements.*

The most interesting point is the make-up of the working party. It was to include, as well as Vosper Thornycroft men, representatives from their customers, i.e. the ship owners, and the unions. Therefore, the company decided that, if things were wrong within its walls, the customers should have the opportunity of saying *what they were*—a unique approach within UK management and an extraordinary one within the world of ship repairing.

The working party was made up of:

1 *A chairman*   An outside consultant acting as a catalyst.
2 *Ship repairers*   Two senior members from Vosper Thornycroft.
3 *Trade unions*   One officer from each of the following (all with members in the company's yards)—Transport and General Workers Union; Boilermakers Society; Society of Woodworkers, Engineering and Foundry Workers.
4 *Owners*   A senior member from each of the following: P & O Lines; Fyffe Lines; Cunard Lines; Cunard International Technical Services.

The working party got down to work quickly and effectively and their initial analysis came under two headings—attitudes and problems.

Attitudes

The main attitudes of the three main sections of the working party were:

10 The owners were wanting value for money This was particularly critical as an issue because of the high proportion of
cost-plus work. They wanted to be able to have more work
done by the ship's crew at sea, and they wanted invoices
earlier and in more detail so that they could be easily
checked and analysed for their own purposes.

*The unions were concerned about the need for better facili-
ties and greater control over sub-contractors* Naturally they
were also concerned with the long-term conditions and security of employment. So often in the UK the involvement of
the trade unions is only asked for at a time of conflict, when
there is a wage claim on the table. In this instance they were
in right from the start discussing with customer and employer the future of the company.

*Vosper Thornycroft wanted to achieve earlier payment and
to reduce working capital tied up in the business* They also
naturally wanted to increase productivity and to share this
benefit with the owners. They, too, also wanted to build
better industrial relations within the company.

Problems

The problems were identified as:

Industrial relations The complex nature of the work, the
history of casual labour, and the difficulties of communications within a sprawling area like the docks all contributed to
a then difficult situation.

Productivity Higher productivity was restricted by the quality of the facilities and the effectiveness of management as
well as by the attitudes of labour which I mentioned at the
beginning of this study. It was necessary, in a situation where
a major proportion of the work is on cost-plus, to find a way
of increasing productivity without damaging profits.

Work booking and preparation of detailed invoices These
were considered major problem areas. A ship's overhaul involves many hundreds of items of work, some of which can
be specified before the ship arrives at the repair yard, but

many of which only reveal themselves when the ship is 'open- ed for surgery'. Ensuring that all the work done is recorded accurately and swiftly so that invoices can be prepared in good time is a major headache.

Other problem areas indicated were the involvement of ship's crews, the control of sub-contractors, and the varying work load—sometimes large peaks, other times long periods with little work available.

The working party then set up various reference groups and working parties to tackle these identified areas; in particular they attacked the work booking and invoicing area. They also instituted a full management development programme for all levels within the company from foremen upwards. The organisation of the Repair Division and its interface with the ships' owners and staff were revised and new marketing opportunities were explored. Other project parties looked at areas such as industrial relations, wages, communications, overtime and restrictive practices plus the scope of the work which could be done by ship's crews.

The basic model for Project Management

Let's look again at the basic model (see Figure 1.2) for project management.

The Steering Group The committee of senior managers, normally including a director and usually chaired by the Chief Executive who decide the problem areas and the methods to be used for solving them. The objectives are defined and quantified in terms of functional requirement, time and cost. The Steering Group sets up the Project Team.

The Project Team In this instance the working party of union members, ship owners and members of Vosper Thornycroft. Along with the Steering Group they decide the objectives of the project and such items as the time-scale for completion and the budgets for any necessary expenditure. The team is empowered to obtain assistance or information from any other part of the company; in fact it operates in the same way as a consultant, for example, getting facts, design-

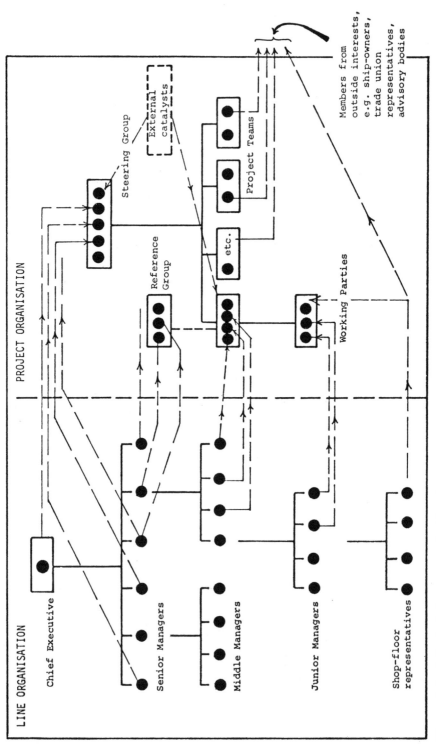

Figure 1.2 A Project Group organisation in a company

Yr/Qtr/Mo																

Description of project

Project Manager	In co-operation with	Decisions as to implementation according to plan	Date & Sig.
			Project No.

Figure 1.3 Project plan for evaluating the time spent on project group or working party assignment. This plan is purposely left bank for the reader to reproduce for his own projects

ing alternative strategies, making evaluations, and recommending procedures to the Steering Group. The team is disbanded when the project is completed.

Reference Groups and Working Parties In Vosper Thornycroft these were the teams of people set up to look specifically at problem areas. This is where the budgeting objectives laid down by the Steering Group for the main project team are so important. All must be quantified in financial terms, and as some of the project team may have to work full-time on certain aspects of the problems, working parties may have to be recruited from other jobs within the company. Sometimes the project absorbs a great deal of time; it is important therefore to have its efforts financially evaluated. Figure 1.3 shows a Project time plan that can be used to aid evaluation.

Another interesting point at Vosper Thornycroft is that after six months the outside consultant was able to leave the assignment, handing over the chairmanship of the project group to John Rix. This meant that even after the consultant left, the management organisation was geared to change. Project management has in fact left the company with a permanent way of tackling problems—and it has meant that the work of the outside consultant within the company has been as effective as possible in both the short and long term.

Conditions for producing change

The most important thing to remember is that it is easy to pay lip service to this kind of management development. It is too easy to form a committee instead of a project team, and I do not mean a committee run along the functional lines of those outlined in other studies. *The Project Team institutes all investigations and then controls the implementation.* So often with a committee the investigation deteriorates into mere paper work and lack of enthusiasm because no-one but the top man has the power to initiate anything, let alone be accountable. Within Vosper Thornycroft this never happened, and it is a credit to their senior management that *responsibility and accountability were handed down the line to the Project Team who implemented the procedures and controlled the recommendations that had been decided upon.*

In looking back at this company over four years, one can see that this approach has been very successful and has formed the basis of something which continues to serve more than just a useful purpose. Specifically it has been possible to reduce the cash tied up in work-in-progress and unsettled invoices from nearly three and a half million pounds to under one million.

Many areas of difficulty in the field of industrial relations at Vosper Thornycroft have been resolved—difficulties that are still causing massive conflict within other comparable industries. A productivity agreement has been operating for over three years and it has increased earnings, improved security of employment, raised productivity and reduced many of the restrictive practices common in the shipbuilding and ship repair world. This has helped the owners to benefit from work done by their own crews at sea. Comparisons have been made and lessons learnt with ship repairers in other UK ports and on the Continent, and new markets have been opened up, both in ship-repair and other heavy-industry areas. The management of the Ship Repair Division has been re-organised and the successful programme of management development has proved to be a feeding ground for the growth and development of much hitherto latent talent within the company, and succession has been secured.

Project management has provided the company with an effective way of bringing ship owners, repairer and unions together to deal with issues which affect them all, and to seek improvements and create opportunities out of the services given. *Crisis management* is thereby avoided.

The success of the Vosper Thornycroft example of project development is due to many factors, but perhaps the most important are:

The status and constitution of the working party and the attitudes of its members, which have meant that important problems can be discussed frankly and can lead to recommendations for actions over which they know they have direct control.

Also, in any kind of programme for change it is essential, as all the studies indicate, that the support of top management is not only seen to be effective but seen to provide its own form of commitment. At Vosper Thornycroft the senior management were prepared to give not only whole-hearted backing but also visible action and confidence.

The principles stand, wherever and whatever the project, and it is essential that the following is stated and understood:

Company policy
Company objectives
Project objectives
Project organisation
Terms of reference
Plan of action
Communication procedures
Management control system
Information network
Procedures and management tools
Updating, review and feed-back systems
Resources and responsibility

In view of the shipbuilding and ship repair problems within the UK it is pleasing to be able to give credit to an organisation like Vosper Thornycroft who are accepting the challenge of *change* with all its pros and cons, especially in a field long notorious for its traditional outlook. Various reports over the last year have been flooding onto the market referring to the future of British shipyards. In view of the international interest and national importance, some lessons should be learned from this approach, particularly from the consideration given to *involvement*, not only of the trade unions but of the ship owners themselves. Perhaps one of our failings is that when we do consider the future of an industry, whether it be British steel or British ships, the views of the customer are not sought let alone considered. The old order changeth yielding place to new—so now that we've got the ships, and we've got the men, let's make sure that we've got the money too.

Case Study Two
Design and Print
Sussex

To change the name, and not the letter,
Is a change for the worse, and not for the better.

Book of Days, ed. Robert Chambers

I would like to thank Stanley Phillipps, Managing Director, and Michael Quibell, Sales Director, of Design & Print for offering me every facility when in their company. Also David Atherfold who taught me about off-set litho presses.

My thanks also to Bob Capes who supervised the assignment and as such provided me with a great deal of background information, as did Bill Shirley, Graham de F. Ross and Bill Rickards.

Traffic came to a halt recently in Shoreham, near Brighton, when a new printing press three times as versatile as any the company had owned hitherto arrived at the works of Design and Print. Imported from Germany, the £21,000 Koenig and Bauer Rapida two-colour, offset-litho rotary press weighs five and a half tons, and was acquired to meet the growing demand for high-quality full-colour sales brochures and other printing requirements from industry and commerce. The hope is that the new machine will boost the company's turnover.

The Design and Print company is a wholly owned subsiduary of Evershed & Son Limited, a dynamic food distribution group centred at Shoreham-by-Sea in Sussex. The subsidiary company was acquired by the Evershed Group in 1940 mainly to satisfy its own printing requirements, e.g. simple letterpress, point-of-sale leaflets, posters and price lists. Today, apart from the two-colour Koenig and Bauer, they have

18 a number of Heidelberg presses and, with in-house artist facilities, Design and Print can offer a wide range of high-class colour work mainly in the small-booklet, brochure and house magazine market. Companies like Solarbo, Haden Carrier, Woodall-Duckham and Dunlop Nordac are some of the many concerns using this printing firm.

The printing industry in the UK competes fiercely for both business and labour, and this is especially so in the Brighton area. When managing director Stanley Phillipps sought new business in the early 1960s, he had to be competitive and still pay wages comparable with the other local printers. In 1965 he invited Evershed's grocery consultants to install a conventional payment-by-results incentive scheme. According to Phillipps 'you either pay blood money or incentives'... in the tough competitive world outside Design and Print blood money and incentives were to become painfully synonymous.

A couple of years after the first introduction of the payment-by-results scheme Phillipps brought in another consultant, this time a marketing specialist, since it was obvious that the company would need to increase turnover to match the inevitable rise in productivity. Productivity did increase and so did the sales turnover—from £70,000 in 1965 to £160,000 per year in 1971.

From about 1968 though, the incentive scheme got out of hand, mainly through lack of consistent attention. Values were not maintained, technological changes took place (mainly through the decision to purchase offset-litho presses), earnings of work-people became inequitable, apathy increased and as costs rose productivity dropped. At the same time as all this, there was a landslide in the UK economy; thus sales margins had to be trimmed if turnover were to be maintained. The net result was a dramatic plummeting of sales margins and the profitability of the company looked like this:

    1969   10 per cent profit on sales
    1970   5 per cent profit on sales
    1971   2½ per cent profit on sales

The most obvious weakness in the company was the incentive scheme; they hadn't done anything about it. Workers in one department, for example, were getting up to $66\frac{2}{3}$ per cent bonus on their weekly wage rates but in another department only 10 per cent. As well, the company was handling some 4000 printing jobs a year involving changes in the mix

of work undertaken by Design and Print since the incentive
scheme had originally been introduced. Taken with improvements in plant and more efficient manning, the standards which formed the basis of the incentive scheme had long become outdated.

It was then that Stanley Phillipps decided to go on a Printing and Publishing Industry Training Board (ITB) course called *Progress to Profit* which was run by PA Management Consultants. Phillipps decided that a radical change in management/worker 'thinking' and 'relationships' was vital if the company was to attain anything like its former level of prosperity and assure its continued well-being. 'I used to think you had to be a printer to run a printing works... now I'm convinced you have to be a manager' said Phillipps after attending the PA/ITB course. There were few alternatives facing the company. These were:

1 Scrap the existing incentive scheme and return to a fixed payment scheme.
2 Update the existing scheme.
3 Find an alternative payment scheme which would have full worker support.

The third choice was the one adopted but instead of devising a scheme 'in isolation', it was felt by all parties that a better and more lasting solution might be found with the full involvement and participation of all the staff in the company. There was to be no question of charging in with a package of pills for all the ailments and leaving the patient worse after the 'cure'—often the result of a consultant's prescription. Instead it began by getting everybody who would be affected by a change deeply involved in it, embarking on a participative 'management fundamentals' programme. This aimed to secure mutually beneficial solutions to employee and employer problems through discussions with all concerned.

Logical stages of the 'management fundamentals' programme

1 Awareness of the existing situation.
2 Understanding of any existing problems (in any area).
3 Recognition of the need to change.

4   Education by parable and case studies of management principles and concepts.

5   Early action in areas where action could be implemented.

6   A building-up of confidence.

7   Appreciation of the problems faced in running a business.

8   The development of a payment scheme which would aim to secure continued prosperity for the company and its employees.

The task of finding an alternative payment scheme was stated as a prime objective at a mass meeting on Day 1 of the assignment. The employees were then divided into groups—and within each group was a cross-section of those represented:

Management and administration staff

Works employees

Seven almost identical 2½-hour sessions were held for each group, with two additional sessions for the management and administration staffs. In the first sessions each group discussed the basic fundamentals of management theory, e.g. setting objectives, planning, cost control centres, budgeting and so forth. A variety of teaching aids were used, including text book parables and cartoon films. It wasn't until there was a point of common language and understanding that everyone began to discuss the specific problems at Design and Print.

If we look at the guide-lines on profit (see Appendix A, p141) it can be seen how basic the information is. This is necessary when teaching shop-floor employees as this is probably the first time many have met this type of education.

Recently I was working within a large motor car combine which had some months previously been involved in a serious strike. I talked with a shop floor employee about his thoughts on the strike. His attitude at the time was 'The Company has made X million pounds profit in the UK alone for the previous year—we only want an increase of 30 shillings a week and they're complaining. It's the bloody shareholders that are keeping all 'em profits as well as 'em on that mahogany corridor'. The point is well taken: the company in question had made a considerable profit, a point that the press didn't fail to note and nourish. What the shop floor, and possibly the trade union representatives, did not understand was the basic concepts of profit and loss and that a company has more costs to its trading account than just the wage bill. The pains taken at Design and Print to explain for example the economic facts of life could prove an example well worth pursuing in other companies such as that particular motor car combine. Naturally the education programme would be on a larger scale but it is possible even in the largest of concerns where units can often total as many employees as those in Design and Print altogether.

As well as 'Profit', other sessions at Design and Print included such teachings as:

    Anatomy of management and conflicting objectives

    Planning and performance

    Controls

    Job enrichment and management style

    Pareto (the importance of the vital few).

Additional sessions for the management group covered:

    Controls

    Action meetings

    16 ways to wreck a meeting

    Selling ideas

    Analytical thinking and the use of time.

Apart from the guidelines to a session on profit (Appendix A), guidelines that can be used for the 'Anatomy of Management' are given in Appendix B, p144.

As I mentioned earlier, the finding of an alternative payment scheme at Design and Print was stated as a prime objective. Following agreement as to how the scheme should operate (see Appendix C, p148), and after discussions with trade unions, the scheme was launched on an experimental basis. Design and Print are continuing to work in conjunction with the National Graphical Association (NGA). The payments experiment which has been introduced relies on frank discussion and full co-operation between management and the shop floor in order to develop the best ideas for everyone concerned. The experiment was originally for a six-month trial period but a further three-month trial period has recently been agreed with the NGA. The fundamentals have been agreed and the skeleton pay structure has been clothed with actual figures.

Appendix C indicates the specification that evolved from the sessions on the new incentive scheme. Basically it is a group payment scheme developed on a value-added concept.

Essentially, payment rises for any increases in a House Achievement (HA) factor which is calculated every four weeks. The HA factor, after taking account of the machinery invested in the company, compares the ratio of pounds value added to pounds wages paid.

The central point of the scheme is the value-added concept —a simple method of calculating bonus by relating the company's output to its resources. Another attraction of this scheme is that clerical work is minimal compared to the many hours needed for calculating bonuses on the old scheme. It may be worth mentioning at this juncture that value added is *sales* less *materials*; net value added (NVA) is *sales* less *materials* less value added attributable to *machines*. The operatives can see how successfully they have done by seeing the NVA go up and wages remaining consistent. The House Achievement plan is graphed and placed on a huge notice board so that everyone can see how he, and the others, are doing.

Figure 2.1 shows an example of the kind of graph that appeared on the board and the important point is that everyone understands it, not only because of their involvement in developing the scheme but because of their basic knowledge of payment systems obtained through the management fundamentals programme.

From the series of discussions it emerged that the management of the company had seldom been on the same wavelength as their employees—a situation not peculiar to Design and Print! There was a feeling among the workforce that the company was being run 'by the seat of the pants', and there

---

Figure 2.1

Data from which the graphs are constructed every four weeks is:

Period	A Net value added, UK £s	B Wages in deliveries (ex bonus), UK £s	C HA factor (4 weeks)	D HA factor (12-week period moving average)	
1	3400	1270	2.677	3.100	
2	3912	1224	3.196	3.173	
3	6695	1493	4.484	3.381	
4	5459	1469	3.716	3.568	28% increase
5	6493	1587	4.091	3.908	
6	5696	1625	3.523	3.943	
7	6984	1516	4.607	3.975	

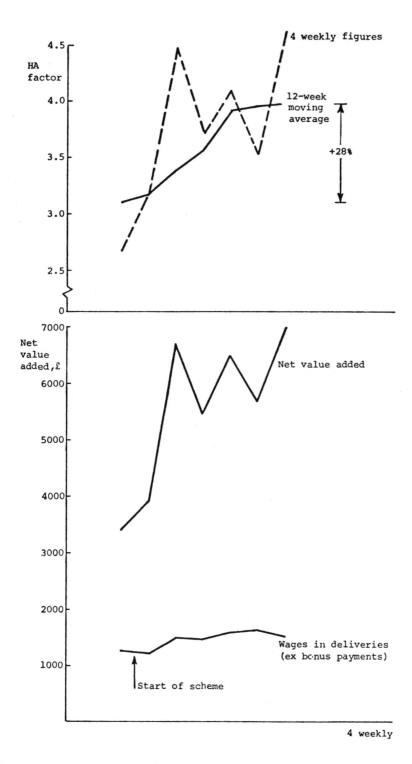

was a lack of adequate co-operation and co-ordination. There was also a lack of information systems, e.g. priorities within Design and Print seemed to change without explanation. There was also little credit given for good work and, as there were no performance reviews, the individual felt that he was involved far too little.

A variety of other criticisms and suggestions also emerged. For example, 'apprentice training is far too inadequate' and 'a new tape machine is needed for the bindery'. Plus 'the guard and clamp on the composing room saw are inadequate and dangerous' to the final 'there should be fewer overhead people'. Naturally all these matters had to be acted upon as had the prime objective of the whole exercise—the task of finding an alternative payment scheme.

Some of the on-going features of this participative management scheme are as follows:

1 A joint productivity committee of management and union members at which all aspects of the business are actively and openly discussed, e.g. sales order book, production figures and machinery purchases.

2 Graphical representation within the works of key factors concerning their scheme:
   a net sales;
   b net value added;
   c total hours worked;
   d wages paid (in goods delivered);
   e the HA factor.

Owing to action taken during the management fundamentals sessions, which involved the total company approach to improving overall prosperity, the effects of the new wage scheme in its first six months were:

1 Profitability (expressed as a percentage on turnover) is in excess of the previous 'high' achieved in 1969.

2 'Productivity' has increased by over 25 per cent.

3 Employee bonus payments have increased by as much as 60 per cent on occasions.

The situation in terms of productivity and bonus increases is, according to more recent reports, still indicating a healthy growth. According to Dave Atherfold who joined Design and Print in 1967 when things were badly wrong, and who now spends most of his time on the new two-colour Koenig and Bauer press, 'It's not just the machine that will get things moving to £250,000 worth of business—it'll only come if everyone pulls in the same direction'.

Printing, like the ship repair industry, is not an industry used to being in the vanguard of change. But participation has, in fact, paid off—as the company results show. And there is a commitment to the new structure because the employees were able to discuss among themselves as well as with management such 'fundamental' questions as:

> What should be the make-up of the new pay packet?
>
> What part should the bonus play in it?
>
> Should merit money be paid on top of this?
>
> Should the scheme be a group one?
>
> Should it apply in different forms in different departments?
>
> Could any scheme be trusted? (On this point the graph helps the operatives to check the figures and know that they are in fact correct.)
>
> Should the sales representatives be involved in the same scheme?
>
> Etc., etc.

Employee participation has helped get everyone in 'on the same wavelength'. Even if nothing else had happened that alone would surely have been a 'change for the better'.

Hellermann Deutsch (Bowthorpe Group)

East Grinstead, Sussex

*Inque brevi spatio mutantur saecia animantum
Et quasi cursores vitai lampada tradunt.*

*(And in a short space the tribes of living things are changed,
and like runners hand on the torch of life.)*

Lucretius, *De rerum natura* (translated by Bailey)

David Burt, Director of Administration, Hellermann Deutsch (of the
Bowthorpe Holdings Group of Companies) has my lasting thanks for
every facility and hospitality he has given me when working within his
company. I am grateful also to many members of the staff, in particular
Ron Reed the tool-room chargehand who taught me all I know about
the life of a connector and relay!

A quotation including 'the torch of life' is more than apt for
the Hellermann Deutsch company. The company makes electronic parts for the aircraft and space industry, specialising
in cable connectors and relays—components on which lives
depend. These are used in aircraft like the controversial Con-
corde, in space shots, three miles underground on mining
equipment and in life-savers such as heart and lung machines.
It can be appreciated, therefore, that the failure of a connector or relay could cause an aircraft to crash, a multi-million
dollar space shot to be ruined, or heart, lung and kidney
machines to fail.

The company is largely the creation of its present Chairman, Jack Bowthorpe, who began it in a garage in London in
the 1930s. He began by cutting electrical wiring into standard

lengths and selling these to the then growing aircraft industry. From this came the demand to supply connectors and to make specialised cables and switches—until today when this Bowthorpe Group, with a value of £20,000,000, has eleven companies within the UK and an international network of companies and distributors (see Figure 3.1).

Hellermann Deutsch (a company within the Bowthorpe Group) opened in East Grinstead in 1964 with only 20 employees. Now it has five factories and employs just over 550 people, two-thirds of whom are women. Many of the key assembly and inspection functions are carried out by women who have proved that they are more dextrous than men and better suited to work on delicate electrical component assembly.

A century ago an industrialist considering the location of

Aden	Cuba	Iraq	Paraguay
Algeria	Cyprus	Japan	Phillipines
Arabia	Denmark	Jordan	Portugal
Argentina	Dominican Republic	Kuwait	South Africa
Australia	East Africa	Lebanon	Spain
Belgium	Ethiopia	Malaya	Sweden
Bolivia	France	Malta	Thailand
Burma	Germany	Mauritius	Trinidad
Canada	Greece	Mexico	United Arab Republic
Ceylon	Grenada	Netherlands	United States
Chile	Guyana	New Zealand	West Africa
China	Hong Kong	Nigeria	
Colombia	India	Norway	
Costa Rica	Iran	Pakistan	

Figure 3.1 Bowthorpe Group overseas holdings

a site would choose one near available raw materials or near an energy source, such as coal. If he was very fortunate he would choose a site that had both these factors plus good transportation facilities like the canals. He had few labour recruitment difficulties then, as men from the surrounding country-side provided industry with their unskilled labour. Supervisors and skilled trades were not needed in abundance.

A century later the reverse is the case, for not only has the industrialist got to consider available labour supplies but also the attractiveness of the town to his key personnel. The proximity of raw materials is no longer a prime concern as they can be brought in bulk cheaply from many parts of the world, and even energy can reach most parts of the globe via electricity, pipeline or in bulk-oil shipments. It is usually the end product that is expensive, fragile and difficult to transport; therefore many industries considering re-location today choose to go nearer to their market.

Hellermann Deutsch decided to move to East Grinstead for a number of reasons, the main one being the supply of suitable labour. Also, most of the 'assembly industry'—aircraft, electronic and sophisticated electrical equipment manufacturers—is situated within 30 miles of London, and the major exceptions, such as the British Aircraft Corporation at Filton, are easily accessible to East Grinstead by road and rail.

The finished product is very small and consequently easy to ship, as is the amount of raw material in the product. Transport either way was therefore not too much of a concern.

If an employee leaves his job, whatever the reason, the loss to the company is as real as the loss of a customer or contract. It is considered so important within the Bowthorpe/Hellermann Group that the personnel function is represented on the Senior Board. At Hellermann Deutsch itself a member of the Board has the line responsibility for the personnel department, which is given the same weight of importance as sales, engineering, accounts departments, etc. It was in 1968 that Hellermann's realised that a serious manpower problem had arisen, with the turnover for females at 62 per cent, and 28 per cent for males—and that out of a labour force of 380. Escalating training costs and serious recruitment difficulties were causing major boardroom scrutiny and it was considered essential to establish just why there

were such high turnover problems, and why, despite the
labour availability in the area (which had been a major factor
in choosing East Grinstead) their recruitment record had
been poor.

There was, of course, a great deal of supposition and emotion, but very few facts which could have decisions based on
them in order to create change. Solution of the problem was
urgent for these main reasons: the industry is a life-line one
and therefore depends on highly skilled and high-integrity
performance from the employees; but when there is a high
turnover this can affect morale. A large proportion of the
total labour time is apportioned to in-line as well as final inspection. Girls with desk microscopes may make checks as
many as eight times on the final 15-stage assembly programme, each sub-assembly of which has itself been checked
through its various stages of manufacture.

The thousands of different metal components are checked
by a variety of sophisticated pieces of equipment for accur-
acies of greater than one thousandth of an inch. From speaking with the employees at Hellermann Deutsch it is apparent
that everyone who works there knows that if one connector
in a thousand proves faulty, not only is their reputation for
the highest quality in jeopardy but that human life may well
be in danger.

As a connector contains little raw material, the real manufacturing cost is in labour and in the high training costs involved in imparting the specialised knowledge that lies behind
the development of a connector. The training time can be as
much as 12 weeks and some of the girls, like Sally Brackenbury, who come straight from school also require an 'experience period' of between 12 and 20 weeks before output and
operation quality reach the required standards. One can
therefore appreciate the indirect cost levels if individuals are
not really 'qualified' for six months and if the turnover—as
it did in 1968—reaches 62 per cent.

A detailed manpower investigation was begun, and many
facts which were previously unrecognised emerged. The turnover figures were not uniformly spread. There were departmental, as well as age anomalies; for example the turnover in
the 15-21 age group was higher than in the 21-25 age group.
The greatest improvement in the stability of the female
labour force occurred between 25 and 35 and this same
group was also identified as being the most stable in terms

of attendance and work performance. Terminal interviews suggested that many married women were leaving the company because of domestic difficulties probably caused by an attempt to fit in with the company's working hours. As a result of the manpower investigation it was possible to build an identikit of the ideal female operator and, together with a job description, this formed the basis for selecting personnel who would be compatible with the company's environment. The Personnel Department were also able to use this information in an attempt to pitch the main recruitment appeal to married women between the ages of 25 and 35 who had children at school in the area. Another advertising campaign was put into operation. Apart from specifically trying to attract females to the company, the company also appealed to the town and its wider potential workforce. This was done through the two local newspapers in which, at least once a quarter, major features appeared on the electrical industry and on contracts awarded to Hellermann Deutsch which affected both the company and the town. Every month there was something in the news about the company, whether concerning relays or 'human' stories... this in fact still occurs to this day. Discussions were held between the Personnel Department and the female employees on the practical problems they were encountering. Hours were the most common saga of complaint; therefore they were made much more flexible, with the company running shifts from 8 a.m. to 1 p.m. and from 1 p.m. to 5.30 p.m. to make it possible for 'double jobbers' to maintain a working life as well as a housekeeping role. This move produced both a higher productivity during the shorter working sessions as well as a lowering of the labour turnover figure.

The attempt at 'compatibility' has been maintained and is continually being improved on. Expertise has built up on 'operating', for example, paired or 'back-to-back' shifts where two operators agree to work a morning and afternoon shift to give a 'one operator day'. These teams are often neighbours and frequently assist one another with chores like babysitting and child care, especially after school. There is also consideration given to periods such as school holidays and production control have been able to implement these considerations into their procedures. Today there are exhaustive records kept of manpower movements, turnover statistics and reasons for leaving. By selecting the right person for the right job the female turnover has been drastically reduced from 1968's 62 per cent to a cumulative figure of 28.7 per cent in 1975.

Manpower management has been improved by carefully monitoring facts which provide the background for decisions that management can make to improve practices and procedures. Much of this better understanding comes from personnel statistics (such as those indicated in Figures 3.2-3.7) which are circulated to line management each month. These figures illustrate a typical management brief for a range of cost centres. Each departmental head and line manager is called upon to give reasons for retention difficulties and the performance of his various departments, whilst the management team as a whole looks for trends and pointers towards action that they need to take to balance the work force.

Naturally it would be most desirable to have 100 per cent full-time operators, but Hellermann Deutsch acknowledge the

PERSONNEL STATISTICS: Month..*April*..Week..*14*....to Week..*17*....

1 Labour turnover percentage for previous 12 months including month..*April*.

Cost centre	Numbers employed		Percentage employed in dept.	Labour turnover, %	
	Male	Female		Male	Female
110	18	13	8.2	16.6	30.7
116	1	8	2.3	–	–
125	2	26	7.4	–	53.8
130	7	4	2.9	42.8	–
135	4	7	2.9	25.0	14.2
140	9	43	13.7	33.3	30.2
142	–	11	2.9	–	36.3
150	12	16	7.4	50.0	73.3
151	20	12	8.4	25.0	41.6
152	5	–	1.3	–	–
155	8	1	2.3	–	–
160	7	1	2.1	42.8	100.0
165	1	13	3.7	–	30.7
170	3	–	0.7	–	–
300	17	6	6.1	5.8	–
400	15	17	8.4	26.6	23.5
430	2	3	1.3	–	66.6
145	5	–	1.3	–	–
800	36	15	13.5	27.7	60.0
162	7	3	2.6	–	–
	179	199			

Figure 3.2

realities of the supply and demand situation for female labour in South East England as well as the changing needs of their female work-force. From practice, errors and experience they have discovered that the benefits from co-operative planning of working shifts are very high in terms of volume and quality—plus, of course, the operator's own satisfaction in balancing her particular needs.

The process of change throughout any company, as all the case studies aim to illustrate, relies upon the understanding of all parties concerned. This can be considerably encouraged through an effective communication structure—'representative' participation.

2 Personnel movements for April compared with the same period period the previous year

	This year			Last year		
	M	F	Total	M	F	Total
No. employed end of previous period	180	196	376	170	180	350
No. employed end of current period	179	199	378	171	180	351
Net increase/decrease	-1	+3	+2	+1	-	+1
New engagement this period	3	9	12	4	5	9
Terminations this period	3	6	9	3	5	8
Divisional transfers increase/decrease	1		1			
Net increase/decrease	-1	+3	+2	+1	-	+1
	%	%	%	%	%	%
Labour turnover percentage year to date	10.1	13.1	11.6	4.1	11.6	7.9
Projected annual labour turnover	30.2	39.2	34.9	12.3	35.0	23.9

3 Analysis of leavers by length of service

	This period			Same period last year		
	M	F	Total	M	F	Total
Under 3 months		3	3		1	1
3 months - 6 months		3	3		2	2
6 months - 1 year	1		1	1	1	2
1 year - 2 years				1		1
2 years - 4 years	1		1			
4 years - 6 years						
6 years - 10 years	1		1	1	1	2
Over 10 years						
Total	3	6	9	3	5	8

Figure 3.3

Figure 3.4

4 Analysis of leavers - reasons for leaving

Reason	Staff This period	Staff YTD	Works This period	Works YTD	Staff This period	Staff YTD	Works This period	Works YTD	TOTAL
01 Dismissed - unsatisfactory performance						2		1	3
02 Dismissed - timekeeping or abseteeism									
03 Dismissed - misconduct									
04 Dismissed - redundancy		2							2
05 Dismissed - retirement									
06 Dismissed - medically unfit									
20 Better prospects elsewhere	1	4	1	2	1	2			8
21 Dissatisfaction - pay									
22 Dissatisfaction - hours of work					2	2			2
23 Dissatisfaction - job content	1	3							3
24 Dissatisfaction - other terms of employment		1						1	2
25 Dissatisfaction - environment									
26 Dissatisfaction - supervision									
28 Transport problems				1					1
29 Accommodation						1			1
30 Medical				1	1	1			2
31 Pregnancy						1			1
32 Domestic								2	2
33 Retirement									
34 Leaving area		1				3		4	8
50 Death						1			1
51 Other reasons		1					2	4	5
27 Dissatisfaction - other reasons									
TOTAL	2	12	1	4	4	13	2	12	41

An attitude survey in the firm revealed anomalies in the overall communication and information networks in the company and organisation charts were subsequently drawn up and published for each department. Although these are excellent devices (if looked at), the over-riding principle remains that the individual employee must be able to identify where he or she fits into the company and the communication pattern. Figure 3.7 is displayed throughout the company on every noticeboard. It uses a standard motorway colour scheme, road classification and town or city identification to indicate the speed of information, the directional flow of information and the proximity of the information centre to the individual. An important express-way is also the works council and committee, and constitutions exist for these which have been thrashed out democratically by elected members of the company.

An example of a typical council meeting is reproduced as Appendix P, p185. Particular reference is drawn to item 7 on the agenda which illustrates the involvement of the workforce in a matter normally reserved for the rights and discourse of managers only!

Ron Reed, the charge hand in the tool room, has been involved with the works council for 14 years and he feels that it does prevent the grapevine from getting out of control. Of course one should always recognise the futility of trying to kill the grapevine completely, but it is management's responsibility to ensure:

1   That the grapevine does not turn all molehills into mountains.

2   That the grapevine does not exist as the main source of company information.

5 Vacancies - outstanding, filled, authorised

	This year		Last year	
	Staff	Works	Staff	Works
Number of vacancies end of last period	19	12	11	8
Number of vacancies end of this period	20	8	7	6
Net increase/decrease	+1	-4	-4	-2
Vacancies filled this period	6	6	7	4
Vacancies authorised this period	7	3	2	3
Net increase/decrease	+1	-3	-5	-1

Figure 3.5

6 Vacancies - age analysis (April)

Cost centre	Age in weeks - outstanding vacancies													Total	Over 12 weeks Detail
	1	2	3	4	5	6	7	8	9	10	11	12	Over 12		
110				1									1	2	Bonding operator
116															
170															
125										2	1			3	
130	2													2	
135															
140	1													1	
142															
150				2						1			1	4	Stock control clerk
151							1			3				4	
152															
160															
165													1	1	Canteen assistant
162	1													1	
300													1	1	Draughtsman
800		1	2	1			4							8	
400	1													1	
143															
Total	5	1	2	4			5			6	1		4	28	

Figure 3.6

Ron Reed felt this had been eradicated by the formal communication links which are offered through the communication chart.

Did he and his colleagues feel that it was an adequate substitute for the Trade Union? There is no bar within the company to any man or woman joining a trade union if they wish, and in fact many of the works council are trade union members in their own right. All discussions on pay and conditions of employment are, however, the responsibility of the various divisional committees.

A number of the employees thought they would be better off with the union, after all the grass is always greener, etc., etc., but on the whole their main reason for this sentiment was that they considered the union better at negotiating with management than the works committee and council. This has been realised... and management have made considerable efforts over four years to achieve credibility and independence. Council members have training programmes carried out by specialist consultants to improve their abilities in discussion, negotiating and communication. This happens without loss of morale and confidence, and the training programme includes managers and supervisors taking short outside courses, and a series of discussions with functional or communication groups discussing any failures and breakdowns in the system. This is a constant process within the company and it is felt by both management and people like Ron Reed that most of the difficulties have been exposed; there is an appreciation that communication has a high priority within Hellermann Deutsch. Again there appears a consistency within all the case studies of visible management support and leadership. Management was committed to change, but realised that it could only come about through all the parties having an understanding of *what* was happening within the company as well as *why*. The resultant dialogue has caused a tremendous change in an operator's daily function, her environment in the company and the relationship between her job and her family and her home, *all of which are intrinsic to the job satisfaction of the married female employee.*

However, all this would carry little credibility unless the company stood by its ability to provide its service to customers. 'Hellermann means reliability' said Sally Brackenbury, and the dependability of this statement plus the efficiency of customer service depends upon the employees' involvement

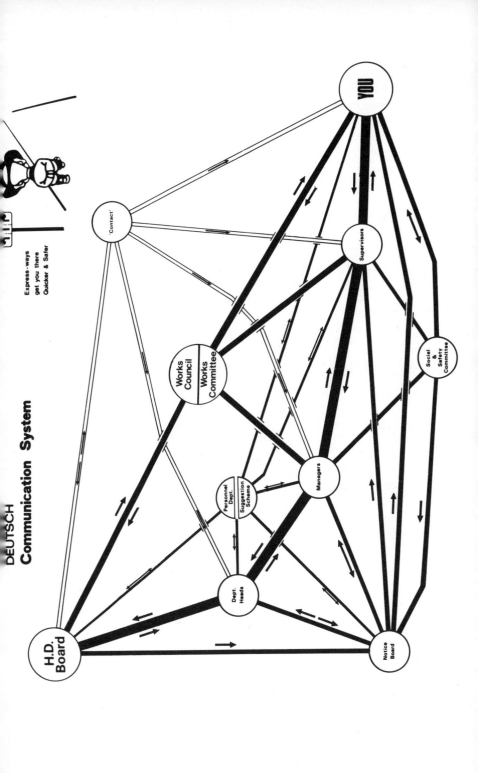

DEUTSCH
Communication System

Express - ways
get you there
Quicker & Safer

YOU

Supervisors

'Contact'

Works Council / Works Committee

Social & Safety Committee

Managers

Personnel Dept. / Suggestion Scheme

Dept. Heads

H.D. Board

Notice Board

and understanding of their role in the company. It is all the more vital in a life-line industry.

Now that change has become an every-day occurrence, further activities can occur. Jobs are rotated in order that female operators can contribute to the 'whole' of the connector, as opposed to a 'part'. On-the-job training and retraining is, therefore, a major activity within the company. For example, employees can make valid comments about proposed assembly line changes and the important point is that they know they will have a feedback from management—which must come within seven days. At this moment in time, 1976, the employees are having a major say in work layout—planning a new factory opening this year.

Their sense of importance is also enhanced in the organisation through their seeing the connectors installed in the end product: this is usually done through photographic exhibitions. They appreciate that in making the connector the copper and aluminium comes to Hellermann Deutsch by way of Zambia, Chile and Canada, bauxite (the raw material of aluminium) from Guyana or Jamaica, with its refining probably having been done in Norway. The plastics used are made from petroleum, possibly refined on Southampton or Tees-side, while the oil itself would have come from the Middle East. Into the plastic plugs are inserted the connectors, plated with gold from South Africa. This understanding of the source of the raw material and a realisation of the value and technical difficulties in gold plating, metal work, milling fluorinated silicone and machining phosphor bronze, together with a myriad of other technical procedures, contributes to the appreciation that each connector and relay is of great value.

The management of Hellermann Deutsch realised back in 1968 that they had to get people to care about being involved in their work. By dint of trial and error the philosophy that emerged remains one of constant attention to detail and to change, with insistence on the involvement of everyone in the company.

Facts alone tell you nothing—only people do, as it is only through people that colour can be added to facts. Therein lies much of the secret to worker participation.

Case Study Four
Sun Life Assurance Society
London

*The highest and best form of efficiency is the spontaneous
co-operation of a free people.*

Bernard Baruch, *American Industry at War*
(A report of the War Industries Board), March 1921

I would like to thank both Peter Bairstow, Deputy Actuary, and Tony
Howell, Assistant Personnel Executive, of Sun Life Assurance Society
Limited for giving me every help in the compilation of the study.

Each year more and more firms move from towns to country-
side and from cities to development areas. A book on co-
operation and change should contain a study that portrays
business relocation being achieved by Socratic methods
rather than by decree.

The Sun Life Assurance Society Limited is one of the UK's
leading assurance companies, with funds exceeding £500 million. It has a national network of offices and over 2000 staff,
of which approximately one half work in the London Head
Office. Sun Life is at the forefront of an industry that is
having to change fast to meet the demands of today—and the
future.

The relocation of the London Head Office to Bristol, 120
miles to the west, is an example of 'change' which has
demanded the most effective use of management support systems: communication and accurate and instant information
services; knowledge; motivation; training; understanding and
co-operation—not to mention time.

A prime reason for relocation must be cost. It is considered that Sun Life require 100,000 square feet for their Head Office staff. In 1975 office rents in the City of London were in excess of £10 per square foot and a saving of up to £8 per square foot could be made by moving out of town. The rental alone would therefore account for a yearly saving of approximately £750,000. Rates are lower out of town, as are most overheads; thus the straightforward economic argument for relocation is easily won.

There are also the actions of Sun Life's competitors. Approximately 35 insurance and finance houses are reported to be considering 'moving out' or have already taken steps to do so. For example the Prudential has already moved many staff to Reading while the Pearl Assurance Company is planning to move to Peterborough. It is imperative in the world of insurance to hold your bonus in a competitive market and to do this you must hold down your expense ratio. Reducing costs like rentals will mean that for Sun Life policy holders their bonus will be as valuable and hopefully higher than if they invested with an alternative insurance concern.

If cost is the prime reason for relocation, people must be the prime consideration. It is the time and effort Sun Life have injected into the personnel aspect of this move that is worthy of comment. Before I discuss this in greater detail I ought to mention why Bristol was chosen as the new Head Office location, as opposed to Croydon or Northampton which are much nearer to the Metropolis.

Bristol has a valuable communication network, with excellent motorway facilities, good railway service and an airport. It is also a good catchment area, being surrounded by south Gloucester, Bath, etc. To move within 20 miles of Croydon for instance, would not bring equal economic benefits—after all the Croydon area is a catchment area for London, with rentals much higher than those in the provinces. Bristol, though, can further attract major employers by offering accessible transport and catchment facilities; it is possible that Sun Life will want to obtain between 500 and 600 youngsters to work in their new Head Office. It is unlikely that even the most hallowed of employers could leave London with all of their teenage staff.

Let me return to the 'people' aspects of the relocation.

The control of the relocation was under a Senior Executive of Sun Life, Laurie Cottrell, who is Deputy General Manager.

A Relocation Committee was formed with the primary function of co-ordinating all matters concerned with the move. Three people sat on the committee:

1   Laurie Cottrell, who was responsible for the co-ordination of policy decisions.
2   John Nicholls, the surveyor responsible for the new building itself.
3   Tony Howell, the personnel executive responsible for the 'people' aspects of the move, as well as their furniture and fittings.

Subsequent to the initial announcement of the move and the reasons for it, a circular was despatched in Summer 1973 to all staff, announcing the intention that between 1974 and 1978 the Head Office would be relocated to Bristol, and indicating that approximately 90 per cent of the staff would be affected.

A management information system is an important foundation in *any* programme for change. In Hellermann Deutsch, for example (Case Study 3), one will recall there was a great deal of supposition and emotion but very few facts that could have a decision based upon them in order to create changes. The reasons indicated in the Sun Life circular letter were based on decisions taken upon factual analysis and not merely on instinct. Figure 4.1 contains an extract from this circular letter.

Prior to these moves a study group of three, two Sun Life personnel and an outside computer expert, had been reviewing the company's computer needs and their expected requirements over the next ten years, since the existing computers were nearing the end of their useful life. It was decided that Sun Life would transfer from a magnetic tape to a magnetic disk system. The CYBER computer system was chosen (a family of machines manufactured by the US firm, Control Data) and it was decided to site it from the first out of London with the relocated departments. Any technical transitions are bad enough on their own, but when relocation becomes involved as well it is a tremendous job.

Accepting the introduction of more machines, whether they are computers or updated automation in a factory plant,

RELOCATION TO BRISTOL

1 Outline of the problem

As a result of researches carried out in recent months, including the questionnaires completed and returned by Chief Office staff, we are now able to give some more background and information about how we are at present planning the move of the Chief Office staff to Bristol.

In planning this move there are various constraints placed upon us which givern the extent and timings of the move. Some of these constraints are:

i We are at an advanced stage in negotiations for a suitable permanent building in Bristol in addition to Temple Gate House. Construction of this building has not yet commenced and this will enable us to ensure as far as practicable that the building can be planned to meet our foreseeable needs. The building is not, however, likely to be ready for occupation until the summer of 1975 at the earliest.

ii There will be a phased transfer of our computer systems but it is unlikely that the transfer will be complete before the end of 1976 or early 1977. Until we have some practical experience on the Cyber, it is extremely difficult to predict with any degree of precision when projects will be completed.

iii In moving to a new location we must bear in mind the question of the recruitment of local staff. In the ordinary way, the summer months of the year will be the best time.

iv The varied problems in moving a substantial number of our present staff from London to Bristol.

v The likely pressure on schemes work during the next 2-3 years.

vi The necessity to maintain service at a high level.

2 Proposed extent and timing of the move

It is the Management's view that it is in the long-term interests of the Society and of its staff that we move a substantial proportion of Chief Office to Bristol. It is the intention, however, to retain part of Chief Office in London, particularly as there are obvious advantages in some aspects of our work remaining in London.

Based on our present plans, at least the following departments or areas will remain in London:

(List of relevant departments)

In view of the constraints we have to face, it is difficult at this stage to give an indication of the timing of moves of all Chief Office departments. However, we expect:

a No major moves until the summer/autumn of 1975.

b Departments for whom systems are first developed on the Cyber will be amongst the earliest to move - these will include departments responsible for policy writing and premium collection.

c No moves of schemes departments until 1976.

d   A phased move of departments in the accounting and schemes area over a period of years.

e   The major moves to be completed by 1978.

3 Moves of staff

The results of the questionnaire were in general most encouraging, particularly for the senior staff and the male staff at all levels. Nevertheless, there are some staff who for personal reasons are unable to go to Bristol in the near future or even at all. We shall, of course, deal sympathetically with those staff who have genuine difficulties, and we expect to see a fair amount of interchange of staff, not only between departments in Chief Office but also between departments and branches, particularly branches in the London area. It will be appreciated that even after the move of the majority of the Chief Office departments to Bristol, the rump of Chief Office left in London together with the London branches will require substantial numbers of staff.

Some branch staff from many parts of the country have already indicated there willingness to transfer to the Bristol Office in due course. In order that we may plan ahead, would Area and Branch Managers please forward particulars on the accompanying form of any staff who would like to be considered. It is appreciated that personal circumstances will alter over the years and steps should be taken to ensure that Personnel Department are advised of any changes that might occur.

Figure 4.1 Extract from a circular to all Sun Life staff, dated 27 July 1973

is always difficult.

It is easier for younger personnel who have been born in a computer and automative era, but many older employees have in the past viewed the introduction of sophisticated equipment with apprehension. They had to be taught to use computers as a tool and not as an enemy. At Sun Life this has meant over the years extensive training programmes, re-training and appreciation courses which have been most effective in creating new attitudes. These programmes have to be stepped up when new computer equipment is introduced, leading in many cases to revised office systems.

In an industry where so much of its efficient customer service has at its foundation a reliance on the computer, it is important that all staff have an appreciation of this machinery. As computer moves were on this occasion linked to departmental moves, it provided Sun Life with the opportunity to reinforce this appreciation down the line. In fact the relocation was looked at in a socio-technical manner—as the technical side was being reviewed and moved, the social needs and fears of the staff were also taken into account by the senior management.

We see in other studies how the initiative for change has, as it always must, take place from the top. It is doubtful whether, without this senior commitment, a process for change within any organisation could be activated.

Project teams

Participation by the staff themselves in various aspects of the move was evolved through the formation of *Project Teams*. The teams not associated with the new computer systems were co-ordinated by Tony Howell and they looked at specific problem areas, for example:
1 Inter-departmental relationships affected by the move.
2 Loading of paperwork/more effective storage/filing.
3 Job loading caused perhaps by the phasing of the operation in having, say, one department in London, another in Bristol.

These project teams were similar in construction to those outlined in the Vosper Thornycroft study which dealt with project management. Sun Life's O&M Department was used extensively to provide the various project teams with information and expertise.

'Action' meetings

A project team's gathering could be named an 'Action' meeting. Such a meeting is not allowed to deteriorate into verbose discussion. Instead, deliberations are, hopefully, more purposeful and positive, and bear a sense of priority.

Action meetings are appropriate for all levels of employees. They usually replace less fruitful meetings or information gatherings which are already being held to discuss the same subjects. They are conducted similarly to the 'briefing' group.

Basically they examine
What has to be done?
What is being done?
By whom and when?

It is important that these meetings be *brief,* for wherever they are held—whether in a situation where a production

track has to be stopped or in a shop that has to be closed for
half an hour say on a Monday morning—they cost money.
Communication always costs money, but it saves a lot more
when it is effective. And to be effective, organisations similar
to those mentioned in this book may well have to hold ele-
mentary communication exercises and effective speaking
sessions.

The meetings are convened by each manager for the people
accountable to him. Thus a Production Manager will confer
with his Foremen, the Sales Director with the Salesmen; the
Managing Director with Departmental Heads and so on, from
the top to the bottom of the hierarchy within a company.

Action meetings are so important that I want to state some
requirements for their success.

Procedure

1   They should be chaired by the person for whom the
    controls are prepared.
2   The chairman should be appraised of the facts behind
    the control results. For the meeting to be a success the
    chairman must do his homework and must be well
    briefed.
3   The meetings should be confined rigorously to apprais-
    ing facts and making decisions. Involved discussions of
    detail should be held elsewhere. Any counselling of indi-
    viduals which may be necessary should also take place
    elsewhere.
4   The agenda, which also forms the minutes, can conveni-
    ently take the form of 'Action Statements' which then
    act as both the agenda and the minutes with a minimum
    of work (and on the same piece of paper).
5   The first subjects to be considered at any meeting are
    those overdue from the previous meetings. By this auto-
    matic follow-up outstanding items get priority attention.
6   Meetings should be short, decisive and to the point.

Chairman's attitude

The effectiveness of action meetings depends very much on
the competence of the chairman. If the meetings are to be

successful (and to a large extent their success determines the usefulness of the whole control system) then the *chairman has to learn how to conduct them.* The chairman's attitude should be:

1 Positive—by encouraging suggestions for improvement (and listening to them). Post-mortems are only valuable in learning lessons from the past so as to do better in the future.
2 The chairman should be stimulatingly curious without being offensive.
3 The chairman should avoid directly making a fool of members. Disciplining should be done away from the meeting. In extreme cases the chairman may engineer a man to make a fool of himself in front of his fellows.

Other facets of Action Meeting chairmanship are no different to chairing any similar meeting and include:

1 Ability to keep the meeting to the point.
2 Flexibility in accepting points of view other than his own.
3 Getting sound decisions made.
4 Engineering people to commit themselves to take action.
5 Instilling a sense of purpose—even urgency—into deliberation.

How often though do companies institute works meetings, plant or office committees, where the chairman (let alone the participants) has no discipline, familiarity or knowledge of the conduct required to make such a gathering effective?

The reader will recall again from the Vosper Thornycroft study that an important criterion for any project team is that it should be *accountable.* Quite often this does not occur as some managers in their covetous positions do not *delegate.* This can occur for many reasons, all of which can be remedied, for example:

Perhaps no-one to delegate to	Do we need someone?
No-one experienced enough	Train them
Not enough personal time to delegate	It takes time—analyse use of personal time
Tradition not to delegate	
Can't trust a person	Better get another person
Fear of competition	
A job has to be done immediately	Should these jobs go to someone else?

What often seems to me to be needed is a widespread change
of attitude to enable such managers to genuinely accept new
management methods. We can see from the studies in this
book that participation necessitates a successful change of
attitude and behaviour and that this depends upon the close
attention to certain key factors. To get maximum improvement from an individual manager it is essential that he knows

1   What he is expected to do.
2   How to do it.
3   He has confidence in his ability to do it.
4   Why he is supposed to do it.
5   When and how he will be accountable.

The first staff within Sun Life to be moved were Data Processing followed by the New Business Division responsible for
policy and record production. In 1975 the first two Premium
Collection Departments moved. Prior to the initial move a
mass meeting was held for the data-processing staff where
again the intentions were spelled out. A number of opportunities and options presented themselves:

1   Staff who would be able and willing to relocate.
2   Staff who would be needed to remain at the London
     Head Office for a period of time to man task areas like
     pensions schemes or to act as link people between
     Bristol and the City.
3   Staff who would not move and who wanted to stay with
     the company. For them retraining would be offered, for
     example as insurance salesman or in other aspects of
     Branch work, or in Head Office departments remaining
     in London.
4   As departments moved any 'spare' personnel could be
     redeployed in Branches or certain London-based Head
     Office departments.
5   There was the opportunity of natural wastage.
6   In the 'unhappy' event of not being able to redeploy an
     employee a very benevolent redundancy scheme was
     negotiated with the internal staff association. The
     present Government redundancy payments, although
     recently doubled, are still appallingly inadequate and it
     is to the credit of Sun Life that they negotiated such a
     generous redundancy payment—for example: aged 55
     and over, one could leave with a full pension and a large
     terminal payment.

The pattern adopted for (1) and (2) above was that all staff were personally interviewed. The main purpose of this meeting was to solve any personal problems staff might have, e.g. geriatric parents, or children's school.

One can appreciate the 'involvement' that was already being realised.

1   There was involvement from the Relocation Committee in terms of support.

2   There was involvement through the use of the employees themselves on Project Teams which were used to solve any particular problems that could be highlighted.

3   The involvement of the employees' representatives in the Staff Association in negotiating conditions for the employees who would be relocating and for those who would have to leave Sun Life. The Association was involved from the outset in the policy formation of the relocation. It was used extensively in the communication process between management and the employees.

The Staff Association was also involved in developing the scales and allowances payable for the relocators—for example:

1   Fares for two visits and up to seven days' hotel accommodation in Bristol.

2   Weekend visits to Bristol for wives and boyfriends, etc.

3   Once transferred a holiday given to help with settlement and to acquaint with the new town.

4   All transfer fees and expenses incurred paid and good disturbance allowances.

5   Legal fees, stamp duties, etc. paid.

6   Generous mortgage and house purchase facilities.

7   Miscellaneous expenses, e.g. replacement of furniture and fittings up to £750.

8   New school uniforms up to £50 per child.

9   Temporary accommodation paid for up to four months in order to allow time for house hunting.

10   Furnished flats available to single staff as a pied-à-terre until they find their feet.

Training and development

Sun Life give a very high priority to training, and the relocation programme has inevitably increased the burden on those responsible:

1   Trainers themselves have been trained in the techniques of various aspects of on-the-job training.

2   A previous clerical work measurement programme has been of value in determining the clerical manning levels possibly required in Bristol and is of value to the personnel and training department in considering training requirements over the period of the relocation, i.e. between 1974-78. (The material in Appendix E I have found of value when aiming to illustrate the basic concepts of performance measurement— and vital understanding in clerical work measurement programmes.)

3   Tremendous emphasis has been placed on induction courses both for London-based staff and the new recruits being sought in Bristol. You will see from Figure 4.2 (the New Entrants' Course) the inclusion of computer appreciation that I discussed earlier, and this at a clerical level within the organisation!

4   There were various management development courses held with emphasis on human resource training. This was considered important by Sun Life, as insurance is very much a 'people' industry. These courses also contained some of the management fundamentals that have been covered in the other case studies in this book as it was thought necessary to have regard to the views of some of the older members of the organisation. The resistance to change is a natural human reaction and whenever change programmes are introduced into an organisation this 'resistance' must be taken into account. Very often this resistance (due more to fear than any other factor) is soldered in a person's feeling of 'no confidence' either in himself or in those advocating the change methods.

The most effective way of curing resistance to change, as has been witnessed in all the case studies, has been through education. Sun Life has proved similar and they have included in their training programmes similar subjects to the profit/loss series in Design & Print (Case Study 2). For the readers' interest I offer in Appendices D and E, pp 150-58, material that can be used by organisations when considering such training in basic management fundamentals. In fact managers, both line and senior, were being taught the concepts of econ-

Day	9.30 - 9.45	9.45 - 10.45	11.00 - 11.30	11.30 - 12.00	1.15 - 3.30	3.30 - 4.15
1	Introduction	Office work flow	Underwriting	The computer and how it affects the Society	Practical session, e.g. use of telephone: a. Reference manuals b. Calculating c. Dictating d. Memo writing	Discussion Group problems at work so far

Day	9.30 1 10.00	10.00 - 10.45	11.00 - 11.30	11.30 -12.00	1.15 - 1.45	1.45 -2.30	2.45 - 3.30	3.30 - 4.15
2	Indoor work at the Branch TV	The things we sell	The Outdoor Man Tape/slides	Pensions Business made simple	The world of commerce	Faces to remember Slides	Staff careers and prospects	Action points

CLOSE

Figure 4.2 New Entrant's Course : Provisional Programme

omic survival. This in turn offered an appreciation of the eco- nomic reasons for relocating. I have discovered that the training material in Appendix D on 'Budgets, Budgeting and Budgetary Control' can be very useful for teaching such economic concepts.

5   Training also brought home to all management levels the fact that relocation was *not a myth*. What happens in many organisations is that relocation is talked about for years and when it happens no one believes it! The 'prophets of doom' were not allowed to exist for long.

6   Training and retraining was also necessary for the newly recruited and existing data processing staff transferred to Bristol. The computer manufacturer gave various teach-ins and courses on the new machine and general computer training was organised including courses taking advantage of the video-tape techniques.

7   Training was given to the project teams to aid them with the tasks and problem areas they were involved with. It was easy for many to understand the technical changes occurring, but not so simple for many to consider the sociological changes.

Major areas of consideration

To conclude I want to outline the major areas that were considered by Sun Life to warrant effort and effectiveness.

People

At all times people were given priority—the prime consideration. Staff had to want to accept the 'change' programme, and it was only through their learning the justification and merits for such a change that attitudes, at all levels, began to alter. The company 'bent over backwards' to help people understand relocation: especially important when dealing with Head Office staff who had never envisaged moving. There is no doubt it came as quite a shock—the thought of moving from the City to Hammersmith would have been bad enough, but London to Bristol seemed at first to be a disaster.

It is all very well to encourage people to change, to ask them to depart from their accepted habits of life, and to work harder in order to achieve something, as has been done (or been attempted) throughout all the case studies. But this attitude, which is healthy, must be encouraged from the top. It must be *visible* encouragement—otherwise the management of demotivated personnel, perhaps who have almost grasped the goal of self-fulfilment, is made that much more a difficult process through the disinterest and laziness of senior staff. [This is particularly relevant to the Leyland South Africa case study (Case Study 7) mentioned later in the book.]

Involvement

This married with the 'people' consideration, and Sun Life went to enormous efforts to *involve* people in the change programme. For example:

1 With the effective use of the project teams.
2 With computer installation appreciation: this was given to all user departments so that people were interested in the success of the system and its subsequent long term development within Sun Life.

Apart from day to day chores people were asked to *think*— and to think of every eventuality. It is worth remembering that learning and growth are two of the more powerful motivators.

Phasing

The relocation is being done over a period of four years. Some may consider this lengthy but it avoids a number of traumas. For example, in the longer term one discovers that lengthy phasing is beneficial from the point of view of choosing your labour market timing. It also aids redeployment.

The long period also gives Sun Life the time to allow people to re-adjust to the move. From personal experience I would say that a relocation move being planned and implemented over three/four years is wise, especially when the move is from the City of London to the west and northern

regions, both areas to the Londoner abounding with myths of
drowse and drab. Completely unfounded of course—but only
time and experience proves the contrary.

Development of new systems

I have briefly discussed the development of the computer systems, but the relocation would (and does) provide management with an opportunity to build its familiarisation into the
long-term philosophy of the Sun Life company.

Jobs would be changing radically over the next ten years,
therefore management also had an opportunity to relook at
future manning. Jobs themselves could be looked at in depth
and job enrichment could be built from the outset into the
job descriptions of the tasks being founded in Bristol.

Staff turnover also occurs in high numbers through people
being bored with their jobs. There are many 0.23 standard
second jobs in an insurance office and tremendous scope
exists for people doing all of a job instead of merely *part*.
The opportunity to look at this in more detail over the next
four years is immense.

Training

I have covered this earlier but it is important that management always have the time to train people in new skills being
required of them, whether they be technical or socio-
oriented. In this way confidence in coping with the variables
and eventualities could be improved.

As with all the case studies in this book relating to involvement and change, it has been made apparent that there is a
great deal of untapped management and employee talent that
has never been given the opportunity to flourish until exhaustive and fundamental training approaches have been put
into operation. Training courses, such as those mentioned in
this study, at all times have produced a great many suggestions and ideas for improving effectiveness and performance
within organisations generally, as well as changing people's
attitudes. Within companies very often there is no outlet for
people to make their ideas known, and although suggestion
schemes go some way towards allowing this, they do not

54 always allow the individual to 'let off steam'. I have witnessed how action meetings as illustrated in this study can for example act as a safety valve and as various management levels can be involved no-one has to wait months for feedback; *it is immediate.*

When feedback is not expeditious work of whatever nature becomes a killing activity. When will managers realise that *feedback* is a powerful motivator?

Whilst discussing training I have found too that the upper levels of management who have normally been exposed to a certain amount of management training previously in their management careers, assist considerably in explaining difficult concepts to persons who have never been exposed to management training at all. A mixture of people from vertical levels rather than just a cross-section of the one level is not only a good thing, but a valuable exercise. Often such mixtures provide a very great deal of enthusiasm and stimulation. In fact what I have discovered with 'vertical' training is that rather than being mute, the lower levels of management do respond to the training programme very well and the level of discussion is always relevant, honest as well as enjoyable— with many useful ideas being expounded. What should *not* be allowed to happen is for the impetus and enthusiasm which has been created during any training programme to be dissipated for want of adequate follow-up.

Being fed the correct food of information, delegates and participants usually usher forth with the correct food for thought. Then a demise occurs in the myth that people should not be involved with any change activity because 'they don't have a clue what it's all about... and anyway they're not damn well interested'.

The new building itself

There are of course the problems that can always occur with contractors and the UK weather, resulting in late completion of a building. There are also the problems that arise from varying occupancy in different buildings at different times.

With a Head Office still in use until 1978 there is no maximum economic return in the short term, and therefore tempers and frustration can become fraught. The training programmes cover these unforeseen circumstances, and people appreciate the problems that can, and do occur with phased moves of this nature. Understanding is more than half the battle.

Design consultants have worked very closely with Sun Life on the lay-out of the building in Bristol. A lot of thought has gone into designing the most effective layouts for work purposes and the project teams have subscribed numerous ideas on this. Motivation is not possible when job descriptions are straight-jacketed and nor is it possible when work areas provide no climate for the 'job content' factors to be pursued.

Costs

As regards the financial aspects Sun Life would expect to effect savings in respect of office rental, rates, reduction in London Allowance, reduced staff turnover and, possibly, reduction in manning levels due to the introduction of more sophisticated systems.

From 1974 to 1978 there will, of course, be the costs of moving, refurbishing the new offices and generous assistance to staff in moving house, but these will be non-recurring. In addition there will be costs in the development of new systems and the temporary extra increase in staff in departments leading up to the transfer of work to Bristol. It is possible that communication costs will be higher, but these must be viewed in relation to the substantial savings anticipated with rental and rates.

The great benefit to staff will be improved travelling, working and living conditions, including Flexible Working Hours. This should, in turn, mean better, fitter and happier staff, leading to increased business efficiency and output.

Co-operation

The spontaneous co-operation that has resulted through the various introductions to change and training programmes has paid off, for without it the process could be much more traumatic. Understanding why there is a need to relocate and having a say in the relocation has brought tremendous co-operation from all work areas. Once this involvement occurs, one is that much nearer to satisfying the most mature need of

56 all in an individual—his dignity.

All in all the motto for the Sun Life Assurance Society looks like being true to its word:

'We can brighten up your future.'

Fred Olsen Lines

Millwall Dock, London

You'll never get change, and you'll never get this kind of trust and co-operation in a company when you have managers who are figureheads.

A member of the Works Committee, Fred Olsen Lines, London

I am grateful to Gordon Morris, who was the Divisional Manager of Fred Olsen Lines at Millwall Dock, London. Also to the Works Committee members—Jack Connolly, Fred Moore, Alex Coveney, Jim Lear and Sid Newton—who all contributed to my enjoyable stint in Dockland.

At Millwall Dock in the heart of London's East End can be found one of Europe's most modern and stream-lined port terminals. It belongs to the Fred Olsen organisation and is centred in its own dock/terminal complex which was built in 1967.

The Fred Olsen Lines fleet of multi-purpose vessels makes it one of the most modern floating 'warehouses' on the North Sea. The main features of these multi-purpose vessels are:

1   Equally suitable for roll-on/roll-off, lift-on/lift-off and truck-to-truck methods of loading and discharging cargo.
2   Hatches in the upper and 'tween decks are as large as possible to permit the handling of large cargoes and optimum stowage of containers—and, with the 'tween-deck covers, are capable of being folded back to provide almost single-decker openess whenever required.
3   A total cargo space of 220,000 cubic feet and a dead-weight of 2700 tons on a gross tonnage of less than 1600.
4   Laden speed of 15 knots.

In the UK Fred Olsen Lines is divided up into five divisions: Cargo Operations; Agency; Ship Operations; Passenger; Ship

Broking. Each Division is controlled by a Divisional Manager, like Gordon Morris who heads Cargo Operations. In his terminal there are between 450 and 500 personnel, involved in such operations as clerical work, maintenance and accounts, and including some 240 dock workers.

This approximate number of 500 employees exist to serve clients who want cargo moved across the oceans, and to do this faster and cheaper through high productivity and efficiency. To help with part of this objective the Fred Olsen Centre covers 32 acres, with berths for five ships. There are also extensive warehousing facilities and lock-up areas for valuable and high-duty shipments. The lay-out of the warehouses and the large canopies facilitate continuous delivering and receiving even in bad weather. There are 80 fork-lift trucks with a maximum capacity of between 5000 and 8000 lb, 30 large pallet-handlers and a container-handler cum large fork-lift with a capacity of 25 tons. Three mobile cranes with capacities of 630 and 100 tons are in operation continuously. (It is actually a combined cargo and cruise terminal, but for the purposes of this study we are only involved with the cargo operations.)

The 240 dock workers are represented in the Fred Olsen organisation through their works committee (labour) whilst the clerical and office committees represent the affairs and working life of other personnel in the terminal.

Often only lip service is paid to works committees and I was at first sceptical about the influence of this one. However the company's reputation for first-class productivity and efficiency is due to the high level of industrial relations between the management and the terminal work-force. This is especially impressive when one considers that this company is surrounded by a dockland not renowned for harmonious labour relations.

There are no ranks or titles within this organisation; everyone is on Christian name terms, therefore I was not surprised to meet with the works committee representatives as Jack, Fred, Alex, Jim and Sid. This Works Committee has been the main force of change, so allow me to detail its composition.

There are ten members—five from management and five from employees:

1   They hold office for two years; two from each side retire one year and three the next, although they can offer themselves for re-election.

2   The chairman and vice-chairman are elected from the management side in one year, and in the next from the employees.
3   The secretary and deputy are elected from the group not represented by the chairman and vice-chairman.
4   The committee meets on the first Friday of each month in works time at 8.30 a.m. or, when circumstances require, at other times which are convenient.
5   Six members must be present to form a quorum, of which one must be the chairman or secretary.
6   An agenda is drawn up and distributed to all committee members at least three days before the meeting, and only items appearing in the agenda are discussed.
7   An account of each meeting is published, the company giving every assistance in the printing of minutes and so on.

Unlike the practice in a number of companies the minutes are not just placed on a notice board for decoration but are also distributed with an account of each meeting to all employees with their wages (an example is given in Appendix F, p159). A copy is also sent to the trades unions (the Transport and General Workers Union and the National Amalgamated Stevedores and the Dockers' Union).

Significantly, the preamble to the AGREEMENT between the trade union and the Fred Olsen Company states:

'the prime objective (of the agreement) is to establish the Olsen terminal as the most efficient in the Port of London and manned by a well-trained and highly skilled labour force. It is mutually agreed that the maximum utilisation of manpower with the efficient use of cargo handling machinery is an essential feature to the success of this enterprise and is tended to increase productivity.'

Works councils and committees which involve direct worker participation in the actual running of the company strike me as very un-British—perhaps that is because I don't see too many of them running and operating in the UK yet. All too often they have deteriorated into loo-paper and half-penny-on-the-canteen-tea issues, as opposed to much more demanding matters, e.g. bridging the gap between worker and management. (A good example of this kind of discussion can be found within the Volkswagen organisation in Wolfsburg, Germany. Their works council [the *Betriebsrat*] would discuss at fortnightly intervals what management and unions are doing *for* their employees as opposed to doing *to* them [see my earlier book, *Not for Bread Alone*, Business Books, 1973].)

Within the Fred Olsen company job content was discussed as vivaciously by the Works Committee as were conditions of work, and the *use* of people was as important an agenda item as the *treatment* of those same people.

I'm not advocating that we in the UK should have a legal framework for works' councils such as Germany and other countries of Europe live with. More days' work are lost in the UK through voluntary absence, bad timekeeping, uncertified sickness, certified absence due to sprains, strains and nervousness, plus industrial accidents, than are lost through industrial disputes. The statutory intervention of the Industrial Relations Act could not and did not solve these problems, and it is these that are the great disruptors of UK industry—particularly in mass production. A 30 per cent absenteeism factor in a car plant for example, brings as much disruption in terms of costs as does absence of components. The Industrial Relations Act may have cured some of the UK ills associated with unofficial and wild-cat stoppages but did it make any improvements (as had been hoped) in the harmony between management and shop floor? In other words, I see little example of statutory intervention in industrial democracy becoming a breeding ground for worthy examples of good human relations; likewise, if worker participation were to be legally imposed on companies, perhaps through amendments to the Companies Acts or, for example, the Trade Union and Labour Relations Act, I think it would fail. Adding to present laws to demonstrate to workers (and management) that they *must* share an active interest in their company will have little, if any, effect if a gulf of alienation exists within that company. Rather, the *them* and *us* image could deteriorate into further estrangement. Compulsory works councils and committees (similar to some in other countries) might not even result in a psychological improvement unless relationships between managers and managed already offer encouragement and optimism.

These were some of the thoughts I had when with the management and Works Committee at Fred Olsen Lines. The five committee members mentioned once had a reputation in dockland for being the most militant of dockers—perhaps they still have! One tends to always associate militancy with bloodymindedness, irrational thinking and no common sense whatsoever. This certainly was not the case with Jack, Fred, Alex, Jim and Sid. The most down-to-earth common sense came through at their committee meetings.

Let me briefly explain what Fred Olsen has done to *prove* to its employees that the company are genuine when they say 'the employees are the company'.

Motivational opportunities

Growth through recognition and identity

Once a week briefing groups are held with the Divisional Manager. The briefing group is a 'brief' face-to-face encounter on a regular formalised basis within works hours during which information can be passed down to the grass roots level in an organisation and questions asked can be answered by the person leading the group. The Divisional Manager talks with up to 30 men during one hour from 7 a.m., i.e. from the start of the day shift. The senior management are there with their employees involving them in the terminal operations, discussing various issues arising from day-to-day events in and relating to the company and their job contents. The briefing group is a splendid way of relating the needs of the company to those of the individual employee—and vice versa.

Growth through learning and advancement

As well as the motivation that accompanies the identity each employee derives from communication involvement, there are also mammoth training schemes allowing all employees to attend day release courses at technical colleges to further their industrial education in the Port Transport industry. Added to this there are in-company management development schemes, plus group-training schemes. On-the-job development and training is an essential factor in the motivation of the individual.

The Works Committee which is totally involved in the day-to-day running of the company is responsible for organising and improving the standards of work, and co-operates in the introduction of new techniques and work methods. There is a great deal of job flexibility and rotation which can be a tremendous asset in this industry as in others. Not only does it prevent the employee from getting bored and, therefore, not giving his best, but it allows management to cope with both increased work flows and the demands of crises. It may be that someone doesn't want to drive a fork-lift truck around all day therefore he can be moved somewhere else. As the committee said *'No one likes to think he is a robot'.* Naturally this flexibility will have to be accompanied by an increase in job training which, as I have said earlier, is itself a motivational factor and is something the company prides itself on. A lot of dock work is already done in groups (gangs) and there is mounting evidence to prove that people do work and produce better when working in groups. This is also highlighted in the GLC case study. However, as the group is a tightly knit social community, it is difficult to gain individual employee flexibility without giving due regard to the group. This consideration is part of the task of supervision, itself well trained in Fred Olsen Lines through the management development programme which covers the areas of human relations and group behaviour.

Through the co-operation of the Works Committee it has been possible to gain something at Fred Olsen Lines that is still being aimed for at other wharves in the UK—namely, this force of men at the terminal who have become fully flexible and mobile in any cargo-handling operation.

Standard work conditions

Another point worth mentioning is that some of the wharf activities I have seen in other terminals have not been accompanied by the high standard of morale that I encountered in the Fred Olsen Terminal. Perhaps this is due to some of the standard work conditions that had been introduced by management in an attempt to prove to the employees that 'we're all in this together'.

There is only one restaurant, which is heavily subsidised and where all the staff eat (it is considered to be the best in Dockland!).

There are excellent recreation facilities, and the amenity centre is second to none for its showers, changing rooms, lockers, plus the habitual taped music: all a very pleasing change from washing your hands in a bucket of filthy water (if you're lucky) on one of the vessels in port.

There is one car park and an emphasis on single status which has eradicated many of the old dockland communication problems. In the company, 'if you have a complaint you know exactly who to take it to, and you can go right away and you know it will be dealt with'. The briefing group system of course encourages this; there is great emphasis on not allowing wounds or sores to fester but rather dealing with grievances at source through better supervision, and through a works committee that is accountable to its members for satisfactory solutions to Dockland problems.

Another reason why morale is that much higher in Fred Olsen Lines than elsewhere in Dockland is the fact that the piece-rate system of wages has been abolished. No payment system can be without its strains and injustices, but there is no question that going on to a fixed, stable basic weekly wage contributes to harmony within the organisation. Knowing there is a fixed income contributes to the security of the employee, and the company has a free life-insurance scheme while a pension-scheme is available to all employees.

I was sceptical at first—three committees in operation—clerical, office and this one, labour. There is also a Social and Amenity Committee (that's the one that concerns itself with the canteen tea!). There is also an Equipment Committee recommending equipment which could be bought, should be bought and which is most suitable for the men. Not even a piece of machinery would be bought without the people who were to use it having been involved at the very beginning in its choice. But the committees do work; 'Management do not pay lip service to this sort of thing. If they just asked us what we thought, then went ahead and did what they wanted any-way—where would that get us? Certainly not change, but back to the old days where there was no trust between us, the dockers, and 'em'.

If one looks at Figure 5.1 it can be seen that management and the Fred Olsen Lines' Works Committee concentrate on making all the items in the outer ring correct. How we *treat* people well is by making sure that all the factors in the outer ring are maintained to a satisfactory standard in the work place. When not satisfactory there will be *complaint* until they are corrected to everyone's satisfaction. As people expect more from the standard of both their working and home lives these factors will continue to warrant replenishment and will constantly have to be brought up to date and remain at the highest possible standard.

However, Fred Olsen Lines are also deliberately developing the 'motivators' illustrated in Figure 5.1.

How we *use* people more effectively is by ensuring that all the factors in the inner circle relating to the job content are also maintained to a satisfactory standard. When not satisfactory there will be complaints, and the absence of motivational opportunities brings different and more costly symptoms.

The sort of *industrial sabotage* that I mentioned earlier in the Vosper Thornycroft study, once known as the English disease, has spread its infection throughout other countries— apathy, laziness, carelessness, emibttered militancy, bloody-mindedness, plus poor timekeeping, absences and what has become the colloquialism 'bad morale'. No amount of legal action based on the framework of an Industrial Relations Act will stop this kind of malignancy if the factors in the inner circle of Figure 5.1 are neglected or ignored. It is far too easy to pay lip service to these concepts: what matters is that they should be developed into the organisation's way of thinking and operating in every-day running of the company. As the Works Committee at Fred Olsen Lines said to me at our last meeting, 'You'll never get this sort of change, or this kind of trust and co-operation in a company when you have managers who are figureheads. The only figurehead we have here in Olsen is what we have on every ship!'

And that is so often what company figureheads are—the bust on the bows of a sailing ship.

Certainly there is patronage in Fred Olsen Lines as in so many companies who have used it as a means of obtaining labour from their employees—almost like prostitution. However as fringe benefits become more and more of a costly carrot and trade unions will not allow management to use the stick, perhaps we can take some note of Fred Olsen Lines, who have combined the patronage with the participation to obtain the productivity.

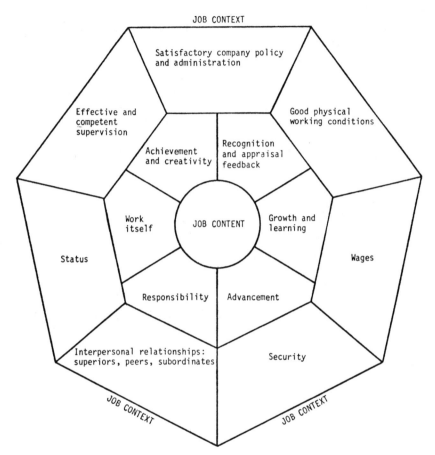

Figure 5.1 MOTIVATION TO WORK: an illustration of what motivates individuals to work. The inner circle is job content and the motivators, whilst the outer circle is the job context and the environment in which the job is done. Reproduced from *Not for Bread Alone – an appreciation of job enrichment* (Business Books, 1973)

It is in fact this company's deliberate attempt at building the 'motivators' into an individual's work life that probably typifies the strongest foundation of all for industrial democracy.

The old battle cry that we used to hear from the dockers as they walked through the gates under the auspice of a wildcat strike 'We don't know what we're out for but we're not going back 'till we get it' has, at least in this part of Dockland, not been heard since 1967.

That alone proves that change through participation—in an industry which never easily made friends with change—has in fact paid off.

Greater London Council: Housing Maintenance Department

Tempora Mutantur nos et mutamur in illis.

(Times change and we change with them too.)

John Owen 1560-1622

I would like to acknowledge my appreciation to Mr Bert Graham, the Assistant Director of the GLC Housing Maintenance Department, and to Arthur Dennis, Maintenance Superintendent at Mottingham who provided me with all facilities in the District. I am also grateful to Jack Newby who supervised the assignment and provided many background details.

Housing maintenance is not something that would fill one with awe, but when the housing authority in question has more than 200,000 dwellings which need to be kept in good and habitable condition the task becomes formidable. Even more so when one is aware that the Greater London Council (GLC) is the largest municipal housing authority in the world, and employs in housing maintenance alone some 4000 men operating from eight district centres—each with a housing stock of between 13,000 and 30,000 dwellings. Each year tenants report some 800,000 defects, covering the whole range of household repairs and requiring the services of carpenters, plumbers, bricklayers, plasterers, electricians, painters and glaziers. There are also mobile teams of drain and dust-chute cleaners, fencing and boarding-up workers, and gardeners.

In addition to building maintenance there is also the planned maintenance of both structure and ancillary parts, including such work as the periodic inspection of high rise blocks, resurfacing of courtyards and estate roads, large scale replacement of fencing, external and internal painting plus redecoration of all vacant dwellings. Added to this is the routine maintenance of all services, e.g. inspection of water and space heating, mechanical ventilation and lifts, cleaning of drains and gulleys and the replacement of defective parts such as window joinery and external cladding: the problems of condensation, mould growth and structural troubles due to design defects, thermal movement or settlement of foundations add to the lists.

Most of the estates in which the houses and flats are grouped are in the Greater London area but there are also 15 cottage estates outside the area and 18 groups of old peoples' bungalows in various seaside towns.

The dwellings are of many types, ranging from one-room bungalows to maisonettes and flats in modern tower blocks up to 33 storeys high.

There also exist groups of mobile houses and temporary bungalows plus property bought for eventual demolition or development, but which is occupied for a limited period. There are also the associated amenities such as landscape features, estate gardens, playgrounds, clubrooms, administrative offices and works departments, which all have to be maintained under the Maintenance Department.

The basic objectives of the GLC are to maintain the fabric of the buildings, to redecorate part of the interior of the dwellings, and, where possible, to improve the standard of fittings and equipment within the dwellings. From the work I saw, it was apparent that the council aims at a very high standard, one far in excess of that imposed by statute; its efficiency and standard of maintenance would embarrass, perhaps shame, many private landlords with considerably fewer tenants.

The annual housing maintenance budget is planned as part of the GLC's overall financial strategy for the allocation of resources to all its manifold services and responsibilities. Within this context the maintenance estimates provide for expenditure by the various trades concerned in day-to-day maintenance, for contract expenditure on routine works and for major reinstatement works and special schemes.

One can appreciate the size of the problem by viewing the finance side and perusing the estimated expenditure on dwell-

ing maintenance. During 1973/4, for example, the estimated
expenditure was as shown in Figure 6.1. These figures are
likely to have increased in inflationary years like 1974-6.

The painting and decorating figure may seem unusually
high in the expenditure list but it is not incongruous when
one considers the painting and decorating programme. External painting, for example, is planned on a five-year cycle and
over 40,000 dwellings are completed each year. Also, once
every five years the GLC redecorates the hall, landing and

Painting and decoration	£5,760,000
Other repairs and renewals	£8,100,000
Upkeep of gardens	£880,000
Minor improvements including miscellaneous estates work	£710,000
Repairs and reconditioning of acquired properties	£600,000

Figure 6.1 Estimated expenditure for 1973/74

staircase of all houses and maisonettes, and the hall and one
bedroom of flats and bungalows—and even, in some cases, the
inside of the window frames. The GLC also helps its disabled
and very old tenants by arranging all the necessary redecoration. Current policy is also to redecorate a dwelling after it
has been vacated, prior to being re-let. The tenant is responsible for the redecoration of the remainder of the dwelling,
however even bearing this in mind in no way deters the popu-
lar concensus that Council tenants like 'to be looked after'.
The gardening expenditure for example includes mobile
teams of gardeners who move from estate to estate on regular
programmes of grass cutting, plus the maintenance of shrub-
beries, privet hedges, and garden features. Hedge clipping and
splitting is an important item, particularly on cottage estates,
while defective trees are replaced and even plant propagation
is carried out in nurseries. Currently an additional 7000 new
trees are planted every year.

The first block of permanent dwellings was built before
1900, thus improvement programmes additional to the maintenance programme take a massive slice of the Council's resources. The Maintenance Branch assist by including in their
programme such items as the provision of modern slow-burn-
ing appliances and gas ignition which came in under the pro-

visions of the Clean Air Act. Added to this is bath replacement and the installation of wash basins where required, while properties built between 1919 and 1939 require installation of water heating systems. Understandably, preventative maintenance is often undertaken to reduce some of the long-term maintenance service expenditure. Maintenance standards are established and agreed as illustrated in Appendix G, p162. These standards are reviewed annually.

The Central Office for Housing Maintenance has at its head Bert Graham, the Assistant Director, whose prime job is as a co-ordinator, or supervisor. He is the driving force behind the organisation, co-ordinates all work of the districts and instructs the same eight districts on policy and technical matters. This includes the monitoring of various programmes of work, e.g. measuring the work done each week against the Council's service standards; monitoring external and internal painting programmes; servicing programmes; preventative maintenance programmes; inspection and budgeting control.

Bert Graham has a team of specialist officers dealing with modernisation, rehabilitation, special works, heating, electrical and horticultural activities, and liaises with the Director of Electrical and Mechanical Services over all electrical and mechanical equipment, including boiler houses. Each of the eight districts have, as I indicated, a housing stock of between 13,000 and 30,000 dwellings and in charge of each district is a District Officer responsible for both the management and day-to-day maintenance. Each District Officer has a Senior Maintenance Surveyor and a supporting staff of Technical Surveyors, Superintendents and work study assistants. The operatives and the supervisory staffs are responsible to a District Planning Foreman. There is also a stores organisation for each district, supervised by a Stores Superintendent, and finally a Transport section. The Maintenance Surveyor is responsible for all the types of work which I have indicated so far in this study, within his District.

Arthur Dennis is the Maintenance Superintendent at Mottingham District, which covers a number of boroughs including Woolwich, Greenwich, Bexley and Wapping. There are 24,000 homes to be maintained in his District, and 463 men under Arthur Dennis are responsible for the maintenance.

Originally there was within the District a 'building-industry' type bonus scheme which had been in operation for some years. Like many similar bonus schemes it was disliked

by both management and the trade unions because under it
pay seemed variable and 'unfair', and because efficiency was
poor. The GLC asked for external consultants to complete
a survey of the situation which stated that a fair bonus
scheme should be introduced based on Work Study.

No changes were made within the GLC for a further thirteen months. As has been witnessed in other case studies this
delay is not unusual. Resistance to any form of change is
quite natural and the time spent over that thirteen-month
period, January 1966 to February 1967, in the GLC, as in
other studies, was spent *talking*—with management, men, shop
stewards and trade unions, teaching them to understand the
principles of such fundamentals as the work study scheme
that had been proposed. It took two years for the assignment
to be completed as can be appreciated from the GLC background that I have indicated. When work started the original
manpower total was 6500 operatives, and they were working
from many workshops scattered throughout the GLC estates.
Planning and control of work flow was naturally difficult—as
indeed was supervision, since it was a time-consuming job discovering where each man was!

During the course of the assignment, the management
structure was changed, work planning offices were set up and
the men became organised in the main into groups of 5-15.
They were provided with transport and junior supervisors
travelled with each gang.

Figure 6.2 indicates the organisational structure for the
District office and its relationship to the GLC central office.

Now in each District there is a Planning Office under a
Maintenance Superintendent, like Arthur Dennis. He is
responsible to the Senior Maintenance Surveyor for organising all direct labour work, such as repairs of minor defects
reported by tenants and which would require the services of
carpenters, plumbers, glaziers, electricians, etc. He is also
responsible for work resulting from regular inspections of
estates, and ensuring that developing maintenance problems
are detected in an early stage, for as I mentioned earlier the
only way to ensure reductions in long-term maintenance expenditure is to practise preventative maintenance. A Maintenance Superintendent is also responsible for ensuring that the
painting schedules for the Forth Bridge are carried out, plus
such things as routine maintenance of services, like the clean-

ing of dust chutes, drains and gulleys, etc. In these responsibilities he is assisted by a District Planning Foreman who has special responsibility for labour, materials, safety and plant, and also by a queries officer who supervises the planning clerks. They ensure a speedy and organised flow of the written requests for work to be carried out. It is this office which prepares the weekly programmes of the mobile trade-gangs, and statistics are prepared weekly on the GLC computer showing the current work load, outstanding jobs and any arrears of work, and also identifying any jobs not completed within the service standards.

Districts are divided into sectors, and generally in each sector there is a mobile team of carpenters, one of plumbers and one of bricklayers. There are also mobile teams of drain and dust chute cleaners, glaziers, electricians, gardeners and where justified, special teams to deal with fencing and with the boarding-up of empty houses against vandalism. In Mottingham District alone there are seven miles of fencing that need to be maintained.

Each mobile team is supervised by a chargehand of the same trade and all the work in a sector is controlled and organised by a sector foreman. Working according to the schedules mapped out for them in the planning office, each team moves through the sector carrying out the jobs on each

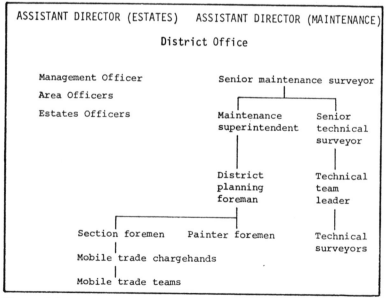

Figure 6.2

group of properties until all repair work is completed, before moving on to the next group. This organisational structure allows a two-way communication and information network to exist; before it was implemented, people worked very much on their own. Now, however, the 463 men in Arthur's District know exactly who their boss is and where he is, and grievances which used to become mountains simply because they were harboured for considerable periods of time can remain as molehills—for there is immediate access to a member of the management team, whether chargehand, sector foreman or Arthur Dennis.

The working group has its benefits also... when simply a random member of the work force, it is understandable that the individual feels his identity is lost in a sea of bureaucracy, and that the only way to be noticed is to sabotage the machine or the man who made it. This can be done with success in a number of forms ranging from absenteeism to 'down tools', from a carelessness with the end product to a 'don't care' attitude resulting in apathy and disinterest. Working within closely knit groups one can at the very least relate to other individuals within the group and absenteeism on a Monday morning is less frequent as 'it's your mates you're letting down, not the GLC'. Having a hierarchy of autonomous and manageable groups is also a boon when passing GLC information and policy 'down the line'. True participation cannot evolve unless such a two-way communication and information process exists—and is both expeditious and effective.

During the assignment, for example, the number of men was reduced to 4611 from 6500. This was done through natural wastage and to date the numbers have reduced further to around 3500 who all carry out an increased work load. Consultants are often greeted by a company's employees with contempt, as it is considered that they come accompanied by numerous redundancy notices. This fear of security being threatened, as well as the natural fear that exists for change as a whole, makes the consultants' job very difficult. To have a group organisational structure such as this one in the GLC, however, allows briefing sessions and training to take place where the exchange of understanding can help make the path of change that much easier to walk on.

In all the case studies it can be seen that change cannot happen in isolation; it must have as its ally commitment and responsibility from the top team of management. The leadership qualities of Bert Graham were appreciated at grass roots level and it was considered that, mainly through his enthusiasm and full commitment to the changes being introduced, were the benefits of the work study assignment as high as they were. The operatives' response to the new incentive bonus scheme was also well accepted, due in the main to the detailed and lengthy communication and negotiation procedures lasting just over twelve months in all. The net financial benefit achieved through the work study assignment was £1,703,700 per annum, and the actual reduction in wages paid was £1,669,000 per annum. A recent check showed that if the work was carried out by contractors on a competition-tender basis the additional cost to the Council would be over £5,000,000—vital stuff in the days of council-bashing.

The work study assignment also improved the service to tenants, and this can be measured by the reduction in the work back-log. When the assignment started, there was, in some Districts, a back-log of the order of 10-12 weeks. This was improved to 4-5 weeks. The average target times for dealing with routine non-urgent repairs are five weeks for bricklayers, four weeks for carpenters, three weeks for plumbers, two weeks for glazing and one week for electrical repairs. Emergency jobs are dealt with in 24 hours. The target times are still continuing to improve with most figures and the work back-log is on average 2-3 weeks. In addition, a large back-log of painting and decorating work as well as repairing structural defects has been eradicated.

It was felt however that despite the involvement throughout the Housing Maintenance Districts, it had not been sufficient at intermediate management levels. A programme of work to install Management by Objectives (MBO) procedures was recommended.

There were 90 intermediate managers, and they were all interviewed. Having become acquainted with them during the first part of the assignment both the consultants and senior GLC officers had acquired a fairly deep knowledge of them and their work and a training programme was designed which was to last over a period of about three months. These training sessions were highly participative and involved both the consultants and the GLC officers conducting the various sessions. The concepts behind the formal MBO procedures were explained in detail, and Figures 6.3 and 6.4 show the training courses for the foremen, Senior Maintenance Survey-

FOREMEN - The foremen will be split into three groups, A, B and C; sessions will be from 9.00 a.m. until 4.30 p.m. unless stated otherwise.

Session	Subject	Dates
First	Introduction and Opening Remarks Objectives of Course Communications I: Introduction Personal impact	A - Wed 25 Feb B - Tue 3 Mar C - Wed 4 Mar
Second	Communications II: Persuasion Preparation and content Finding common ground Organisation and Methods: General introduction Case study	A - Tue 10 Mar B - Tue 17 Mar C - Wed 18 Mar
Third	Communications III: Face-to-face technique Overcoming objections Communicating leadership Role playing using video tape Seeing ourselves as others see us	A - Wed 1 Apr B - Tue 7 Apr C - Tue 14 Apr
Fourth	Role of the Foreman: Function and responsibilities Effectiveness and guidance to chargehands Selection, development and training Discipline and sickness procedures Principles Case studies	A - Wed 15 Apr B - Tue 21 Apr C - Wed 22 Apr
Fifth	Metrication and Decimalisation Management Development I: Human aspects Understanding motivation Management and tenant viewpoint: Council's and management's attitude Problems in practice	A - Wed 29 Apr B - Wed 6 May C - Wed 13 May
Sixth	Management Development II: Key Target Areas Performance plans and controls Counselling and reviews Review of Course and Closing Remarks	A - Wed 27 May B - Wed 3 Jun C - Tue 9 Jun

Figure 6.3 Management development course for foremen

SENIOR MAINTENANCE SURVEYORS AND MAINTENANCE SUPERINTENDENTS -
Sessions will be from 9.00 a.m. until 4.30 p.m. unless stated otherwise.

Session	Subject	Dates and times
First	Introduction and Opening Remarks Objectives of Course and Film	Fri 20 Feb (9.00-12.30)
Second	Communications I: Introduction; Language Barriers; Emotional Barriers	Fri 27 Feb (9.00-1.00)
Third	Network Analysis: General introduction; Case study Role of Senior Maintenance: Surveyor and maintenance; Superintendent - functions and responsibilities	Wed 11 Mar
Fourth	Communications II: Finding the meeting place; Listening	Fri 11 Mar (9.00-1.00)
Fifth	Budgetary Control: General principles; Case study Estimating Expenditure: Procedure; Case study	Fri 20 Mar (9.00-1.00)
Sixth	Communications III: Leading people; Application of effective communication	Fri 10 Apr
Seventh	Role of Foreman Disciplines & Sickness Procedures *Course members will each join one of the three sessions on the foreman's course*	A - Wed 15 Apr B - Tue 21 Apr C - Wed 22 Apr
Eighth	Management & Tenant Viewpoint *Course members will each join one of the three afternoons on the foreman's course*	A - Wed 29 Mar B - Wed 6 Apr C - Wed 13 May (1.30-4.30)
Ninth	Organisation and Methods: General introduction; Case study Management Development I: Key Target Areas	Tue 5 May
Tenth	Management Development II: Performance plans & controls Case Study - Visit	Tue 2 Jun
Eleventh	Management Development III: Performance appraisal and development Behavioural aspects of management Review of Course/Closing Remarks	Wed 10 Jun

Figure 6.4 Management development course for senior maintenance surveyors and maintenance superintendents

one of the Maintenance Superintendents on such a course
and he found it both challenging and stimulating.

The opportunity for learning and development is a long-
term motivator (see Figure 5.1 in the Fred Olsen Lines case
study) and as these case studies show, the maximising of the
resources of a company's human assets has a long term pay-
off. Arthur Dennis is convinced that there are many people in
his district who have latent talent, waiting to be released—his
problem is in discovering it. Arthur Dennis himself is a case in
point: for 27 years he was a 'chippy'—a carpenter—before
becoming a chargehand, then acting foreman for 3½ years.
He then progressed through the various foreman stages and
did specialist training before gaining promotion to Maintenance Superintendent. He enjoys 'working for the council' and
has progressed his way through the organisation to his present
position, in charge of 463 men. Having had little basic education and having started life in a basement bed-sit south of the
Thames, he now drives fast cars, lives an English-village style
and has a wife who is a fashion designer. One would expect
the job of Maintenance Superintendent to be very much the
overall-and-boots scene, but it is collar and tie and west-end
shirts (although in Arthur's case his wife designs and sews
them making his appearance extra special). He has days
where he spells badly but states that this is an advantage as it
gives him a good excuse not to write notes and so add to the
mountain of paper work! Communication, he feels, should
be face-to-face and, as I emphasised, with the formalised
group structure throughout the District this can be done with
speed and efficiency.

After the training sessions, job descriptions, key target
areas (KTAs) and performance plans were drawn up with the
managers. At every stage Bert Graham was deeply involved.

The managers soon began to work to their performance
plans (such as the one in Figures 6.5), filled in control docu-
ments showing their achievements in the KTAs, and had the
formal feedback meeting with Bert Graham at regular intervals—initially quarterly, then half-yearly. This must be considered very important as working without feedback is a killing activity. Although an organisation's recognition of
achievement by its employees can be shown by such things as
promotion and salary increase dependent (at least in part) on
past successful performance, all too often many organisations

GLC HOUSING MAINTENANCE BRANCH
Senior Maintenance Surveyor Performance Plan agreed with Assistant Director of Housing (Maintenance) at March 1973 for period
1 April 1973 to 30 September 1973

OBJECTIVE: To maintain the Council's dwellings and estates to the approved standard, prevent property falling into a state of
disrepair and give tenants a speedy and economic repairs service

Key Target Area (KTA)	Performance Target	Method of checking and evaluating
1 Programming and budgetary control	(a) Allocate approved financial budget for 1973/4 into monthly programmes for all central and local contract work. These to be prepared in order of priority and when agreed with the AD(H) to be worked to accurately. These to include preventative maintenance (b) Agree central contract programme with M2 including time phasing of work and starting dates (c) Ensure contract expenditure does not exceed budget provision. Global District budget figure (direct labour and contract) must not be exceeded (d) Ensure correct coding of all expenditure including job ticket support work and specially costed estates	(a)(i) Programmes for April, May and June to be submitted within 7 days of Performance Plan agreement date above (ii) Programme for remainder of year to be submitted by 1 May 1973 (b) Agree with M2 within 14 days of AD(M)'s programme approval in writing (c) Compare monthly computer expenditure print-out with District record of orders and expenditure and ensure no orders are issued if finance not available. Consult M5, Mr Osborne, if there is any discrepancy in the comparison. Consult Mr Osborne, M5, or AD(M) if additional finance is required for any maintenance work (d) Check print-out for correct expenditure heads against your records. Consult Mr Osborne, M5, if any problems arise
2 Planning of work load and servicing	(a) SMS to familiarise himself with revised average service standards (5,4,3,2,1,etc.) and these must not be exceeded. No job tickets to be outstanding over 8 weeks from date of issue. (Lost tickets, computer errors, must be dealt with within 24 hours of receipt of computer print-out) (b) Difficult access cases to be dealt with by appointment	(a) Weekly computer job ticket print-out to be studied in conjunction with forward planning of work loads to ensure standards achieved at all times (b) Out of hours or Saturday working can be agreed in difficult cases by MS

annual estimates of expenditure for building maintenance and services	to comply with the PPBS format direct labour and contract and agree figures with M5, Mr Osborne, by 6 August 1973. Collection of data will be a continuing process (b) To prepare programmes of preventative maintenance in consultation with PMO and briefing officers to comply with PPBS multi-year plan	6 August 1973 (b) Report to MDA on programme by 21 July 1973. Then discuss with PMO and AD(M)
4 Production and quality control	(a) The SMS to study production control data, consult Work Study Officer and to chair Weekly Production and Management Control meetings with senior staff and decide action to be taken to improve efficiency, achieve service standards and a good service to tenants (b) Study direct labour force production and control data on (i) effective performance, (ii) pay performance, (iii) labour cost PSH against MbO target, (iv) total cost PSH, (v) overheads for each trade, (vi) direct labour costs compared with contractor's costs, (vii) non-productive time and lost time, (viii) value for money, (ix) sickness, accidents, absenteeism (c) Ensure that all contractors' accounts are checked in accordance with the procedural note (d) To achieve a high quality standard for all work whether carried out by council staff or contractors:(1)Painting and decorating, (2) Day-to-day repairs all trades including gardening and (3) Servicing work, (4) Major contract work, (5) Estate environmental work	(a) Report weekly to MDA for recording and forward to AD(M). Action to be stated and suggestion for improvement (b) Report weekly to MDA for recording and forward to AD(M). Action to be stated and suggestion for improvement (c) All accounts must be checked before authorisation for payment (d) A weekly check to be made by SMS and other senior staff on a programmed basis and report weekly to MDA for recording and forwarding to PMO for attention
5 Reduction of costs	Management by Objectives target costs to be worked to and action taken to achieve a minimum of 10 per cent financial saving over work study budget as shown in the table (see overleaf). The total financial benefit target to be achieved	Study performance costs weekly and take action to achieve MbO target Labour cost PSH and total cost PSH to be separate objectives for achievement
6 MbO for Work Study and Works Executive staff	To introduce with the co-operation of the MDA, management by objectives disciplines for all work study staff	Job description, KTA, Performance Plans to be agreed with MDA and introduced not later than 11 May 1973

Continued overleaf

Trade	Current work study budget cost/PSH	Current MbO target cost/PSH	Target improvement on direct labour budget cost in 'P's	Work Study Budget PSHs per week	Target financial benefit over six months	Current MbO target on total cost PSH
1 Bricklayers	1.28	1.10	18p	1600	7500	2.75
2 Carpenters	1.48	1.34	14p	1260	4575	3.75
3 Plumbers	1.82	1.64	18p	1200	5600	3.85
4 Electricians	1.67	1.40	27p	314	2200	4.45
5 Painters (ext.)	1.17	1.05	11p	6700	19000	2.25
6 Painters (int.)		1.11	6p	1650	2500	
7 Glaziers	1.27	1.15	12p	357	1100	3.10
8 Fencing	1.28	1.08	20p	1445	7500	3.40
9 Gas servicing	1.13	1.02	11p	274	285	
10 Gardeners (summer)	1.16	1.00	16p	1150	4750	2.15
					£55010	

Figure 6.5

come to rely solely on this reward system. The trouble with
this kind of reward is that once given it becomes a 'right'. A
20 per cent salary increase will, at the very least, have to be
20 per cent when the next rise is due (and in many cases it is
considered necessary to give higher percentage increases when
taking into account cost of living, threshold index, etc.). This
kind of reward system escalates rapidly (how recently 10 per
cent was 3 per cent!) and its motivation is only short term.
Letting individuals know how they are doing, as Bert Graham
does in these feedback sessions to the performance plans, is a
psychological motivator—praise for good work, recognition
for hard work and guidance when work is not up to standard.

The example given of a performance plan indicates all the
motivators being used: responsibility, more demanding work,
recognition for achievement, as well as opportunity for
achievement growth and for learning through more interesting as well as more challenging tasks. These motivators, considered and developed in all the case studies in this book,
reap much greater rewards than those hoped for by relying
on the 'rights' system alone.

The GLC allowed the managers to have a say in setting
their objectives and targets for future action—and this applied
to the first liners of the management team, the foreman level.
The motivator of increased responsibility can soon be shown
by making individuals responsible for aspects of their own
work, e.g. for quality as well as quantity, and that brings the
encouragement of group interdependence and mutual help
rather than reliance on outside supervision and technical
assistance. An increase in responsibility is also shown by
allowing the individual more say and control over the financial side of his job, and on Figure 6.5 this is indicated under
the programming and budgetary control section (Figure 6.5,
KTA-1).

Each Senior Maintenance Surveyor has responsibility for
full budgetory control of spending within his District, and
his feedback is through an overall financial position that is
regularly monitored by the central costing system which fur-
nishes the monthly expenditure figures. All of this responsibility also indicates *trust* in the individual, because in effect
they are now doing and undertaking tasks that were previously handled at another level in the organisation. Of course
the managers were given their necessary tools: training in
management principles, advice when sought, information

when requested. At all times there was the back-up system of the service of management—a support system—which radiated from the complete involvement at all times of the people at the top. In this case the support system comprises people like Bert Graham whose enthusiasm is radiated throughout the organisation to people like Arthur Dennis.

When I spoke with Arthur Dennis about the MBO programme he was impressed. Before, 'there was no concept of measure of efficiency, now everyone knows how well they are doing and there are incentives other than money to come to work for'. He wants his District to be the best, and one way of realising that his ambition is being answered is that a great deal of the talent in his District is providing other Districts with expertise. His people are certainly more involved in their work—as can be indicated when viewing the suggestion scheme. As I mentioned earlier, there are seven miles of fencing to be maintained in Mottingham District alone, and until recently the fences were built 'on-site'. This resulted in battles with the elements; when it rained, the fencing gangs hung around in doorways and got bored. The boredom in turn led to high labour turnover and to the job becoming a seasonal one. Now Bert Greenwood runs a fencing factory—the idea which got a suggestion scheme award for one of the fencing gangs. On rainy days the fencing factory allows the building of fences to continue unabated, with the fencing gangs fully employed.

Ideas which sound like common sense, but of course common sense is never that common.

Summary

The psychological pay-off in the GLC Housing Maintenance Branch has been a greater all-round commitment to the job and an enthusiastic involvement. The financial pay-off after the work study, as I mentioned earlier, is £1,703,700 per annum, with a reduction in wages of £1,669,000. The Department considers that they have achieved further benefits, which can be put at around £300,000 per annum, as a result of the new style of participative management.

If one views the Performance Plan (Figure 6.5, KTA-5) it can be seen that it includes a provision to beat the work study budget of financial benefit by 10 per cent. Figure 6.6

Target - 10% below WS Budget			
Trade	MbO target at 14 weeks £	Actual gain £	Actual loss £
Bricklayer	1115	1382	
Carpenter	1350	2374	
Plumber	1240	2628	
Electrician	490	392	
Painter	7160	8871	
Glazier	890	1100	
Dust/drains	270	768	
Gas appliance	270		185
	13085	17805	185
Net gain is thus £17,620 Target achievement = 135% (£4535 over the total target)			

Figure 6.6 MbO profit and loss account for the fourteen-week period 2 April to 8 July 1973

shows that this target was beaten, e.g. by 13.5 per cent in 1973, and that it continues to improve at the time of writing.

This is how people like Bert Graham measure the success of the MBO participative approach of the assignment. If this order of achievement were maintained in each District, the annual financial benefit attributable to the MBO assignment would be half a million pounds.

As for Arthur Dennis, he measures success by the style of cars that his carpenters, electricians, glaziers, plumbers, painters, plasterers and bricklayers drive to work in, and by their general standard of living. He also measures the success of the assignment by the fact that these same men now 'want to do work rather than dodge it'—indeed times have changed, and the people have changed with them.

Case Study Seven
Leyland South Africa

Change is inevitable. In a progressive country
change is constant.

Benjamin Disraeli, 1804-1881

If we could learn to look instead of gawking
We'd see the horror in the heart of farce
If only we would act instead of talking
We would not always end up on our arse.

from *Arturo Ui* by Bertolt Brecht

I am grateful in particular to Basil Landau, who was Deputy Chairman and Managing Director of Leyland South Africa, and who provided me with every facility in his Corporation, both in Johannesburg and Cape Town. Many thanks also to John Barber, then Deputy Chairman and Managing Director of the British Leyland Motor Corporation, for giving me much of his time in discussing various points.

I would also like to thank the National Development and Management Foundation of South Africa for arranging my lecture tour to that part of the world, and for their marvellous hospitality.

In 1974 the Nationalist Party celebrated 25 years of rule in South Africa, a celebration coupled with a world-wide outcry, mainly against UK companies, concerning the living and working conditions of employees of foreign-based subsidiaries there. It seems correct therefore that a book concerning change should contain a case study on a company involved in the development of industrial democracy in an environment that is vastly different from that outlined in the UK and Australian case studies. It is necessary to expound on the South African environment to some degree before discussing the man-management activities within the Leyland Corporation of South Africa.

Fear corrodes the very foundations of both society and change and although, according to Disraeli, in a progressive country change is constant, the fact is that it cannot happen when *fear* exists. Fear exists in South Africa under the veneer of Afrikaaner self-righteousness; it exists despite the materialistic values of the English society in that country. There is fear of permissiveness, of immorality, unorthodoxy, and most of all fear of new ideas and of the change which inevitably must accompany them. There is fear of the future, and the fear that accompanies non-comprehension—as when 60,000 black employees are involved in illegal strikes. When this happened early in 1973, people the world over were forced to realise that this wave of dispute and unrest indicated that, despite the efficient authoritarian regime, black workers could, and do, organise themselves; a warning to us all that their compliancy could be ending sooner than anyone considered.

'Investing in Apartheid' is a familiar cry to any senior executive such as Lord Stokes, at the time of writing President of British Leyland Limited, whose corporation has investment responsibility in SA. Proposals have been flaunted which demand that UK and USA investment is withdrawn from SA, for if it is not, the proposers point out that the Republic can always claim that its present policies have the support of those companies, and countries, which have invested within its borders. (A tendentious argument to those companies who could also be accused of investing in communism if they trade with Poland and East Germany—as in fact British Leyland does.)

The economics are simple—the UK has the largest foreign investment in South Africa, more than 3,000 million Rand in 1973/74. The USA has less than a third of this figure, and is comparable with that of Western Europe. Besides the fact that South African currency control regulations prevent capital already invested from being taken out, this massive investment gives the UK its highest return on all overseas investments. Some people have advocated a policy of sanctions in the belief that no country in this day and age can exist in total isolation. The costly farce of Rhodesia, with its Boeing aircraft on the tarmac at Salisbury, can prove of little encouragement; and on my last visit I felt that the sanctions had a worse effect on those people whose interests we professed to have at heart, rather than on the white community whom we were aiming to influence, restructure and subsequently change.

The positive side of the economics, and one that British Leyland hasten to affirm, is that if we did not invest in South Africa many blacks and coloureds would be unemployed. Our ability to help these employees is dependent therefore on the continued expansion both of the republic's economy and the profitability of UK companies there. There is no better way that these employees could advance towards a Western European standard of living than on the basis of economic growth, which rests in turn on the supply of investment capital.

If investment is the backbone, sport is the Achilles' heel, and it is suggested that a means of forcing change within South Africa would be to break off all diplomatic sports ties. The central issue is one of white domination and although integrated sport may go some way to improving race and inter-race relations it will take more than this to attack the foundations of the issue. Thus, in 1973, the Pretoria Games were multi-racial and yet the spectators were segregated. Contrast two events, one inspiring hope and promised change— the other despair.

Chief Mangope, head of 2½ million Bantu, spoke to 300 white industrialists at the Carlton Hotel in Johannesburg. It was a memorable event. The fact that this man was addressing white industrialists, discussing rational methods of change and ways of coping with that change, was an extraordinary event within South Africa and it is thanks to the National Development and Management Foundation (NDMF) that it occurred. An event in contrast and causing much despair was when Chief Buthelezi, Chief Executive Councillor of the Kwazulu Legislative Assembly danced with a white woman at a Cape Town press ball, there was an example of deeply entrenched and unchanging attitudes. A member of the cabinet said that the event went 'against the grain' and that 'legislation would be passed so that such a thing should never happen again'.

The battle therefore in South Africa is not just for higher standards of wages and living, but for a certain standard of human right and dignity. The progression from the present low-wage, labour-intensive economy to a high-wage, capital-intensive one requires a massive investment and no doubt the UK's assets could be directed this way, not only in capital

goods but also in more constructive forms like education and
training.

The UK's investment in South Africa must be seen to ensure an increase in working and living standards, and to secure full-time employment for all their employees. Without this it is doubtful whether companies can secure motivation and the subsequent pay-offs, such as commitment from their employees.

The concern for the wages and welfare of the lower-paid African workers has had the attention of many UK investment corporations such as British Leyland who had perused the matter before the 1973-74 spate of press disclosures concerning wages levels below the poverty datum level (PDL). The fact was, there were many UK concerns who *were* paying below the PDL, and a great many more who were paying merely the PDL. British Leyland appreciates that the PDL is the minimum rate which its South African operation can offer—not the maximum—and there is nothing to stop British Leyland's Cape Town plant from offering higher rates still, which in fact it does. There can be little excuse for companies paying starvation wages—they are wrong, whichever country they are paid in. The excuse often given is that UK concerns know very little about their South African operations. We will be discussing later in the study how British Leyland have corrected this situation. The Institute for Race Relations in South Africa say they have always been 'pestered' on good employment practices by US firms, and yet rarely approached by our own UK enterprises—this considering that the former have less than a third of our investment interest in the Republic. The Africans that I spoke with certainly would consider themselves very lucky if they worked for General Motors or IBM.

To help facilitate change therefore we must appreciate that although we cannot expect to change the laws governing PDL in a distant country, a company like British Leyland can ensure that their investment interests are used constructively. For example, they can ensure that the jelly beans and fringe benefits at least are available to the black labour force within their South African plants. The best possible work conditions should be sought and provided.

One person I talked with who seemed to be doing rather appalling arduous work on his back in a gold mine said he would rather work there than in a factory in town as he had far better work conditions than some of his township friends. This I can vouch for—the work conditions in the Orange Free State gold-mine were at times better than I had seen in some London West-End offices; certainly 'loo' facilities were not shared by as many employees as I have seen sharing in some city offices, and beer on tap is something we would have to search for on European shop floors!

Therefore, Leyland South Africa ensure that employees have housing facilities, transport, medical services, pensions and sports facilities. Better minimum wages are far from being the only important aspect of advancement. The scope for improving real standards of living through increased minimum wages is in fact strictly limited. UK corporations should be ensuring that their South African operations are moving away from a traditional labour system which has considered the African employees as both interchangeable and unskilled labour units. As British Leyland are eager to assert, jobs should be objectively evaluated and paid, providing both opportunity and motivation for any worker to advance. An important goal that all companies should be striving for is a uniform wage scale for *all* employees, and one based on objective criteria. As British Leyland South Africa plants are finding out, this is a long haul; but everyone knows that change is not easy.

South Africa must change—if only because their national economy can prosper further when both capital and labour have a shared interest.

Economic partnerships the world over have been achieved with greater success where there has been participation between the capital and the labour. This economic partnership must occur before the emerging pattern of social and political co-existence can be achieved with any success. Economic, social, internal and external forces are putting South Africa into a situation where change is inevitable. It is under way, that I will not deny, but all too painfully slowly, mainly because the forces of internal change are too weak. As all the case studies indicate, *leadership at the top is the main instigator and supporter of change.*

In South Africa party politics become ossified with concerns like 'who students are sleeping with', i.e. 'petty-apartheid', and thus the Government seem more and more unsuited to resolving the conflict between black and white. Chief Mangope said

'We are at this moment at the crossroads—let us take it from there and try to focus our attention on the possible alternatives.'

Development of people, like nations, always occurs through action, never through mere contemplation. What has a company like British Leyland been doing about precipitating and coping with change within its South African organisation—changes which will allow for greater employee involvement?

First of all let's look at the manufacturing industry within the Republic. This sector contributes 30 per cent to the economy, thereby ruining the myth that the Republic's economy is based exclusively on agriculture and mining. In some eyes, like those of Basil Landau, who was Leyland South Africa's Deputy Chairman, industrial development will not take over the gold industry's leading position within 25 years, but could in all probability exceed by far the present earnings of gold. Return on capital invested within South Africa is much higher even than it is in the USA, averaging 21 per cent, with only 12 per cent in the USA. Of course, this comparison is a trite unfair—competition is much more fierce within the US market and price-fixing, whilst totally prohibited in the USA, is merely outlawed within SA.

However, within the motor industry worldwide, my experience has been that where there is a motor car it is aligned to cut-throat competition, which in South Africa is painfully tough—particularly at the time of writing (1975). The component manufacturing market must grow in size and in improved profitability, and British Leyland realise that heavy investment is needed in plant and machinery. The training of labour, whilst a high priority in the company's plants, is both a slow and a costly process. Rising costs, as everywhere, mean that sales must constantly increase, especially in these days of continual economic crisis. This is not always easy if you are waiting for components from the UK, and British Leyland admit to losing on average 150,000 cars a year over the last five years through UK strikes. Profit margins are thus continually under pressure. On top of that, the South African Local Content Development Programme requires that the industry produces cars with a local content reaching 66 per cent by 1976, even with the overall limiting factor of small volumes per unit that are available within the republic's market. Costs of production, with such low volumes and short production runs, are both excessive and uneconomical. It is, of course, a problem that faces all competitors in the South African industry, not one peculiar to British Leyland alone.

Now let us turn to the change programme which British Leyland has been involved with, featuring the operation of an overseas subsidiary, and bearing in mind the above environmental issues dominating South Africa.

The South African operation of British Leyland until approximately 1972 was over-autonomous and it got to the stage where the company was doing badly. It was not until Head Office realised how badly that they stepped in and did some sorting out. A spring-clean included the resignation of six out of eight directors. There was a loss of nearly R10 million on the books, as well as other signs of serious inefficiencies.

British Leyland in the UK was only formed itself in 1968 and there were major jobs that had to be done in the integration of various motor car companies from Rover to Jaguar, the Austin-Morris range, through to Daimler. Overseas subsidiaries were not high up on the list of priorities. British Leyland realised that this was a very vulnerable position to be placed in, and when things in South Africa went sour a new organisational structure was formed. Basil Landau was brought in, and as an efficient and enthusiastic company doctor, both he and Head Office collaborated throughout 1973 to bring together a strong management team. Most of the team were 'local', but there was representation on the board by both Lord Stokes, then Chairman of British Leyland, and John Barber who was then the financial man in the organisation and Vice Chairman.

How could British Leyland ensure that things did not get out of control again with their overseas subsidiary in South Africa, whereby both morale and economics could deteriorate?

When Basil Landau was hired there was an agreement in the form of a long letter which stated exactly on what issues he should consult Head Office London. This missive outlined policies such as personnel, as well as product matters, that Head Office would like to be consulted on. The most important part of the undertaking was to ensure that the South African management were sufficiently competent to be able to deal with such local issues as wages—locally a major emotional issue.

A number of decisions are of course taken at Head Office.

As a motor car company they are virtually a single-product company, which makes them very different from either GEC or ICI, for instance. In a conglomerate, more things, much in the product line for example, can be left to the discretion of local management. Let's take the extreme as an example. If British Leyland make an Austin motor car in order to achieve the economies of scale from a world-wide impact, Head Office must make the decisions on what the Austin is going to look like, and generally how, and to whom, it is to be marketed and sold. If one allowed all the 'local' people to dream up their own products British Leyland would not only lose economies of scale but world-wide impact and a great deal more. Obviously Head Office will listen to what local companies want, and there may be slight variations on a certain product; but in the end the decision rests with central management.

Therefore, the British Leyland overseas policy is that things which affect the entire Corporation are dealt with centrally at Head Office.

Let me move now to the other extreme, that of local issues, such as personnel. With this there has to be much more local autonomy. However, as a Corporation, Head Office will lay down basic policies, such as requiring all employees of the company to be treated decently. How these policies are implemented and maintained is at the discretion of local management. British Leyland must be informed on what is going on and must have sufficient information to judge whether the interpretation of policy at local level is in line with central management's thinking. It is about these local issues that Basil Landau must report to Head Office regularly, so that never again can there be the serious economic manifestation of 1972, or the press allegations of starvation wages and inhuman treatment made throughout 1973-74.

The fact that the South African company once made a loss was due to Head Office not being aware how *badly* that overseas subsidiary was doing. The fact that some UK companies were paying below the PDL was, according to some of the reports made to the Select Committee on this issue, that frankly 'they didn't have a clue what was going on out there'. The British Leyland corporate policy subsequently had an effective feed-back mechanism included in it and this, coupled with the selection and high training of local management, does go some way (in fact a long way), to ensuring a competence within the overseas subsidiary. Like all feedback mechanisms it is a two-way process. Basil Landau reports on the various local issues, and he has access to a UK operation 20 times larger than his own. (British Leyland is ranked 23rd in the *Fortune* list of the 300 largest industrial concerns outside the US, with 164,000 employees in the UK plants alone.) Therefore the feedback mechanisms:

1   Allow Head Office to know exactly what is going on and to have an element of control in the situation.
2   Make available to Landau the expertise of the UK operation.

Of course, Head Office don't know what expertise Landau wants unless he tells them, therefore the letter agreement and the reporting procedure is a formal way of ensuring that local management does tell Head Office. It is always much easier for many large companies to put in Head Office management at local level, but all the more important that this should not be the case in South Africa, for it is a fairly nationalistic country and one where local issues can best be handled by local management. Local management can also cope with the serious morale problems that normally occur when the whole of a top management team is restructured. Of course this can be done better by displaying the 'visible' management supports of commitment, enthusiasm and leadership.

The point of having power is to make changes and we have witnessed in all the case studies that for change to succeed it should have as its main ingredient 'involvement', and especially the major involvement of those people whose lives will be affected by the change. I have included a check list as Appendix H, p165, which people like Landau could refer to when considering implementing any local change policy.

Action meetings and worker participation as outlined in other case studies are becoming the rule of the day in the Leyland South Africa plants in Durban, Elandsfontein and Cape Town. This is a tremendous step forward in South Africa.

One example where the two-way feed-back mechanism between Head Office and local office pays off, is with training. In 1973 Dr Diederichs, then the South African Finance Minister, announced in his budget that there would be wider scope and tax concessions for industrial training in the fields of skills and literacy. In 1974 Mr Botha, Minister of Bantu Administration and Development, outlined considerable det-

ails of his Government's plans for giving urban Africans indus-
trial training. Centres are being established where Africans can learn one or two industrial subjects, e.g. in the use of tools, machines, materials, etc., and this would of course simplify the on-the-job training which has to occur in-company before an African can usually commence work. Basil Landau would assure Head Office that, at local level, they were taking full advantage of the new training facilities and concessions being implemented, and not being lazy in this field. Head Office would advise Landau on the training programmes that could be constituted, as they have all the world-wide facilities of training and trainers who can bring their expertise to South Africa's doorstep.

As I mentioned earlier the forces capable of causing internal change, namely the Government, are painfully weak, therefore much of the brunt must fall on the manufacturing sector to carry out the responsibilities of education. Many would argue that basic education is the priority of the state, and 'on-the-job' skills training the responsibility of the organisation. South Africa must be an exception to this. Although more and more African children are getting the opportunity for schooling this is comparatively recent, and the numbers involved are still comparatively few; the pay-off will not be seen for a decade or so. With corporations like Leyland South Africa the urgency for basic education amongst its employees is not so severe; it has about 1600 coloureds and 700 Bantu. With only that number they can usually find enough who are reasonably well educated to begin with, and only need basic skills training. At Huletts, the South African Sugar Corporation, they have approximately 22,000 Bantu, and one can appreciate the magnification of the situation. With them, literacy training is a priority, for until employees have the basics of education the door remains shut to promotion and further advancement. We have seen from other studies that man comes to work with both levels of need—*physiological*, such as the demand for rewards to give him his food, clothing and shelter; and the *psychological* demands for achievement, responsibility, self-fulfilment, identity and appraisal. The striking employees in Durban in 1973 certainly indicated that they wanted *something*, but didn't necessarily indicate *what*. Lack of motivation militates very strongly against higher productivity. Therefore companies like Leyland South Africa are trying to provide motivation by building into their employees' lives some of the psychological factors. A way of doing this is through the Works Council which allows for worker participation and which is similar to the one mentioned in the Fred Olsen case study. This works committee doesn't merely discuss the standards of the toilets (it can leave that to the international press) but it does discuss what people are to *do* as well as how they are to be *treated*.

Another way of building identity into the employees' working lives, apart from the communication involvement, is through the opportunity to develop and gain promotion. About a dozen *coloured* foremen were appointed by Leyland South Africa in 1973, and more throughout 1974-75.

Supervision is a problem in SA companies. Many of the supervisors are white and are frightened of any change which could affect their hegemony. They envisage the labourers below them advancing through training and the promotional ladder, and eventually making them redundant. But supervision as we know it today must become redundant as a more participative labour force emerges (due to the spread of education), and refuses to tolerate the old 'don't do as you think, do as you're told' dictum. School attendance of black children is increasing by 200,000 per year; already 70 per cent of all Bantu children attend school at some stage and the figures will increase as 400-500 schools are built each year. This classroom revolution will in time exert its pressures on employers—as the aspirations of the new employee change, so jobs must be restructured to accommodate this. Are we not witnessing such a movement already in Europe?

Although traditional supervision may become redundant, supervisors will not, as industry and the acceleration of technology demand that the first-line management skills of development, planning, organising and training are increasingly more important. Many supervisors are capable of producing these talents; all-too-often however, they spend the major part of their day doing things which could be done at a level below them. The red-tape, discipline and control chores all too often take up as much as 70 per cent of a supervisor's time, making him a 'checker' as opposed to a first-line manager. Supervisors in South Africa must be given African-appreciation training in order that they can understand the psychological make-up of the black employees under them. The company does appreciate the importance of this, for where there is misunderstanding or incomprehension over an

African's action, shop-floor tension increases. The promoted supervisors at Leyland South Africa have all undergone supervisory management courses which would also give the latter an appreciation of white man's time!

I include an example of this supervisory training scheme as Appendix J, p173. Just as Landau has a check list (Appendix H) which he considers when implementing change involving human relations, so a similar list is part of the foundation for the supervisory training programme with regard to job relations (see Appendix K, p175).

Appendix L 'Main duties of a Production Foreman' (p177) is given to all the supervisors, and the contents are expounded upon in the training sessions. There is emphasis on the fact that the tools available for a supervisor to do his job are:

Men
Materials
Machines
Time

The teaching sessions on motivation and leadership aid the supervisor to conduct his performance appraisals with more positive effect. So often these reviews deteriorate into personality judgements which tend to become static. A suggested tabular guide for these sessions is given in Appendix O, p184.

I am including two performance reviews for a supervisor and production foreman within Leyland South Africa and throughout there exists emphasis on human relations, e.g. with regard to handling problems and employee management potential (Appendices M and N, pp 180-83). The most important point of all for the readers when viewing the various appendices and training material is to appreciate that these supervisors were not only bypassed within the cultural system in South Africa because of their creed, but, as in many companies worldwide, the role of the supervisor is often misjudged—too often seen as a checker and not often enough as a first line manager who has a valuable role to play within the corporation. Competent and effective first line management is an essential ingredient in closer co-operation between senior management and their work force. These training schemes, coupled with the works council, go an influential way towards the observance of the democratic process in allowing the black people to become a self-respecting and self-reliant community. The works council provides a safety valve. It prevents petty gripes from becoming malicious grievances, which was why and how, for example, the 1973 Durban strikes started.

There is another source of communication open to top management within South Africa. This is the INDABA, which is an African meeting where a group sits down and chats for hours (and hours), this being an annoyance to all who cannot understand their culture. Circumstances such as this could be grabbed as an opportunity to use them rather like the briefing-group (tellingly, the Zulu word for such a management support system is *isibonda*, which means a 'prop').

Chief Mangope said:

> 'the workers in a company or organisation have a feeling of belonging. Only where this working climate has been successfully created; where the worker feels he matters as a person, as a human individual, will he start to identify his interests with those of the company. Only then will he realise that he has got a stake in the progress of the company, and the company that it has a stake in his welfare and loyalty.'

Such a situation would represent economic partnership in practice. This should be an ultimate objective of all UK companies with South African investments, like British Leyland; for, as I indicated earlier, our ability to help all African employees is dependent on both the expansion of the South African economy and on the ultimate profitability of the UK concerns.

With its new thinking along these lines Leyland South Africa has managed to see-saw out of their 1972 loss to a profit of over R4 million at the end of 1974 and this figure is increasing through 1975-6.

Change can never happen in isolation; it is often slow and usually undramatic. Yet there is less to fear from the reactions to explained and enlightened change than there is to fear from the reaction to *no* change.

The real test for South Africa and its management will be in its ability to cope with this change. *The most effective form of education is experience* and it is the experience and example that companies like British Leyland can offer to the immediate environs within the Republic that will eradicate some of the fear and the resistance to change which are blueprints for disaster.

It is this portrayal of *example* which will bear much

greater fruit and be much more influential within South Africa than European debates on the standards of toilets. Business cannot be divorced from living—both must be nobly done—and when this is acknowledged within South Africa then change will be both inevitable and constant. Perhaps then the sky could be the limit as opposed to merely the ceiling. This is what is happening within British Leyland's plants in South Africa.

Summary

Within the last year I have been involved again with Leyland South Africa, and the working conditions for all employees in that factory are well above average, with much better pay conditions and with all hourly paid workers on a pension scheme. At one of the plants, the new Elsies River plant, which was commissioned in January 1974, all the foremen are coloured men who have been promoted from within the ranks through the training scheme I have outlined in the study. Works committees are being reformed with both worker and management representation and these committees are operating successfully. Delegates to these committees are elected from the shop-floor ranks, and as with the Hellermann Deutsch study, this form of employee involvement has in fact paid off, both in terms of ensuring better working conditions and in promoting the motivational opportunities for growth, development, recognition and achievement. British Leyland's South African plants have a right to be proud of their progress, considering the exceptional environment in which the company must operate, in ensuring the dignity of all the members of its workforce.

Case Study Eight
Redfearn National Glass
Yorkshire

Oui, cela était autrefois ainsi, mais nous avons changé tout cela.

(Yes, it used to be so, but we have changed all that.)

Jean Baptiste Poquelin, *called* Molière, 1622-1673

Peter Redfern, Commercial Director at Redfearn National Glass, is owed my appreciation for providing every facility and assistance within the Fishergate plant. I am also grateful to Graeme Robertson who supervised the assignment within Redfearn National Glass and as such has provided me with many background details.

Glass was discovered over 5000 years ago and is one of the oldest man-made materials. While the date and exact place of origin of the very first glass may never be known, it is certain that it was discovered somewhere in the Eastern Mediterranean prior to 3000 BC. According to Pliny, the Roman historian of the first century AD, its accidental discovery occurred at the mouth of the River Belus in Phoenicia—now the Naaman, in Israel. In his *Natural History* he writes... 'The story is that merchants put in there with a cargo of natron (crude soda), and when, scattered over the beach, they were preparing a meal and could find no stones of the right height to prop their pots, they supported them on lumps of soda which they fetched from the ship. When these were melted by the heat and mingled with the sand, transparent streams of a strange liquid were seen to flow, and thus glass was discovered.'

There is considerable credibility in this account if we consider just what glass is. Basically glass was—and is—made from silica (sand, flints or crushed quartz), alkali (natural soda or plant ash) and a stabilizer such as limestone. The shores of the River Belus were famous throughout antiquity for their glass-making sands, but the first records of glass technology come from Mesopotamia in the form of inscriptions on clay tablets. The earliest text found near Tell 'Umar on the Tigris, dates back to the 17th century BC, and presumes a glass-making tradition already well established. Egypt can at least claim the earliest glass furnace to be discovered so far. In 1891 Sir W. Flinders Petrie excavated, at Tell el Amarna, the remains of a glassworks which has been ascribed to about 1350 BC.

Despite the Belus discovery of glass formation by a fusion of chemical compounds and trace elements, the truly scientific understanding of glass and its potential is less than 50 years old, and the automation of the glass industry is a creation of the 20th century. The first thing man found on the moon was glass, and those same men could not have got there without glass—glass enabled them to see it properly in the first place. Warmth, light, entertainment, travel, work, recreation: life without glass would be uncomfortable and graceless. The glass industry today is busy making all the things people regard as their birthright as well as researching into newer ways for using glass and its production. Glass making is one of the world's essential operations, with the UK being the third largest glass producer in the world. In Great Britain more than 75,000 people are employed in the industry, which is located in London, Midlands, Lancashire, Yorkshire, Tyneside and Scotland. The annual turnover in the industry is in excess of £150 million.

The basic material—glass (of which there are innumerable varieties) is converted into a wide range of products including domestic ware, flat glass in many forms, containers, glass for lighting, radio and electrical components, laboratory and optical equipment, glass fibre, vacuum ware, industrial and scientific glassware, stained glass, glasses for bottles, rods and tubing.

The two largest sections of the UK glass industry are those that make glass containers such as bottles and jars, and manufacturers of flat glass (window glass and glass for the building and transport industries). Together they account for nearly two-thirds of the total value of UK production. Domestic glassware, machine-made and mouth-blown, industrial plant, glass fibre and vacuum ware are included in the remainder.

The UK produces about 6000 million glass bottles and jars every year. There are 14 companies involved, several of whom have more than one factory, and one of these organisations is Redfearn National Glass.

Before I discuss just what is a bottle—along the lines of how it is made—let me mention that Redfearn National Glass was the result of the merger in 1967 between Redfearn Brothers Limited, of Barnsley, Yorkshire, and the National Glass Works (York) Limited. In the York and Barnsley areas they have approximately 3000 employees. Nine furnaces and thirty-two bottle forming machines produce some 1250 tons of glass per day, though it varies with the mix of jobs being produced. Their total annual turnover is in the region of £20 million.

Glass bottles and jars are usually made on automatic machinery and all stages of production are carefully controlled. Factories work day and night; over 7500 glass bottles are produced every minute in the UK, and most glass containers are blown by automatic machines fed from large tanks of molten glass, new melting going on continuously day and night. The production process is highly automated from the arrival of the raw materials to the emergence of the finished product.

Increased control over furnaces, hot glass and forming machines, coupled with research, has led to a significant decrease in the weight of bottles without loss of strength. Surface coatings in particular, and other treatments have improved performance and strength, and it is probable that the future development of the industry will lie in this direction. Light-weight bottles are being produced in increasing quantities; 20 years ago a milk bottle weighed 20 ozs, but now they are being made at less than half that weight.

Let us look at a typical background to a bottle in a company like Redfearn. A customer contacts the sales department—he has a new product and he thinks that it ought to go into a new bottle. The sales department finds out whether he wants a special bottle or a standard container, like a jam jar, which can always be made to look distinctive with interesting capping and labelling.

Let's say the packer wants a completely new bottle. Although it will be more expensive it could have a greater impact on the buying public. The packaging designer from the customer's advertising agency is called in to collaborate with

Redfearn's design team. Basically they have to find the best
way of adapting designer's dreams to moulds for the machines. The designs are drawn up by the drawing office staff
and then costings are agreed.

Models and then moulds are made before the bottle is
ready to be manufactured. It will of course be one of thousands in a production run. Automatic forming machines must
produce on a very large scale to cover the costs not only of
machines, and glass, and moulds, but also of course for the
manpower.

The raw materials must be checked, cleaned, drained and
weighed before being mixed and fed to the furnace. Within
Redfearn this is almost wholly done automatically which is
cleaner, more accurate and utilises less labour. The glass furnaces are maintained at a very high temperature. Although
temperatures in the vicinity of the furances are over 100°F
elsewhere in the factory they are much more amicable.

Bottle-forming machines must produce on a large scale to
cover the high costs. It is therefore not considered a profitable exercise if, in the desire to satisfy all customers' needs,
the factory has many short production runs with a high number of mould changes.

After the merger of Redfearn in 1967, centralisation of the
salesforce showed up production-planning problem areas as
well as discrepancies in the liaison with sales function. There
was no selective stock control; a seven-day production plan
prepared weekly was amended almost immediately. There
was no overall production plan, no comparison of sales delivery promises against production capacity. A simple system of
production control was looked for. The initial network
drawn of all inter-related tasks showed an introduction period
of approximately 18 months. The initial findings in the
assignment showed up some of the inefficiencies of the pre-
merger operation. For example, although there were 1500
bottle types available, in a six month period only 327 types
had been made, on 543 occasions. Also on 55 per cent of the
occasions the bottle had been previously manufactured less
than four weeks before—and the gap was often less than one
week.

*The stronger the involvement of those individuals in an
organisation being subjected to change, the greater the
strength of commitment to a change activity.* Activities which
are concerned with long-term development and which focus

on attitudes have a better record of success if these individuals have played a part. It is to the credit of Redfearn National Glass that they appreciated the importance of 'involvement' and the subsequent working party approach that was to be evolved. It was important that such items, as for example those on the list 'killing of initiative' (see Figure 8.1), should remain anathema to the philosophy of such a company.

As we have. seen in other studies the catalysing and evocative approach of project management and the teaching of management fundamentals usually have as their desired result

```
┌─────────────────────────────────────────────────────────────┐
│ 15 WAYS TO KILL INITIATIVE                                   │
├─────────────────────────────────────────────────────────────┤
│ 1  Never take him into your confidence, keep him in the dark │
│    about the real purpose of his work.                       │
│ 2  Make sure that you get the credit while he gets the blame.│
│ 3  Never admit that you might be wrong.                      │
│ 4  Don't give sincere praise.                                │
│ 5  Put him on work for which he is tempermentally unsuited.  │
│ 6  Let him involve himself in a really serious mistake before│
│    you pull him up.                                          │
│ 7  Talk about 'objectives', but make it quite clear that     │
│    conforming to the system is really much more important.   │
│ 8  If he comes to you for real help, give him platitudes.    │
│ 9  Harp on details while ignoring the real issues.           │
│ 10 Avoid giving advance information about changes that affect│
│    him.                                                       │
│ 11 Discourage new ideas.                                      │
│ 12 Make it clear that it never pays to step out of line.     │
│ 13 Discourage initiative, insist that his job is done your way.│
│ 14 Demonstrate that promotion goes to those who ingratiate   │
│    themselves rather than those who perform.                 │
│ 15 Pay him so well that he can't afford to leave you.        │
└─────────────────────────────────────────────────────────────┘
```

Figure 8.1

a plan for action with an establishment of controls and feedback. It was with this in mind that Redfearn's decided to establish working parties whose task was to sort out for *themselves* the systems necessary to install an effective production control mechanism in line with the communications flow chart and network plan. The working party approach decided on is similar to the project management approach which has been described in greater detail in the Vosper Thornycroft study (Case Study One) and it involves the members of the parties being given the tools of their trade in order

```
┌─────────────────────────────────────────────────────────────────┐
│ WORKING PARTY - RECOMMENDED MEMBERSHIP RNG                        │
├─────────────────────────────────────────────────────────────────┤
```

All working parties

A.J.Barton	Chairman
R.M.Bartlett	Secretariat
P.G.Redfern	Director in Charge
P.Upton	External adviser

Forward plan and short-term scheduling

G.Webster	Manufacturing
J.M.Asquith	Sales
R.Winder	Barnsley Production Control
C.Crampton	York Production Control

Stock control

J.M.Asquith	Sales
S.Morris	Barnsley Stock Control
R.Winder	Barnsley Production Control
C.Crampton	York Production Control

Carton provisioning

J.Lowe	Barnsley Packaging Supervisor
T.Bucknall	Purchasing
C.Crampton	York Production Control

Figure 8.2

to achieve an end result or objective. For example, it is unreasonable to expect various employee members to come out with rational and acceptable conclusions if they have no appreciation of the basic fundamentals of management, as well as the concrete knowledge of the particular technical areas involved.

The recommended working party membership at Redfearn National Glass was as shown in Figure 8.2. Each of these working parties had main objectives (see Figure 8.3) and their basic module for the method of working was as shown in Figure 8.4.

The parties met at various times with meetings ranging from 13 in the case of the stock control to as many as 24 in the short-term scheduling party. Once the final recommendations were made to the executive the parties were disbanded. An essential feature with this kind of approach is that there is a constant mechanism for change within the organisation. The act of feedback is important—this could be given by

Forward plan and short-term scheduling

Forward plan To establish the systems necessary to enable the expected customer requirements to be compared with the available manufacturing capacity on a continuous basis for a period of approximately four months ahead so that:

(a) the necessary changes in capacity/order intake can be highlighted;
(b) realistic delivery promises can be quoted;
(c) a forward plan can be applied to the short-term scheduling function as an indication of the expected requirements.

Short-term scheduling To establish the necessary systems to enable an achievable short-term programme of work to be prepared from the forward plan and latest information, to be used as:

(a) an instruction to manufacture;
(b) a basis for progress control.

Stock control

To ensure that an effective stock recording system is in operation.

To establish for a selected stock range, the necessary systems to identify on a continuous basis the forward requirements and on order situation, and to exercise effective control over:

(a) when an item should be ordered;
(b) how much should be ordered;
(c) when further review is necessary.

Carton provisioning

To establish the necessary systems to control the supply of cartons in line with the manufacturing schedule at the lowest overall cost, by equating storage costs, carton availability and procurement costs.

Figure 8.3

Peter Redfern, who was the director in charge of all working parties. He is an approachable man who knows the glass trade, has worked on the shop-floor and has an instant rapport with many of his employees. Any grievances or queries, information needed or advice sought could be given immediately to each working party. Often these parties can deteriorate into committees with a jungle of paper work, and then the enthusiasm rapidly wears off—even more quickly if the employees represented by the working party members feel that management are only paying lip service to the concept. Many of the case studies in this book indicate and endorse the importance of feedback, commitment, involvement

Steering Committee

It is recommended that rather than establish a separate Steering Committee, matters on policy raised by the Working Party should be for inclusion as a standard item in the agenda of the weekly Executive Meeting. Such matters would be discussed with Mr P.G.Redfern and submitted to the Managing Director, prior to the Executive Meeting.

Working Parties

The objective is to install an effective production control system in line with the communications flow chart and network plan. The involvement of external consultants or advisers will be:
(a) to provide the necessary expertise and guidance;
(b) to ensure that the sub-systems designed will be consistent with the objective;
(c) to supervise the overall system installation and to give all possible assistance to ensure its effective operation;
(d) to advise continuously the Managing Director of the rate of progress and where deviations from the network plan may occur.

Whenever possible, meetings of the Working Parties should take priority over other commitments.

The Working Party to have powers to co-opt further personnel as required, subject to due consultation taking place.

Initially, Working Parties to meet once a week and subsequently as necessary.

Meetings to be chaired by Mr A.J.Barton and in his absence by the external advisers.

Secretariat to be provided by PA.

Matters of policy to be referred to the Executive Meeting.

It is recommended that the Forward Load and Short-term Scheduling Working Party should meet at 1300 hours on Fridays and that the Stock Control Working Party should meet at 1030 hours on Thursdays.

Figure 8.4

and a leadership from the top man which is able to penetrate to ground roots level.

It would be easier in the eyes of some people for consultants to be brought in and impose their policy for change within the organisation. But this would only cause resentment and make future changes that much more difficult to implement. The individuals throughout the organisation must appreciate not only *what* changes are happening but *why*. This is even more important after a merger has occurred, when security and stability are threatened.

Bearing in mind the hypocrisy of many a working party meeting—some alas I have served upon—it might be an idea to include a light and satirical list for abusing the type of working party and action meeting that I have discussed in many studies apart from this one. I trust however the reader will consider this list (Figure 8.5) in a positive humour.

Some of the changes that accrued from Redfearn's working parties were:

1   The number of job changes per week was reduced to an average of 17, from 30+ at the Barnsley factory.
2   Fewer delivery promises were broken.
3   A much better and more effective selective stock control was in operation.

---

16 WAYS TO WRECK A MEETING

To be borne in mind when considering Action Meetings, Briefing Sessions and meetings connected with Project Teams and Working Parties

1   Don't let anyone know in advance what subjects will be taken up. (They might come with data, prepared to discuss the matter intelligently.)
2   Send out notices of the meeting at least a month in advance. (Participants will be put off preparation, figuring they have lots of time. They may even forget the meeting.)
3   Alternative: give notice only a few hours ahead of the time through a secretary who knows not one thing about it. (Count on this to cripple meetings by 50 per cent since many participants will be dated up with important customers and won't be able to attend at all.)
4   Announce that the meeting will start 'about' a certain time. (Assures interruptions as latecomers take advantage of vague timings and want to know what's happened so far.)
5   See that the Chairman doesn't study questions in advance, has no sharp idea of the meeting's aim, isn't prepared to deal with loaded questions to stimulate discussion when it gets on dead centre. (Guarantees that when meetings bog down, they will stay bogged down, with no interference from the man at the head of the table because he hadn't thought it through either.)
6   If purpose of meeting is only to pass along information, let everyone think that he is going to be asked for advice and decisions. If advice is wanted, spread the word you're just going to hold a 'hair-down', gabfest session. (Participants will feel like fools when their advice is ignored, or overruled and will resent future meetings. If, however, they think the meeting is an informal one they may sound off at will, and then when asked for careful conclusions, they'll feel tricked and just as resentful.)
7   If the meeting is to make authoritative decisions, invite wide variety from President to janitor. If purpose is education, to broaden everybody's outlook, invite only those on similar jobs who work, eat lunch, play golf together daily. (Meeting is queered from beginning by giving janitor

Continued

to President one voice and one vote each. Little good will result. In the other kind of meeting, participants may learn something new, get a fresh slant and become more useful to the company, if they meet with somebody with a different viewpoint.)

8 Instruct all secretaries to transfer all calls into the meeting room. (Breaks up best planned meetings, interrupting not only people called but everyone else. Call from Chairman's child, telling him to pick up bubble gum on the way home, tends to show how much importance he places on the conference, creates spendid lack of response for it.)

9 Encourage leader to do all the talking instead of drawing ideas out of others. (Make everybody else feel he's useless. Driven into silence by a one-way torrent of talk, they will soon absent their bodies as well as their minds from meetings.)

10 Don't use graphs or charts. (Facts interfere with people who do things by 'ear' and they are apt to lead discussion into productive channels.)

11 Don't let participants indicate what is interesting to them. Stick to cast iron agenda. (People will become interested in discussions about things they feel they should know about. If one person makes the agenda, chances are better of getting a high percentage of duds.)

12 Encourage private cross-talk between individuals. (Very interesting to those who indulge in it; but seldom enlightening to anyone else. Also stumps the chairman in summing up because he hasn't heard enough of the private conversations to get them into the summary accurately.)

13 If leader is talkative encourage someone else to monopolise the discussion. (Helps everyone to learn the long-winded talker's personal philosophy and troubles and all details of last convention he attended, without wasting time on the intended purpose of the meeting.)

14 In solving problems discuss solutions first, facts afterwards. (Increases chances of adopting first solution that comes along without considering the possibilities. May even let you skip over a few facts that don't fit in with your favourite solution.)

15 If the meeting is a training type and you were responsible for choosing one or more of the participants, never ask him what went on or show any interest. (Let him know how little you think of the meetings and give him an idea of how little importance he should place upon them. Discourage any idea that he can help the company while improving himself.)

16 If you have managed to keep your mouth shut during meetings and have contributed nothing to them, spring your opinions on a couple of participants when the meeting is over, demonstrating how the meeting was run all wrong. (Deprives the meeting of the benefit of your ideas, if any, and saves them for the time and place where they'll do the least good. May even tend to build up cliques. And if your ideas weren't very good anyway, this saves you the pain of having their weaknesses exposed.)

The author is grateful to Johnson & Johnson, Chicago, USA, for aiding and abetting.

Figure 8.5

The working party approach has now been extended with equal success to tackle the problems of planning mould manufacture, and in 1975 was being used very effectively to consider the feasibility of expanding the use of a computer. The latter is very important as so often I have witnessed the introduction of a computer and its possible extensive use being viewed as a threat to employees' security—perhaps potential redundancy. The only way to alleviate that fear is for people on the whole to see by experience that this is not going to be the case. More important is that employees understand the decision for the computer's installation in the first place. The decision to purchase a computer is the prerogative of the executive: however the decision as to the extent of its feasibility can be made by those people whose lives the computer will affect: and this can be done through constructive discussions in working parties similar to that in Redfearn National Glass.

The organising and guiding of the working party can be standardised for all projects within any area of development. In Figures 8.6, 8.7 and 8.8 I have summarised the organising of a project, and although this may well have proved a valuable map for the Redfearn project regarding the feasibility of their computer extension, it can also provide a basis for any working party approach.

For people like Joe Atkinson, Jack Crouch and John Mordue, who have spent the greater part of their working lives within the Inspection Department of the Mould Shop at Redfearn's, the merger could have brought with it a loss of identity and the feeling they were becoming smaller cogs in

SURVEY OF THE SITUATION
Problem analysis

1	Find and list problems and suggestions.
2	Collect data concerning the structure and development of the department, the firm, the industry, the market, etc.
3	Screen the problems in accordance with evaluating criteria.
4	List current problems and conceivable development projects.
5	Roughly estimate the results in cash terms of the various projects (calculations of profitability) and other final results in the view of management.

Figure 8.6

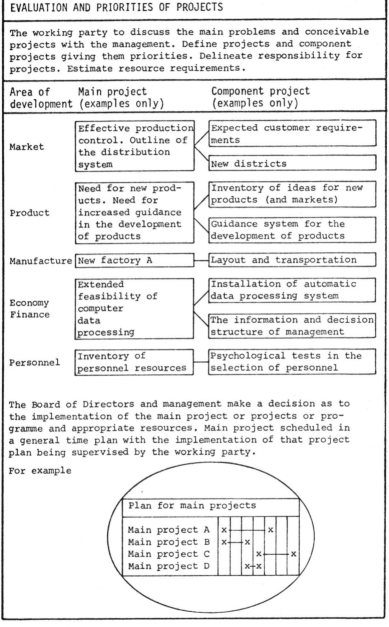

EVALUATION AND PRIORITIES OF PROJECTS

The working party to discuss the main problems and conceivable projects with the management. Define projects and component projects giving them priorities. Delineate responsibility for projects. Estimate resource requirements.

Area of development	Main project (examples only)	Component project (examples only)
Market	Effective production control. Outline of the distribution system	Expected customer requirements New districts
Product	Need for new products. Need for increased guidance in the development of products	Inventory of ideas for new products (and markets) Guidance system for the development of products
Manufacture	New factory A	Layout and transportation
Economy Finance	Extended feasibility of computer data processing	Installation of automatic data processing system The information and decision structure of management
Personnel	Inventory of personnel resources	Psychological tests in the selection of personnel

The Board of Directors and management make a decision as to the implementation of the main project or projects or programme and appropriate resources. Main project scheduled in a general time plan with the implementation of that project plan being supervised by the working party.

For example

Plan for main projects

Main project A	x			x		
Main project B	x	x				
Main project C			x		x	
Main project D		x	x			

Figure 8.7

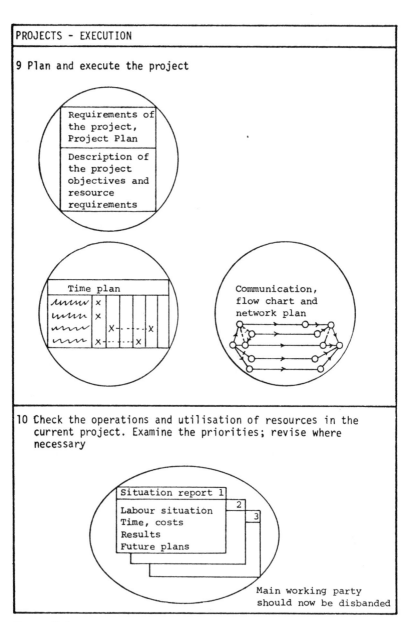

PROJECTS - EXECUTION

9 Plan and execute the project

Requirements of
the project,
Project Plan

Description of
the project
objectives and
resource
requirements

Time plan

Communication,
flow chart and
network plan

10 Check the operations and utilisation of resources in the
current project. Examine the priorities; revise where
necessary

Situation report 1

Labour situation
Time, costs
Results
Future plans

2

3

Main working party
should now be disbanded

Figure 8.8

larger wheels... not an uncommon symptom when a company
expands. Perhaps that used to be the case when the merger
was still a baby. Now employees have experienced that whenever changes are to occur their views will be asked by some
of their colleagues who are members of the working party
developing and implementing the proposals. They are proud
of belonging to a larger and more successful concern such as
Redfearn National Glass, who by using this approach are still
capable of considering the individual and his views.

Really what happened is that the working party came out
with the same recommendations as probably any consultants
would have imposed on entering the assignment. These working parties were allowed to work the problems and proposals
through for *themselves*, and were able to do so with the help
and support of senior management; consequently the implementation of change within the company has been that much
the easier for their involvement and participation.

In the days before the working parties' main objectives
were established, and when the production control system
was not in operation, effectively 'you didn't know what they
were going to do to you next—but now they've changed all
that'.

Case Study Nine

Sydney Hospital
Australia

Tis a lesson you should heed
Try, try again.

William Edward Hickson, 1803-1870

I want to thank F.L. Ritchie, President, and B.A. Herriott, General Medical Superintendent, both of Sydney Hospital, for allowing this study to be included here. I also wish to credit the *Medical Journal of Australia*, who included part of this study in a series on 'Replanning Sydney Hospital'.

In particular I am grateful to Mike Gorman and Len Crawford for sharing their knowledge on hospital administration with me.

As a concluding study I want to mention some of the participative work being undertaken within hospital groups, in this instance the Sydney Hospital in Australia. However, many of the concepts and mechanics mentioned are relevant to all types of business.

With the soaring costs of the national health services worldwide (in spite of many gaps in the service even in the developed countries), this study indicates the considerable potential for improving the value obtained for the money spent by hospitals. The study also indicates that a reduction in cost and greater efficiency came as by-products from improvements made in hospital management for the benefit of patients.

To obtain these benefits in this case study, as with all the studies, there had to be considerable emphasis on training, education, leadership, encouragement and involvement. With these components, attitudes were slowly changed at all levels within the hospital.

Teaching the hospital staff to solve their own management problems has not only brought a review of outlook by gaining their commitment to change—it has ironically proved that hospital staff can make managers who are as good as, or better than, their business counterparts.

At the February 1971, Annual General Meeting, the President of Sydney Hospital announced:

1 That the cost per patient treated was down 33 per cent (Figure 9.1).
2 That during the previous six months 30 per cent more in-patients had been treated than for the same period in the previous year (20 per cent more than ever before in the hospital's history) (Figure 9.2).
3 That nurse wastage was reduced from 17 to 9 per cent.
4 That the number of nursing staff was the same as for 1969.

He attributed these improvements to a management training programme that helped to develop better internal self-management, more effective work load distribution and a consequent rise in morale.

In a time of rising costs and nursing shortages, these are rather surprising results. The story behind them goes back to 1965.

In 1965, the State Government agreed to Sydney Hospital planning for a new hospital. It was soon found, however, that planning a new teaching hospital was much more difficult than appeared at first sight, and no expert help was available in Australia. It was therefore decided to start from first principles and treat the exercise as a research project, the results of which would be available for all hospitals. During planning, it became obvious that, in addition to functional needs, some thought must also be given to the layouts of departments and their relationships one with another. It was also evident that physical layout must take into account the way in which the hospital would be managed and run. How was it to be run?

Investigation showed that nobody has much good to say for the traditional method of managing a hospital. Most people saw plenty of scope for improvement, but there was no precedent for another system; all hospitals in Australia, as in the UK, were managed along very similar lines. It became clear that, along with functional planning, management aspects of the new hospital would require researching as well.

The results of this research culminated in an 'hypothesis'. This advocated decentralisation within the framework of clearly defined and quantified hospital 'objectives', which would distribute a much greater degree of managerial author-

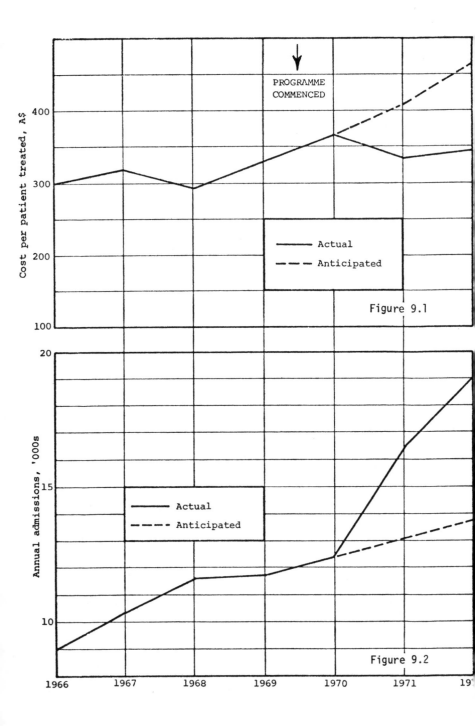

Figure 9.1

Figure 9.2

This hypothesis was published, the purpose being to invite comment and criticism before testing the ideas experimentally in the present Sydney Hospital. The comments received said in effect: 'It looks fine on paper, but do you really think it can work in practice? Nobody has done what you are suggesting'. That nobody has done something before has never been a good reason to Sydney Hospital for not trying a new idea. It was decided to give the scheme a trial.

Approach

A management development programme was planned as three phases.

> *Phase 1* was to be classroom education in management principles.
>
> *Phase 2* applying these principles to the job.
>
> *Phase 3* putting improvements to work to achieve better management results.

The programme required staging. A teaching hospital is too big and too complicated to tackle all at once. But training programmes in individual departments would not have been very effective, because too many departmental difficulties originate beyond departmental walls. On the other hand, to have concentrated exclusively on the hospital's executive officers would also have been of limited value. These people, of necessity, are out of touch with details of current day-to-day work in departments (and it is the small details rather than the big ones that so often cause most concern to people on the job). Somehow it was necessary to involve both top management and departmental staff at the same time.

This was done by going into the departments to learn at first hand what their problems were, and then to trace these problems to their source. Some could be corrected by departments themselves; but others—those caused by other departments, or by the management itself—were taken to the executive group. For this approach to work, it was essential first to educate the various parties in the fundamental principles of management, so that they could have a common understanding of the process—a common 'language' by which to communicate. Further, it was assumed that if the programme of education plus corrective action started in one department, it would not be long before not only would allied departments become implicated, but their staff would become interested as well. Good management should be this infectious.

What follows describes the approach used in the wards; this has subsequently been repeated in modified forms throughout the hospital. It reveals how related departments did in fact become implicated.

Training was undertaken by external consultants and as one of their immediate jobs they had to find out what nurses thought their problems were. In this way they could discuss matters that really interested them. They could also use illustrations from the nurses' own work in their own hospital, to bring management principles alive and hence establish rapport.

The first (Phase 1) training session was for 26 senior nursing sisters (ward-sister level and above) in two groups, each meeting for two hours per week after lunch for eight weeks. The purpose of these sessions was to give a thorough grounding in the simple fundamental principles of management (objectives, planning, control, accountability, etc.). This enabled the group to see their own work from fresh viewpoints. It also provided a common language for the group to communicate both among themselves and with the consultants. The content for some of this grounding is similar to that indicated in relation to other case studies, e.g. 'Anatomy of Management' in the D & P study (Appendix B) and 'Authority and Accountability' in the Leyland South Africa programme (Appendix I).

At first the sisters were polite but detached. This was to be expected; some of them had experienced 'management' training courses before, and nothing much had come of them. Also, it was found that, whereas many members were ready to describe their difficulties, they were less adept at identifying the causes in terms of fundamental principles. They expected to be 'told'. As they were conditioned to didactic instruction, it was difficult to get them to think for themselves from first principles.

Something had to be done to stir the group. Eventually a method of instruction evolved which is better illustrated by the following example (the subject was 'Objectives').

A PA consultant started by briefly introducing the subject. Each member was then given a written 'parable' to read. Parables (case studies) are short, open-ended stories that

present a situation with which members can identify themselves (but not too closely!). In this case, the parable was not
so much about objectives as about conflict of objectives—
situations in which all parties conscientiously did what they
believed to be right, but in which the end result was a
disaster.

The purpose of parable is not to teach, but to set the stage
for learning through discussion. Teaching comes from discussion, not from the parable itself. This is important, because
for people to 'believe' (as opposed to 'understand'), they
must discover basic truths for themselves. The simpler an idea
is, the more difficult it is to 'tell' anyone about it—listeners
jump prematurely to their own conclusions and stop listening. This 'parable' approach has been used with equal success
in other case studies.

The first parable was about a business situation. After the
points had been explored thoroughly, a second parable was
handed out. This time it was an example specially written
from incidents in the group's own hospital. Business and
hospital examples were deliberately mixed throughout training to discourage 'ghetto' thinking about my 'business being
different'. Remember, the subject at this stage was 'management principles' not 'hospital management practice'. This far,
instruction had followed conventional 'Socratic' lines; but
now 'theory' (Phase 1) moved smoothly into 'application'
(Phase 2).

When, from the discussion, it was clear that groups had not
got the essential message about objectives, the consultant
provoked the following exchange:

Consultant: What are *your* objectives?

Group: Good patient care.

Consultant: What do you mean by 'good patient care'?

Group: Everybody knows what that is.

Consultant: I don't, tell me.

Group: We can't, you haven't been trained as a nurse.

Consultant: I see. Well what sort of things do you mean?

Group: (Examples from group)

Consultant: How do you *measure* how well they are being
    done?

Group: You can't *measure* them, you tell by experience.

Consultant: I see. Do you know when, say, one ward is
    better than another?

Group: Oh yes!

Consultant: How?

    Group: By looking.

    Consultant: But what do you look at?

At this point there were plenty of suggestions; everyone had her own ideas. Quite soon with the help of a blackboard, it was found possible to categorise points under five headings:

1   Patient welfare and safety.
2   Patient comfort.
3   Medical records.
4   The ward.
5   The nursing unit.

The sisters even surprised themselves at the consensus of their opinion. It was agreed that the lists on the blackboard might be useful as a guide during ward rounds. At any rate, the idea was worth a try. One sister copied down the information, and arrangements were made to have some sheets duplicated so that everyone could have a go.

The check-list proved to be workable, but scores came out too high (some of the wards were not so good as all that). So the list was modified, more weighting being given to patient conditions, for example, than to the tidiness of the drug cupboard.

After four attempts over several months, the sisters *themselves* evolved a method of assessing the quality of ward management, which now provides a *'Patient Care Index'* for each ward weekly. The procedure was endorsed by the Director of Nursing as part of the hospital routine, and has now been in regular operation for more than four years.

About a year after its introduction, the patient check-lists were modified once more. This time, rather than merely recording what was wrong, stress was laid on what was being done to put it right. Also, the method had extended from the original block-matron/charge-sister level as an inspection device, to the charge-sister/ward-sister level as a training aid. This is a very significant change—a change from authoritarian control by somebody else to self-examination by the individual of how she is shaping up to answering the real problems posed by her responsibilities. The most effective form of discipline is self-discipline.

Some advantages of patient-care assessment are:

1   By focusing attention on matters that senior sisters agree are specially important, it has helped improve the standard of ward management.

2   Replacing arbitrary judgement by systematic appraisal
     has helped to improve staff relationships.
3   Ward sisters find it useful for training nurses. Nurses
     find it useful for training themselves.
4   The Director of Nursing has found it useful for evaluat-
     ing assignment nursing by comparison with task nursing.
5   The tutor sisters are using it for reappraising priorities in
     nursing training.

The description of how the Patient Care Index evolved illustrates several points relating to 'participative' programmes
outlined in all the studies, e.g.

1   Education in fundamental management principles, i.e.
     the real meaning of objectives, planning, control and the
     relationships between them, enables employees to apply
     their own abilities and experience to evolve soundly
     based solutions to their own problems.
2   Management emphasis is 'results orientated'. Partici-
     pants are encouraged and assisted to devise quantified
     measures for the results of the work they do—instead of
     just doing it and hoping for the best.
3   Classroom theory is closely linked to practical applica-
     tion.
4   The causes of local problems are traced to their source.
     When causes are beyond departmental boundaries—as is
     often the case—the external catalyst follows up on be-
     half of the department and gets something done.
5   Attention is focused first on work-face areas and on
     day-to-day difficulties of people actually doing work,
     and then traced back from here.

Linking theory with practice and getting action on behalf
of departments are the most important features. Practice
makes theory real; and a group really begins to believe that
the management programme is worthwhile only when issues
that have been running-sores for years are fixed.

In addition to the question-and-answer type discussion,
other training methods were used: role-playing ('charades'),
tape-recordings and films—including a coloured cartoon made
specially for the purpose. Visitors participated as well!

In the case of the senior sisters' programme, visitors included the Chief Executive Officer, the General Medical Superintendent and the Director of Nursing. They joined role-playing sessions to illustrate how simple data, when properly
used, could lead to useful management action. This had a

very practical outcome: it led to action being taken in the wards to reduce patient stay, improvements to the ambulance service and a number of other worthwhile benefits. This really convinced the nurses that the hospital executive were in earnest. It cannot be over-emphasised how vitally important to the success of a management development programme are some real actions from the upper hierarchy to support their encouraging words. This is another example—as portrayed throughout the studies—of 'visible' management support, commitment and leadership.

Patient care

Patient care has had top priority throughout the programme; every step has been governed by this consideration. Substantial financial and administrative benefits have indeed resulted from the work, but these have been the by-products from improving hospital management in the interests of patient care; they have never been the prime issue.

It was the only way. Had methods of administration or cost reduction been put first, the programme would have had a cool reception, because the people who have most influence on how a hospital's time and money are used—the doctors and the nurses—would not have been very interested.

A major difficulty for the manager of any large hospital is the lack of clearly defined goals to unite the staff in a common purpose. Each department thus largely decides its own priorities. This leads to conflict of interest and misunderstandings, so that throughout the hospital 'communication' becomes a number one problem.

The point at issue is a question of degree. All hospital staff accept good patient care as their aim; but what constitutes good patient care is open to widely differing, and sometimes conflicting, definitions. For hospital staff to have a common purpose, they must first agree on what constitutes good patient care, how it is to be achieved, how it is to be measured and what their own role is to be.

One facet of patient care measurement has been described, but there were some other aspects of interest, e.g. a patient questionnaire on their views about the hospital, a consumer panel for providing patient services, and there was also a food project.

The senior nursing staff, during training discussions, felt strongly that something should be done to improve in-patients' meals. It was decided that a project on food service should be undertaken by the nursing division. This was a big job, so the Director of Nursing agreed to release a senior sister full time for several months, rather along the lines of the project management study within Vosper Thornycroft (Case Study One), or the working party approach featured in the Redfearn Study (Case Study Eight).

Sister Jean Shaw began by learning the elements of work study. An early step was to get the hospital's photographer to take colour photographs of meals, and to note patients' reactions to them. This was done as much as anything to demonstrate to the nursing staff that the hospital executive took the project seriously and supported a thoroughly professional approach. It was found, contrary to general belief, that neither the food itself nor the way in which it was cooked was the main problem. Troubles lay in the way in which meals were ordered and in what happened to them after they left the kitchens. Weighing showed that waste was excessive; less than half the food cooked was eaten by patients, mainly because it reached them cold and unappetising, helpings were too big, presentation was unattractive, and too many meals were ordered—just in case.

Serving hot food was the first priority. In due course, after Sister Shaw and her team managed to resolve a number of difficulties, they were delighted by a compliment from one regular patient: 'That's the first time I've ever burnt my tongue on food at Sydney Hospital!'

Attention to menus, portion control, training in food presentation, a new team method of serving, and, above all, a much better working relationship between wards and the catering staff, all contributed to improvements. Not only were patients appreciative, but the hospital saved A$300 a week in food as well. At the same time, the work in serving meals was reduced by 40 per cent. But the main point is that patients now find the food more appetising. Having been a UK hospital's in-patient, this is one area our own NHS could look at perhaps in similar fashion!

There is little point in getting patients' opinions—via the consumer panel for example—unless there is somewhere useful for the information to go to. The lack of clarity about responsibility which causes difficulty in the first place also makes corrective action difficult; issues get bogged down in interdepartmental committees. To overcome these obstacles, a permanent Patient Care Committee was formed. This committee consists of a small but powerful nucleus (Deputy Medical Superintendent, Deputy Director of Nursing and a Project Sister), and handles all problems relating to patient care across the board, from admission to discharge.

The committee meets monthly and co-opts other staff members as required. Matters considered fall into three groups, as follows:

1   Those relating to day-to-day operations (most of these are fixed by the committee itself).
2   Those requiring a change in administrative procedures or organisation (these are passed to the hospital's executive).
3   Those relating to policy (these are relayed through the executive to the board).

Rostering

Shortage of nursing staff naturally loomed large during discussions on ward management, as it would in any UK hospital. Sydney Hospital had some closed wards because of a shortage of nurses, and so nursing shortage obviously required looking into as a matter of urgency.

Nursing staff were allocated to wards by a rostering sister on the basis of the number of beds (this is the way the Hospitals Commission determines the hospital's nursing establishment). Nurses were allocated according to the number of beds—regardless of whether there were patients in them or not, and regardless of whether the patients who were there were very ill and requiring a lot of attention, or almost well and needing very little. The arrangement caused nurses in some wards to be overloaded ('hard' wards), while other wards were known as a 'push-over'. Thus, part of the nursing staff had cause to be disgruntled, having too much to do, while others could be bored, having too little—two good reasons for nurses leaving their profession.

In view of the very high cost of the nursing time bought each year by the hospital (between A\$1.8 and 2 million), it was obviously desirable to find a way of equating work to nurses. For this, data giving nursing hours (per day) per patient according to the categories of sickness were needed. Plenty of studies on nursing have been published, but despite this, data of the type required did not appear to be readily available. It was decided to carry out a project to get the information. Sister Jean Keneally was given the job.

Sister Keneally started by finding out what nurses did with their time. She found that, by comparison with other hospitals, Sydney Hospital nurses were not overburdened with non-nursing duties. Even so, it was possible to reduce non-nursing work by more than one-quarter. While doing this, Sister Keneally gained valuable insight and background data, which enabled her to take full advantage of some unexpected and very welcome help from Dr McEwin, Chief Medical Director of the Repatriation Commission. The Commission had already done studies along similar lines and made their information available. This saved six months' work, for which Sydney Hospital is indebted to the Repatriation Commission and to Dr McEwin.

Eventually the nursing hours per patient for six categories of sickness were evolved, tested in practice and eventually agreed by the sisters as being fair and reasonable. From these data, the nursing load per ward is now calculated daily to provide a 'Nursing Staff Utilisation Index'. A correct load is indicated by 100, figures above 100 depict overloaded nurses, whereas figures below 100 represent under-employment.

This system was introduced at the end of 1970. Since then, the imbalance between work to be done and nurse availability has been halved. More important, the nursing staff have responded to the fairness of the method, which has contributed significantly to improved morale and reduced nursing wastage.

Ward	Index (high figures are good)	
	Patient care, %	Nurse utilisation, %
A	94	80
B	90	76
C	76	68

Figure 9.3

The management indices described (that is, the Patient Care Index and the Nurse Utilisation Index) are examples of an extremely useful management device, the 'Performance Index'. A brief outline of how Performance Indices are used may be of some interest. Indices representing the results for one week for three different wards (A, B and C) are shown in Figure 9.3. From this information, the following deductions are possible:

1   *Ward A*   The staff are busy (80 per cent occupied) and the patient care score is excellent (94 per cent)—an exceptionally well run ward (the ward sister deserves congratulation).

2   *Ward B*   Staff over three-quarters occupied (76 per cent) and patient care good (90 per cent)—a well run ward (no action).

3   *Ward C*   Staff are not hardworked (68 per cent), and yet patient care is poor (76 per cent)—not a well managed ward (this ward requires investigation).

The figures confirm something already known in a general sense: that fewer staff do not necessarily mean lower standards of care, nor more staff better care. The capability of the ward sister as a manager has an overriding effect. But the figures also provide a 'measure' of just how good a ward sister is as a manager. Furthermore, trends also indicate whether she is improving, or getting worse. This is an example of feedback—a powerful motivator.

The indices do something else as well. They enable a costing figure to be put on management competence. Thus, if the sister in charge of Ward C were to improve to the level of the sister in charge of Ward B, not only would patients benefit, but the hospital could get by with 12 per cent fewer nursing hours. If, say, one-quarter of all wards throughout the hospital were to improve to this extent, the equivalent of A$30,000 worth of nursing time per year would be made available. Indices can thus put a costing tag on the value of training ward sisters how to become better managers.

A word of warning—success in using indices and figures of this type depends entirely on the attitude of mind of the staff to whom they are applied. The approach works only when people are receptive through having been prepared first. Imposing ready-made schemes on the unprepared invites non-cooperation, and possibly hostility. Instead of proving an advantage, they can, if handled ineptly, easily put staff off.

I offer an example of how infectious participation can be— the management style in one area influencing that in another. When the management programme with the nursing staff had been running for about two months, what the nurses were doing began to attract attention in other departments. The heads of the service departments asked whether they could participate in something similar of their own. This is exactly what the hospital was hoping for—in effect infectious good management practice. A programme similar to the wards programme was designed, but instead of using ward example, the presentation was adapted to the service departments. The reaction of the engineers is a good example of what resulted.

The engineers, overloaded with work rather like the GLC maintenance men, had a backlog of 200 jobs—many outstanding six months or more. Ward sisters were having the greatest difficulty in getting anything done, and regarded the engineers as a lazy, incompetent bunch. In their turn the engineers were convinced that the sisters were both unreasonably demanding and a destructive threat to the hospital's fabric and equipment. There was constant strife between the two departments, not peculiar to only the Sydney hospital! Mr Wilton, the Chief Engineer, was sceptical about the management programme at first; he could not see how management theories could provide him with more engineers which was all he needed. However, he was willing to give the schemes a trial and started keeping records of the jobs outstanding, i.e. applying management control principles to his own department. After a time, his figures started to improve. Mr Wilton was perplexed. 'These figures must be wrong', he said. 'They show we are doing more work, but we can't be, I haven't put pressure on my staff. All I did was show the figures to the foreman.'

The point was, of course, that somebody was taking a real interest in the engineers, and they responded. Six months later, the engineers reduced the jobs outstanding to a fraction of their previous number. They have managed to hold this figure ever since, and in doing so have doubled their former amount of work. The sisters so much appreciated what the engineers did that the Director of Nursing wrote a letter of thanks for their better service; this letter was displayed on the engineers' notice board. I cannot impress enough on the reader how important feed-back is, whether it is a thank you letter on the notice board as here, or regular feed-back sessions as with the Fred Olsen Works Council and Redfearn National Glass's working party or Hellermann Deutch's guarantees with the suggestion programme. The important points to remember are that feedback must be *positive, visible* and *immediate.*

The mutual respect that developed throughout 1971-2 has persisted. This was illustrated very recently by an aside from one ward sister at a ward meeting: 'I don't know what the engineers are doing, but they are sure doing something!'

Phase 3 of the programme, i.e. putting new management methods to work in order to get better results—is the most difficult part. Seldom is it as easy as has been described for the engineers. Real management learning begins when people start applying management theory in practice; when they have to face up to real situations and take real decisions with the possibility of being wrong; when they have to insist on action that may be unpopular. The action meeting is an excellent means for training in the reality of management (*q.v.* Case Study 4). It is a useful and flexible necessity applicable to any situation where people are working to a common plan; whether carrying out a managerial routine, or engaged on a project, e.g. constructing a building or introducing changes to management procedures. Their obvious practical value as an aid to getting things done conceals a more subtle advantage of action meetings—their use in management training. Forcing people to think a problem through, insisting on facts, putting someone on the spot to get results by a set date, are part and parcel of practical training in management. Action meetings are the mainspring for any management development and change programme—because, after all, the main aim in developing managers is to get people to take more effective management action leading to more effective management results. To know more about management theoretically is only a starting point. Classroom training, designing procedures and so on are merely means to an end. It is all too easy to teach in the classroom how other people manage, without in fact improving the managerial ability of a group at all.

But at action meetings and briefing sessions used in almost all the studies the 'doers' became clearly distinguishable from the 'talkers'. Those with potential to handle bigger jobs inevitably reveal their capabilities, just as do those who are already square pegs in round holes. The advantages of this precise method for evaluating management talent in staff in relation to their promotability are obvious.

At Sydney Hospital, action meetings are now a regular feature of managing at all levels, from ward sister to executive committee; about 30 different regular meetings a week are being held. Not only are these meetings contributing to a better standard of management today, but as a by-product they are also training more managers for the future, and so ensuring a continuity of high management performance.

Departmental budgets

One ought to mention that the 30-odd departments now covered by the programme all have their own budgets. These budgets incorporate both targets for achievements and reports of results actually being achieved for 'quality' and 'quantity', as well as 'cost' of work done. The first purpose of data is to signal to those on the spot when something requires investigating, then point to where to look for more information, and finally, to indicate whether successful action has been taken or not. For these purposes, absolutely accurate data are not necessary. Provided information is accurate enough to lead to correct decisions, it is adequate. Accuracy thus often takes second place to speed, relevance and the cost of recording. I am a firm believer in controlled disclosure of information.

Ward budgets are a good example. Each sister in charge of a ward now has the data she needs to run her ward as if it were her own 'little hospital'—that is, a measure for the quality of work done (the Patient Care Index), a measure for the quantity (bed occupancy and throughput), a measure for the efficiency with which staff are used (the Staff Utilisation Index) and measures for the cost of labour and materials.

She has targets to work to and weekly feed-back of actual progress for comparison with the targets. To provide these data, special arrangements have had to be made, because the hospital accounting system does not provide information in the form required. For example, it lumps together all nursing, all drugs and all stores; costs are not easily traceable to individual users. To have changed the accounting system itself would have been very complicated, and it has not been necessary. Ward sisters are interested not in exact figures, but merely in their own progress by comparison with targets and with other wards, and whether their own ward, week by week, is doing better or worse. So long as the figures they get are reasonably accurate and so long as they are consistent, the ward sisters get all they require.

For simplicity 'notional' costs have been introduced. For example, staff employed in wards have been divided into six different categories of monetary rate per hour. The hourly cost rates are all-inclusive, incorporating holiday pay and other 'payroll overheads' in addition to the wage itself. The system does not give the precise cost of running a particular ward in a particular week; but this is of no significance anyway. What can be determined very quickly and very effectively is how much it costs to nurse patients, what it should cost, why one ward costs more or less than another, and whether costs are rising or falling. The type of data dissection described is a natural for a computer—had one been available. But it might not have proved any cheaper or any quicker than the hand method actually used.

The 'notional' costs which have been used for staff are also used for ward stores. There is now a hospital price list, in which figures have been rounded to something higher than actual prices. Advantage has been taken in the rounding process to exaggerate differences between prices of products which serve the same purpose, in order to discourage the use of more expensive items when cheaper ones will do—for example, two brands of adhesive plaster, one of which was slightly better, but very much more expensive than the other.

In addition to notional costing, a further simplifcation in ward paperwork has come from a comprehensive imprest system for all ward stores, laundry and drugs. Not only does the arrangement reduce stores work, but it makes it easy to calculate ward costs, and it also saves about half a day a week in clerical work for each ward sister. It was this reduction in paper work which was a consideration also in the Design and Print study when viewing payment and reward systems.

Throughout the hospital, departmental budgets are summarised into divisional budgets—separate summaries for the heads of medical, nursing and services divisions. The Chief Executive Officer now gets a summary of the hospital's vital statistics on one sheet of paper (Figure 9.4) three working days after the end of each month. The data for this are summarised from the divisional information, with the addition

			I Current month	II Variance	III Year to date
C O S T	1 1A	Cost per occupied bed Cost per inpatient treated (Outpatient regulars converted to inpatient equivalent)	$ 40.01 $ 310.82	+8.01 +25% -55.12 -15%	35.74 + 311.18
A C T I V I T Y	2 3 4 5 6 7 8 9	ADA No. Bed days No. Admissions No. Available bed utilisation No. Daily average occupied beds No. Outpatient attendances No. Outpatient registrations No. Average stay No.	530 12,328 1587 87.9% 397.7 17,994 7695 7.8	-18.3 -3.4 +13 +502 46.3 -3.1 -3.4 -2309 -11.7 -1223 -13.7 -3.2 -29	514 105 12 8 39 16 67 8
I N C O M E	10 11 12 13 14 15 16 17 18 19	Hospitals commission Patient fees (raised) Commonwealth subsidy Other Total Total - year to date Patient fees (receipts) Patient fees owing Patient fees O/S days Days Patient fees billing time Days	$ 408 $ 147 $ 16 $ 19 $ 590 $ $ 190 $ 627 132	- - -9 -5.8 -2 -11.1 +3 +18.7 -8 -1.4 +30 +25	328 1,550 150 106 504 139 62 114
E X P E N D .	20 21 21A 22 23 24 25 26	Salaries and wages Drugs Medical/Surgical supplies Provisions Other Total Total - year to date Owing to	$ 488 $ 44 $ 20 $ 25 $ 79 $ 656 $ $ NIL	+19 +4 -2 -4.3 -2 -9 -2 -7.4 -11 -12.2 +2 +3	3,50 4.1 172 20
C A S H	27 28 29	Operating surplus Operating deficit Bank Balance	$ $ 23 $ 42,316	37	
R R & R	30 31 32 33	Available Committed Balance Spent	$ $ $ $		106,583 59,867 150,091 43,503

		STAFF REPORT				
		Movement for month	Annual T/O rate,%	Establishment	Actual	Variance
	35	Admin & Clerical	8	58	166	177	+11
	36	Nursing	40	88	548	503	-45
	37	Domestic	34	194	210	218	+8
	38	Catering	15	188	96	97	+1
	39	Other	20	52	464	449	-15
TOTAL			117	95	1484	1441	-40

Figure 9.4 Sydney Hospital: executive monthly summary available three working days after the end of each month. (Expenditure and income in '000s) *Reproduced from the Medical Journal of Australia*

of data from the accounts department. Formerly the hospital's executive officers were in the very difficult position of having inadequate management information with which to make decisions in carrying out their responsibilities. Now, not only do they have good information about their own departments, but they are also in a position to contribute usefully to discussions about each other's. Whereas formerly the divisional heads tended to speak very much from the point of view of their own divisions, they now collaborate as a tightly knit team.

As can be judged from results quoted in the first section of this study by the President of Sydney Hospital, the executive meetings have become tremendously effective. Full credit for what has been accomplished must go to the staff generally, but also in particular to Mr Beer, the Chief Executive Officer, whose enthusiasm and leadership have been an inspiration acknowledged by his colleagues. Similar credits you will recall were directed at Bert Graham in the GLC, John Rix at Vosper and Peter Redfern at Redfearn for displaying such support characteristics of enthusiasm and leadership vital in both originating change programmes and motivating employees to want to contribute to such changes.

I have made little mention of doctors and paramedical personnel as a group in relation to the programme. They were the last groups to become involved. The importance of their participation was not overlooked. However, until more basic matters had been attended to, and success had been demonstrated in other areas, it was thought premature to involve the mass of medical staff directly in the programme. This is not to say that the General Medical Superintendent and his deputies were not involved from the outset. Not only did they participate in seminars for the ward sisters, the executive, the middle-level administrative officers and chief technologists, but they also investigated, for example, bed stay and the sources of drug costs. It will be appreciated then that when one discusses 'employee' involvement it indicates involvement at all levels within the organisation.

Improvements in other management areas made appropriate some more concentrated attention for the medical division. Heads of the medical services departments were involved in discussions leading to results measurement and management control for their departments. The junior medical officers sought help with their own management problems.

Visiting medical staff have also played—and continue to
play—an important part in the programme.

Through the introduction of a planned patient care procedure, doctors pre-arrange tests and consultations, where
possible, before admission. This has contributed to a dramatic
reduction in length of stay from 11.5 to 7.5 days, and better
utilisation of beds, while at the same time helping medical
departments and nursing staff to plan their work more
efficiently.

The introduction of management to medical staff has
taken a slightly different course than with the sisters and administrators. Because of their working conditions, their commitments outside the hospital, and the lack of definition of
the management role within the hospital, it is rarely possible
to bring them together to form management seminars or the
like. Instead, the introduction of projects suggested by themselves is used to demonstrate how management can help in a
very practical way.

As interest grows and spreads, then parables are used,
either with individuals or small interested groups, to convey
the fundamental principles behind what is being carried out
in practice. At the outset it is necessarily a very unstructured
approach. Only when the doctors really want to become
more closely involved is any attempt made to establish
formal meeting grounds or committees, as in the case of staff
specialists.

The aim is first, to demonstrate that management is relevant to the professional's job, and that it can help the doctor
in his service to his patients. Secondly this approach gives the
doctors an insight into how a hospital is managed, so that
they can better utilise the services on behalf of their patients.
At the same time they really understand the competing
demands placed on these services. Finally, since the system is
always open to improvement, doctors can spot weaknesses,
understand why they occur, and have the insight to make
constructive suggestions for correcting them.

Multidiscipline projects

One of the basic objectives of the management fundamentals
approach in all the studies is to break down communications
barriers between individuals and groups and so reduce as far

as possible the negative effects of conflicting objectives. Ultimately, multidiscipline projects become a major feature of any programme, whatever organisation is involved.

In a hospital, many activities require the involvement of more than one profession. Writing in the Royal Melbourne Hospital's 1971/72 Annual Report Dr Yeatman, Medical Superintendent, described a number of such projects undertaken as part of the programme carried out at his hospital:

'In the past year an appraisal has been undertaken of a number of activities of the hospital. It became apparent that many problems existed where a number of departments were required to operate in harmony in the patient's interest. For example, co-ordination of the efforts of a number of departments was required in order to achieve the speedy admission of patients. The services of the Admitting Officers, Accounts Department, Medical Records Department, Medical Orderlies and the Ward team were all closely involved....

Clear direction was required from a forceful Executive to improve administrative control systems, to obtain regular feedback of information to streamline a number of procedures of the hospital.

But perhaps the most worthwhile results are coming from a number of project teams, made up of representatives of various hospital departments. These teams were formed for the purpose of solving particular problems.

One team has the task of developing an appointments system for out-patients. As a result, a Central Appointments Desk was established and charged with making all out-patients appointments within the hospital. There has been a substantial improvement in the system in the short period since the formation of the Central Appointments Desk. Besides the patients, many doctors who refer patients to the Out-patient Department of Royal Melbourne also are benefiting.

Another of the project groups has been trying to reduce the waiting time for patients booked electively for admission. The administrative procedures necessary before admission have been smoothed considerably, but delays still occur when beds are not available for patients arriving for admission.

The Casualty Radiology Service was reviewed by a project team with the aim of improving the system of sending

films and reports to the wards with patients on admission.
Within the limits of present staff and facilities the team
was able to ensure that nearly two-thirds of all patients
X-rayed in Casualty had their films reported on and sent to
the wards in company with the patient.

The Out-patients Pharmacy team was able to change
their staffing rosters and improve their dispensing methods.
This reduced the waiting time of patients by two-thirds to
an average of less than half an hour. We believe that a
better patient service has resulted from the work of these
teams and are confident that these improvements will
continue.

Other developments in the Out-patients Department include the rescheduling of Surgical Clinics and the establishment of an Anticoagulant Clinic in conjunction with
the Department of Haematology. A relatively simple individual patient appointment system has been introduced for
surgical clinics. Already it has resulted in a reduction in
waiting time for patients.'

In seven general hospitals world-wide where programmes
are now underway, multidiscipline projects follow a single-
discipline start, the objective being to give each professional
group a common understanding of management before bringing them together on a mixed exercise.

However, in two mental hospitals—Viborg Hospital in Denmark and Callan Park in New South Wales—a multidiscipline
approach was used right from the start, and psychiatrists,
mental nurses, administrators and community workers have
worked together on the initial stages of the programme.
Vertical approaches do ensure that at least each level within
the hierarchy is committed to change. So often one tries to
change attitudes only in a horizontal level of the organisation—change cannot occur in isolation. At Viborg this vertical
strategy has been largely responsible for a 40 per cent reduction in bed requirement and confinement of patients.

Apart from management training of the type already outlined, there are two specific training programmes that the
hospitals regard as particularly important:

1   Preparing the up-and-coming sisters for the heavy res-
     ponsibilities they face when promoted to take charge of
     a ward.
2   Teaching staff at all levels throughout the hospital how
     to deal with patients (clerks and engineers must know

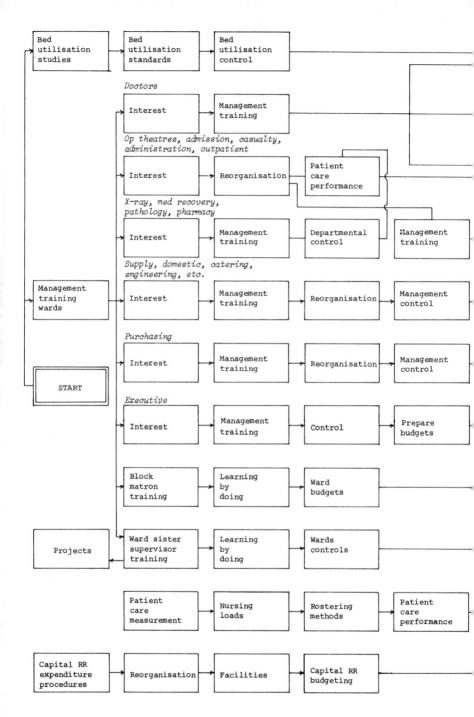

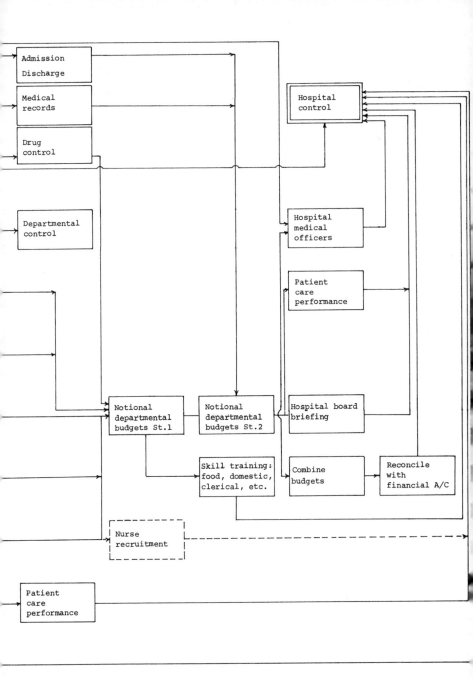

Figure 9.5 Sydney Hospital Management Development Programme

this, as well as doctors and nurses).

An outline of the various 'change' training programmes in this hospital is shown in Figure 9.5.

Summary

For something so complex and diffuse as a project to change the management style of a teaching hospital, it is difficult to decide what have been primary issues and what merely secondary. However, it is believed that an initial decision to direct the weight of attention to two matters simultaneously: (*a*) to the attitudes of mind of departmental staff and (*b*) to the management methods they employed have been very important. This partnership has occurred throughout every study in this book.

Departmental heads and their staff, more than anyone else, determine the quality, quantity and cost, in this instance, of the work done by the hospital. More even than knowledge, it is their attitude of mind which determines what will be done and how well it will be done. If, in addition, they know what to do (managerially), one is a long way towards a good job being done; but if they are not interested and do not want to know, then no amount of streamlined procedures, reorganisation or training avails us. Stimulating interest has been the first priority throughout as Figure 9.5 indicates. Motivation and commitment therefore go hand in hand, forming the true basis and solid foundation for participation and involvement.

Because people are motivated by what they themselves want to do, one had, somehow, in this study for instance, to get staff to see their jobs in line with patient needs. In practice this proved not too difficult. The reason, perhaps, is that hospital people get great satisfaction from helping patients (or helping their colleagues to help patients) and these objectives are, of course, the hospital's objectives. Because it was a hospital they were really very fortunate in being able to provide strong job satisfaction for their staff so closely aligned to their objectives as an institution. Business people do not get the same satisfaction from making profits for shareholders. One makes this point because too many hospital administrators dwell so much on hospital disadvantages; there are some very real advantages as well.

In the past Sydney Hospital, in common with other hosp-

itals, has undoubtedly traded too much on the interest and
fulfilment their staff get from their work. As in the UK, they
have underpaid and overworked willing horses as nursing and
medical militancy in the UK is indicating. Perhaps even more
important, they have not paid enough attention to their
management 'housekeeping', hoping that, because a spirit of
service prevailed, somehow management problems would not
arise, or if they did, that they would sort themselves out.
The same is true with many of the case studies be it shipbuilding or printing. Of course, problems seldom sort themselves out, so interminable committee discussions tried to
patch up and make do with what the hospital, in this instance, can now see was at root managerially unsound.

It is greatly to the credit of this Institution and of all the
case study organisations and their executives here described
that they not only appreciated the need for change but the
need for maximum employee involvement in the change programme. Consideration for, and the participation of the
'employee' are still seen as luxuries by many organisations
which they feel they cannot yet afford. It is becoming painfully obvious that they are necessities we cannot afford to be
without.

APPENDICES

Appendix A

SUGGESTED GUIDELINES ON PROFIT

The book, *Facts About Business: Why Profits?*, published by Facts About Business, 5 Plough Place, Fetter Lane, London EC4A 1AN, is of particular value to me when giving this training.

PROFIT

What is profit?

The general aim or objectives of all business organisations is to make what is called a profit. But what is a profit? Why is profit accepted as the objective of a business?

First of all, we can define company profit quite simply by saying that it is the amount of its revenue from sales remaining in the company's hands after it has met all of the costs of operation. It is what is left after the company has:

1 Paid all its employees their wages and salaries.
2 Paid all the people from whom it has bought goods and services (paper, ink, outwork, etc.).
3 Paid certain legal costs of operation such as rates, training board levy, NHI contributions, VAT, etc.
4 Made provision for maintaining plant and replacing it when worn out.

Why does a company need to make more than just enough to cover its costs? Because the first duty of a business is to survive. It cannot meet its obligations to its customers, to its employees or to the people it owes money to unless it *survives*.

But survival involves risks. Any company wants to keep on surviving in the future—and the only thing certain about the future is its uncertainty, its risks. A business must produce the premium to cover the risks of being in business. The only source from which this premium can come is from the money that's left after all operating costs have been met, i.e. from profits.

Some of the premium needed to cover risks is used to build up reserves of money within the company.

Some of the profit is used to pay shareholders a return on the money they have invested in the business. This also helps guarantee the survival of the business. The fact that the company *can* pay a dividend creates public confidence. On the basis of this confidence, the public in turn permits the company to continue to use its money, and supplies more when the business needs it.

Finally, any company exists in a community. The company can thrive only if the community thrives. The community thrives only if certain things are done by government. For example, people must be educated, the country must be defended, citizens, including organisations, must be protected from the anti-social behaviour of some of the members of the community.

A company pays for the provision of these community services through taxes.

To summarise these points: a *minimum* profit (or surplus of revenue after meeting all the costs of operating the business) is needed to

1   Cover the future risks of the business.
2   Enable the company to continually survive intact as an organisation capable of producing wealth.
3   Enable the company to finance its expansion, either through building up reserves, or by being able to attract investments from the public.

As a final point, profit is the final test of business performance. It measures how sound the business is, and how effective it is in doing what it sets out to do.

What is the process for making profit?

What is the operating process that results in a profit for Design and Print? In outline, the steps are:

1   The company meets customers' needs for print by selling them printed work at a price.
2   Customers provide the company with income by paying for their jobs. The sum of all the payments can be called 'Company Revenue'.
3   The company incurs costs in obtaining this revenue—it pays wages, buys paper and ink and so on. We can call the sum of these costs 'Company Operating Costs'.
4   If we subtract Company Operating Costs from Company Revenue, we can call what is left 'Company Contribution'. This is a contribution to cover other company costs and a contribution to profit.
5   Examples of costs which the company has to meet in addition to operating costs are rent, rates and office salaries. The total of these costs can be called 'Company Overhead Expenses'.
6   If we subtract Company Overhead Expenses from Company Contribution, what is left can be called 'Profit'.
7   Some of this profit is used to pay taxes. Some is used to pay a dividend to shareholders. What is left goes into company reserves.

How are profits made?

The process just described shows how money flows from the point where it comes in 'over the counter', to the point where the company's balance sheet is produced.

It does not tell us anything about how the profit is actually *produced*. How are profits made? Profits are dependent on:

1   How many people we sell print to.
2   The quantities of print sold.
3   The prices we charge.

4   The costs of paper, ink, wages, etc.
5   The costs of premises, presses, managing the business, etc.
6   Other costs such as spoilage and rework, and the losses on sub-
      standard work for which the full price cannot be charged.

None of these things 'just happen'. They do not come about because of
the way we *record* our business. They only come about because somebody in the business *does* something to *make* them happen:

1   The number of sales depends on: (*a*) how many customers *we* can
      persuade to do business with us, (*b*) how good *our* service to cust-
      omers is.
2   The prices depend upon what *we* decide to charge.
3   Costs depend on decisions *we* make. For example, the costs asso-
      ciated with machines depend on what type of machines *we* decide
      to buy, on how many machines *we* decide are needed for our
      business, on how many shifts *we* decide to run the machines, and
      at what speeds *we* decide to run them.
4   Spoilage depends upon the quality standards *we* set, the training
      and instructions *we* give, at what stages of the process *we* place
      checks, and upon what type of checks *we* introduce.

The point of all this apart from things outside our control, is that
nothing can happen to our profit unless *we* make it happen:

1   Either by doing something that makes it increase.
2   Or by doing something that makes it *decrease*, i.e. taking the
      wrong action.
3   Or by *not doing* something that we should do, so that profit isn't
      as much as it should be.

Whether or not the company makes a profit depends on action *we* take.

ANATOMY OF MANAGEMENT

Managing

Definition: 'Getting things done through people'. Managing involves:
1   'Deciding what has to be done' (analysing and planning—handling *ideas*).
2   'Getting people to do it' (training, motivating and controlling—handling *people*).
Management is to do with *ideas* and *people* and the inter-relation between the two.

Management techniques

Cost accounting, work study, market research and so on, are management techniques—tools for managers. To apply them properly one must first know how to manage.

Intention into results

A manager starts by making up his mind what he wants to do (with an *intention*) and he wishes to end with a *result*. There are three ways of converting intentions in to results:
1   Irresponsible delegation.
2   Using people as machines.
3   Partnership in decision and doing.
Only the last is true managing.

The process of managing

The six phases of managing are:
1   Objectives (intentions)
2   Policy
3   Sub-objectives   } Thinking
4   Plans
5   Action   } Results   } Implementing
6   Control
The last two apply only when we put plans into effect.

Phase	Word	Definition	Example	
			Public Service	Business
1	Broad objective (long-term goal)	Required end result	Beautifying city	Make profit
2	Policy	General course of action. Guide lines for decision	Protect trees (also: reduce litter, clear slums, etc.)	Specialise in making precision springs
3	Objective (sub, short-term target, goal)	Points to aim at in reaching end result	Prevent tree destruction	Expand automotive valve spring business
4	Plans (programmes)	Practical details of how objectives are to be reached	Gazette tree preservation orders	Develop new spring for X Motor Co.
5	Action	Putting plans into effect	Enforce legislation	Make samples
6	Control	Ensure action accords with plans	Inspect trees and prosecute offenders	Test samples and follow up on quality and cost

Objectives

The word *objective* can be confusing because it means different things to different people. Thus the main *objective*, the 'Intention' or the 'Ends', of one man will often be a 'Sub-objective' (a step along the way or a 'Means') to his boss. For example, framing legislation is an end in itself to a lawyer, but it is only a 'means' for a city councillor in beautifying the city. Making a new spring is an end in itself, the *objective*, for a production man, but only a *sub-objective* towards making a profit for the company's directors.

Confusion about objectives, because it leads to wrong emphasis on priorities, is at the root of many management difficulties. So often too much attention is given to MEANS before the END, or the purpose, is clear.

Implementation (putting plans into effect)

Implementation involves:
1   *Resources*   Factories, money, knowledge, customer goodwill, personnel.

2   *People's attitudes*   The qualities differentiating people as human beings from 'personnel' as obedient slaves or automata.

3   *Control*   Procedures for ensuring that people carry out plans properly, or where necessary, for adjusting the plans themselves to accommodate reality.

Because *control* compares what people are actually doing to *plans*, it gives the means of either correcting people's actions, or adjusting the plans themselves, or both.

   Control should thus be the focus of a manager's job.

The director and the executive

Managing implies two types of work:
1   *Policy making*   Broad objectives; Policy; Objectives; Monitoring.
2   *Policy execution*   Objectives; Plans; Action; Control.
This is attended by two groups of people: *directors* and *managers*. What follows here relates primarily to managers, i.e. to the job of the executive.

Executive essentials

Summarising, the executive's job roughly embraces:
1   Accepting an objective defined by policy makers, e.g. earning a specific profit.
2   Sub-dividing the objective into *short-term objectives* or sub-objectives, e.g. budgeting.
3   *Planning* how these objectives will be reached, e.g. planning a sales campaign.
4   Organising and directing people to *implement* the plans, modifying the plans themselves where necessary to secure the required result (co-ordinating advertising, sales, production, accounting).
5   *Controlling* activities to ensure that things go according to plan (follow-up departmental progress).
6   *Informing* the policy makers on matters relevant to their duties.
These things are not accomplished single-handed so the executive is also very much involved in communicating, deciding priorities, resolving personal differences and generally motivating a group of people to work together for a common purpose.

Planning	Without proper planning the wrong things will be done, or the right things the wrong way; people will work at cross purposes and control will be impossible.
Controlling	Control ensures that people carry out plans properly and it helps them to learn in the process.
Training	Management results depend on people; on having the right sort of people and in training them properly. Whenever the results are improved it is because people have learned how to do their jobs better.
Communication	Communication relates together the components of the business system.

Appendix C

SPECIFICATION FOR A NEW INCENTIVE SCHEME

As produced for Design and Print, Sussex

This Outline Specification has been produced from notes taken during Discussion Group Sessions. It is intended to represent the outline of the incentive scheme which the employees of Design and Print would wish to see in operation.

This specification in no way implies any agreement at this stage between management and unions. It does provide a basis for further development work.

It was agreed that any new scheme must be subject to a *trial period*, and should continue only as long as it is of mutual benefit to all parties.

It was agreed that any new scheme should be on a company-wide group basis.

The general feeling was that all personnel should be included (except the two Directors, Mr Phillipps and Mr Quibell); one or two of the office girls did, however, express doubts as to whether they personally would wish to participate.

It was agreed that the outline of earnings under the new scheme should be:
- (*a*) Nationally Agreed Minimum Grade Rate.
- (*b*) Nationally Agreed Extras.
- (*c*) Bonus.
- (*d*) Responsibility Money.
- (*e*) (Possibly) Merit Money.

(*a*) Nationally Agreed Minimum Grade Rate is self-explanatory.
(*b*) Nationally Agreed Extras cover such things as machine extras, etc.
(*c*) Bonus—the points agreed were:

Bonus should be based upon a company-wide calculation in the form of

$$\frac{\text{Company Output (£)}}{\text{Company Resources (£)}}$$

Bonus should be calculated at intervals of 1, 2 or 3 months.

It should be paid weekly.

It should be expressed as an hourly rate.

The hourly bonus rate for an individual should be related to his/her basic rate.

It should be paid on all attendance hours.

There should be a minimum fallback bonus level (or a house rate).

Possibly a stepped (or banded) incentive approach might be employed.

(*d*) Responsibility pay should be paid in recognition of supervisory and/or other special duties.

(*e*) Merit money—a need was seen under the group scheme outlined above, for some recognition of exceptional contributions by specific individuals. However, the use of merit payments to recognise such contributions was viewed with concern by many group members, their main fear being that such a scheme would be devisive and reduce group co-operation. It seemed to be the general feeling that if a merit scheme were to operate, then the decisions on who should receive merit money should be taken by the management. At this stage, merit money should therefore be regarded as an 'optional extra' to a new incentive scheme.

BUDGETS, BUDGETING AND BUDGETARY CONTROL

If you have built castles in the air, your work need not be lost; that is where they should be. Now put the foundations under them. (Thoreau)

Introduction

The basic aim of a budget is to set levels of costs or expenditure expected to be incurred in a period of time so that actual costs incurred may be measured against the forecasts. A standard of performance is thus set up which also serves as an important management control.

If the budget is to be a meaningful expression of standards of performance to be achieved in the period in review, it must be built up in detail from the bottom of the organisation. It is vital that people responsible for achieving results, participate in the preparation of their own budgets, and that the budgets are not just imposed from the top. Obviously major changes in policy and fund availability must be notified from the top and the budgets will have to be set in accordance with any given parameters.

At the local level of budget preparations, it is important to examine critically and systematically the amount of spending. Decisions on positive specific action, to reduce the amount required, or minimise any increases in expenditure, will have to be taken. 'Once off' or unusual items of expenditure in the current period and in the review period will need to be identified.

All known and forecast factors should be taken into consideration. For example, some important local works may give rise to a significantly increased expenditure forecast in one particular area; the prospect of a wage increase for a particular industry may indicate an increased budget overall or in a special work area, and so on.

The financial effects of action decisions and non-recurring events must be estimated so that adjustments may be made to the current period's data which will be serving as a basis for setting up the expenditure levels in the review period. It cannot be over-emphasised that each period's budget presents a different set of problems which must all be critically examined.

To be an effective tool the budget must not simply be a reflection of the '10 per cent more than last year' attitude. This approach is totally inadequate. It leads to the continuation of inefficiencies; it encourages spending 'because the money is available'; 'because the budget has got to be used up'. This attitude does not encourage management to think critically and constructively about what it has to do and how best it should be done.

The result of all this is a plan of action for a period, usually a year, a statement of budgeted expense totals for each type of expense, together with a summary of the assumptions which have been used to compile it. Expenditure to be included in the make up of a budget will broadly fall into two classifications: variable and fixed. Each of these types of expenditure will now be considered.

Variable costs

These are developed from calculations of two key factors:
1   Cost rates per unit of output for each class of resource.
2   Estimates of the volume of work to be done in the period.
Unit costs are obtained by considering all aspects of the activity by:
  Work method
  Labour requirement
  Pay rates
  Material requirement
  Material costs
  Plant to be used
  Plant hire rates
and so on. If standard costs are available these may be used for budgeting.

An example of building up a budget item using unit costs, standard cost, known factors and other variables follows. It will be seen that a detailed examination of all elements is needed to get a good working forecast.

Example: assume an earth fill of 20,000 cubic yards for foundations for new works, to be completed within 2 weeks:
  Equipment to be used—bulldozers.
  One bulldozer costs £10 per hour working (1) or £4 per hour idle (2). (1) includes depreciation, fuel, operator's wages and maintenance. (2) includes depreciation and maintenance.
  Normal working week—40 hours.
  Effective utilisation—90 per cent of normal working week.
  Standard rate of output while working—100 cubic yards per hour.
From the above information it is possible to prepare a variable cost budget for the particular item of expense as follows:
  Volume to be shifted, 20,000 cubic yards.
  Output per hour per bulldozer, 100 cubic yards.
Therefore 200 bulldozer hours are required, equal to 5.5 effective working weeks.
  Thus 3 machines will be required: 2 for 2 weeks, 1 for 1.5 weeks.
  36 hours normal costs at £10/hr =   360
  4 hours idle costs at £4/hr   =   16
                                   £376 per bulldozer per week

  5.5 weeks × £376 = £2068.
Thus:
  Budgeted costs for this operation = £ 2068
  Actual costs for this operation   =   2140
  Excess costs for this operation   = +   72 or +3.4 per cent
                                               over budget

This variance will show up on the management report for the period in which the expenditure occurred. The variance may be within the acceptable limits, or if not must be explained. Labour and other variable cost budgets will be prepared in this detailed way.

The significance of this method is two-fold:

1   It encourages greater attention to be paid to what costs are actually likely to be.
2   It provides the essential element—the measure—in the cost control process, as well as providing the standard of performance.

Fixed costs

This budget element differs from variable costs completely in that the expenditure likely to be incurred is well known and the quantum established either from historical data or from exact statements of future needs, coupled with known prices. Salaries, rents, office equipment hire, telephone rentals are examples of fixed costs. They may be subject to change, but the change is known well in advance, and these costs are not subject to variation in output. Some semi-variable costs such as printing and stationery, phone calls, etc., may for convenience be included with fixed costs. These are items where fairly accurate forecasts of useage can be made, and cost, in these cases varies with useage.

In preparing a budget a detailed analysis must be made of the type of cost entering into the expenditure of the operating unit. Such an analysis will:

1   Separate fixed, variable and semi-variable costs.
2   Make us examine closely our plans and needs especially in respect of variable costs.
3   Make us realise that much of our forecasting is intelligent guess work, but make these estimates as fact supported as possible.
4   By becoming involved in the process of forecasting costs, accept the fact that we have a standard to meet, and make all concerned with the expenditure of money become conscious of getting value for money and good performance.

Budgetary control

The sum of all the budgets of the branches must be compatible with the overall intention of the department so that the whole budget is the financial expression of the work proposed to be done in the year. The reviewing of the budget undertaken at branch and departmental level is a vital step in the budgeting process not simply to ensure that the proposed spending is likely to be acceptable to the board, but also to ensure that

1   The assumptions, predictions and plans for action on which the budget is based are reasonable.
2   A good degree of budgetary control is maintained, with possibility of action available to improve results.
3   Acceptable revisions are made in order to achieve the desired

results and to improve presentation and actionability for future
years.
4   The budgets are fair statements of standards of performance, by
which all those responsible for costs may measure their performance.
Comparisons of budget with actual expenses will be a simple matter.
The new chart of accounts will provide great flexibility in allocating
expense according to responsibility therefore budgets drawn in accordance with the expense account codes will be reported upon in the same
terms so as to achieve control and action on variances.

Responsibility accounting

Budgets should be prepared by the individuals who will be responsible
for achieving them. The object here is partly to make use of the knowledge of those who know most about the detail; but, more important, to
ensure that managers and their subordinates eventually regard the
budgets as their own intentions.

The more 'grass roots' level the budgeting process starts from, the
better chance there will be of obtaining realistic results. Cost control at
branch level will be more effective with the greater involvement of
lower echelon staff.

Budgeting also requires the provision of management control information—a feedback system which compares the performance and effectiveness of operating with the plan. This provides the opportunity for
re-appraisal and adjustment to plans.

It will be appreciated that we are talking about flexible systems,
about guides and not strait-jackets. We are talking about better decision
making and more effective monitoring of progress. This is a move
towards facilitating the whole complicated business of running an
enterprise—not to make it more restrictive and difficult.

Much of the point of budgeting and analytical budgeting in particular is that it is concerned with management effectiveness. It is better to
do the right job moderately well than to do the wrong job superlatively
well. Of course it is better still to do the right job superlatively well, but
analytical budgeting procedures assist in determining priorities and with
a proper feedback system help management to monitor performance.

To summarise, budgeting is a technique that provides
1   The statement for action this year.
2   Feedback of information on progress.
3   Involvement of all persons responsible for costs.
4   Control, appraisal, re-direction.

Appendix E

PERFORMANCE AND MEASUREMENT

Performance

1 Definition

Beware of the word, it has several meanings—*you* may know what you mean but others may not, e.g. 'high performance' car (powerful) and a 'good' theatrical performance (enjoyable).

Our meaning:

$$\text{Performance} = \text{A ratio} = \frac{\text{Output}}{\text{Input}} \quad (\text{'Efficiency'})$$

That is, what we get out of something for what we put in.

Examples:

1   A shopping expedition. We all like to spend 'wisely'—we relate what we get to what we paid for it. We are pleased with a high performance, e.g. good 'value for money'.
2   Cigarette machine (a box); put something in (coins); get something out (packet of cigarettes). We don't have to know about its insides to know whether it 'performs' satisfactorily.
3   Lawn mowing. We have to know how big the lawn is and the time taken, before we can assess performance.

The ratio of output to input is called an *index*. Typical performance indices used in management are:

Labour cost *per* hour.

Stock Turnover *per* year.

Sales *per* month (or per year, etc.).

Profit *per* cent (%) (on sales, or funds employed).

*Per*formance, i.e. achievement, is commonly expressed as a *per*centage.

2 Why is 'performance' so important?

Absolute quantities are meaningless in themselves—there has to be something to compare them with. Performance simplifies this comparison.

Examples:

1   *Labour turnover* 'We lost two people' doesn't mean anything unless we know in how long and out of staff of how many. To lose two people out of a staff of ten in one week is significantly bad. To lose two out of 1000 in a year is miraculously good.
2   *Profit* A company earned a profit on sales of £10,000 last year. Is this good or bad?

If the company earned £10,000 on £50,000 sales (average profit 20 per cent) it would have done vastly better than if the

£10,000 had been earned on £100,000 sales (2 per cent profit).
We know from experience (our yardstick) that 20 per cent is good
and 2 per cent is poor.
3   *Building progress*   How is the builder getting on with your
house? I see the walls are going up. Before we answer we need to
know (*a*) what the builder's programme is, (*b*) how much brick-
work has been done and (*c*) a comparison of (*a*) and (*b*).

3 Performance and measurement

A figure for *per* cent (or *'per'* anything else) is a *ratio*, a mathematical
shorthand. Before we can use the shorthand we must put numbers on
('Quantify') what we are talking about. Contrast: 'I can mow my lawn,
which is fairly big, in an afternoon' with 'I can mow a tennis court (320
square yards) in 30 minutes'. The former is a vague statement, the latter
is precise.
     When we can quantify (put numbers on) things we get two advan-
tages:
1   It forces precision and eliminates argument (arguments stem from
     differences of opinion).
2   It enables useful comparisons to be made, i.e. comparisons
     between different situations and comparisons between the actual
     event and a standard of performance.

Measurement

Performance indices are important to a manager. They depend on his
ability to measure results. But measuring results can be such a tricky
business that the subject of measurement itself is worth looking at.

1 What do we mean by 'measurement'?

We mean 'expressing things in numbers'. Lord Kelvin said: 'When you
cannot express it in numbers your knowledge is of a meagre and unsatis-
factory kind'.

2 What is a 'measure'?

For example, when recruiting staff, you see whether applicants
'measure' up to your requirements. Requirements for policemen?

Height	How tall?
Weight	How heavy?
Intelligence	How bright?

Reasonable uniformity in recruits is easy if one man is doing the recruiting, but suppose you have two different recruiting sergeants: one small
and very intelligent, the other big and a bit dull. What is likely to
happen? Small man will tend to recruit small bright policemen, the big

man will tend towards big dull ones.

How do we get uniformity? By *measuring*

Height	Feet and inches (or metres)
Weight	Stones and pounds (or kilogrammes)
Intelligence	I (Intelligence) Q (Quotient) test

3   The practical problems of measuring

How do we measure:

Height	Ruler—easy
Weight	Scales—more complex
Intelligence	I (intelligence) Q (quotient) test—more complex still

Supposing we added 'Conscientiousness'. This is so complex we can't measure it—yet. It is a subjective assessment; however this can be useful, especially if regularised, e.g.

HIGH CONSCIENTIOUS

↓

COMPLETELY IRRESPONSIBLE

The *Queen's Regulations* for the Royal Navy state:

1105 3   Hair, beards, moustaches and whiskers are to be neatly cut and trimmed and, so far as practicable uniformity in length is to be established.

How much accuracy do we need? The purpose of data is to help make decisions which lead to appropriate *action*. Provided data is sufficiently accurate to lead to the right decision, further accuracy is irrelevant. If we can only trim beards to ½ and inch, there is no point in specifying length to 1/16 of an inch.

4   What measures do managers use?

Profit	£
Sales	£
Expenses	£
Labour turnover	Number
Complaints	Number
Faults/accidents	Number
Delays	Weeks
Production volume	Tons
Absenteeism	Days

Accuracy

The standards and targets on a management control statement are a convenient shorthand for expressing our intentions. If these figures are not reliable it means that we are not expressing our intentions clearly. Numerical control forces a discipline. On the other hand, the act of expressing something in numbers does not necessarily mean we know any more about it, it may be merely that we fool ourselves with a spurious accuracy.

However, because it is convenient to do so and because it disciplines our thinking, figures ($, tons, feet, units, hours, dates, etc.) are very commonly used. For some subjects this may at first sight appear impossible to do. For example, how does one measure an intangible quality like 'Reputation'? The answer: by looking for an indirect tangible measure, e.g. number of enquiries (because of reputation).

What accuracy do we require anyway?

The sole purpose of management data is to help make decisions which lead to appropriate *action*. Provided data is sufficiently accurate to lead to the right decisions, further accuracy is irrelevant. Figures need only represent events to the extent we can take action. Provided they lead us to the right conclusion that is all we require. In any case, data itself seldom tells us the answer—it points to questions we should ask to discover the real situation.

Very often we are merely interested in whether something is getting better or worse, bigger or smaller, or whether there is 'enough'. Precisely how much smaller or how accurately enough is often immaterial to our decision.

At the same time we must be careful to guard against vague, inaccurate or confusing information or be lulled by pseudo accuracy. For example look at the irrelevance of expressing to an accuracy of one part in a hundred, something that is erratically variable to one part in ten!

Conclusions about accuracy of data can be summed up thus:

1   Do not allow an inability to get mathematical accuracy prevent data being used—some is almost always better than none. As G.K. Chesterton said, 'If a thing is worth doing, it is worth doing badly.'

2   But always try and make data as accurate as possible consistent with its purpose and the cost of getting it.

3   Read into data all it can reveal but do not try to read beyond what is there.

4   Remember that results are influenced by many factors beside those selected for control.

Typical performance indices

The following are real examples of performance indices used successfully for management decisions:

Quotation achievement	Machine utilisation
Orders overdue	Material yield
Customer complaints	Clerical staff cost
Staff turnover	Return on funds
Labour cost per hour	Stockturn
Programme achievement	Profit

Market penetration

Output per hour

Overtime worked

Labour performance

Sales cost per £ of sales

Drawings completed per week

Reject rate

Overdue accounts

Stock levels

Sales value

Accounting ratios (Liquidity, etc.)

Mark-up

Sales per square foot

Deaths per 1000 patients

New accounts opened

Items out of stock

Market share

Calls per day

MINUTES OF A TYPICAL WORKS COMMITTEE MEETING

FRED OLSEN LINES: WORKS COMMITTEE MEETING

Present: J. Lear, G. Morris, A. Coveney, F. Moore, W. Makin,
S. Newton, J. Connolly (Chairman), G. Lane (Secretary).
Letter of resignation received from P. Shea who regretted that he must
leave the Committee. This was accepted.

Matters arising from previous minutes:
Holidays   Notice to be displayed on Board reminding members of
minute of 14 November.

'Men are expected to take one week's holiday between January and May,
weeks 1-21; bookings will be taken up to Friday 15 December on a first
come first served basis. Maximum number allowed away in any one
week is 20 men.

Position of these bookings will be reviewed after this date and if necessary any man who has not booked this one week will have dates allocated to him. It should be noted that men are not restricted to one week
only during this period, if desired, more than one week can be taken.

All other holidays will be booked on a first come first served basis
and maximum during final period, September to December, will be 20
men.

All holidays not booked by 14 September will be subject to allocation from the first week of October.'

Bookings for this first week are not coming forward and men are reminded that situation is to be reviewed after 15 December for this first
week to be allocated if necessary. Holiday booking forms are available
at the Labour Desk.

HGV licences   Further discussions on difficulties in obtaining licences
and report on outcome of visit to Licencing Head Office at Acton and
information obtained there. This matter was left on the table 'till next
meeting whilst further enquiries are made.

At the present time the working way of a member of the Terminal
Force being positioned with the driver of the vehicle should continue.

This man must be drawn from a position apart from the hatch where
item is being loaded so that number of ship-side men is not depleted
whilst vehicle is being brought to the ship side.

Familiarisation of working ways   A number of complaints were made
of both Management and Terminal Force not abiding to the laid down
working ways.

(*a*) Short manning on *MS Borre* on second shift on Friday 24 November at the Forward Port and excessive manning at the aft port on
Black Watch on second shift Wednesday 22 November. Both these
matters were discussed.

(b) Gas truck had again been used for transporting sets of pre-slung pulp and had been turned over, causing excessive damage to the truck.

(c) That a few men were objecting to being re-allocated after receiving their initial allocation from the labour desk. These men must appreciate that allocation is prepared by noon of the previous day and therefore there are always likely to be changes. These members of the Force are reminded of the Flexibility clause of 'The Agreement' and that when necessary they must accept these new orders.

Safety awards and conference   One day Safety Conference arranged by Thurrock College had been a success and worthwhile attending. Letter of appreciation to be sent to Organiser.

The 'Bronze Medal' for Safety awarded by the British Safety Council was collected on behalf of the Terminal by G. Morris and H. Aylett (Safety Officer).

It has been decided by the British Safety Council that this will be a yearly award so we must in future aim for a 'Gold Medal'.

Letter has been received from Peter Shore MP, apologising for being unable to attend at the Guild Hall to present our Award. G. Morris has replied to this letter with an invitation that he visits the Terminal.

Reefer production   This matter is still being progressed in an attempt to improve method of loading and therefore the production.

Baggage—Victoria Coach   It was agreed that with full compliment of passengers four men are necessary for this job and therefore should be allocated. It was also stated that some maintenance is required to the lower stage of the baggage conveyor used for this operation.

AGENDA

1 Ship working ways
  (a) Hanging deck—Canary service—Bad plates
  (b) Variation of work—Winch drivers
  (c) Munck Crane—Maintenance
  (d) Floormen No. 1 Shed
  (e) Work position—22 December
2 Communications:
        Channel flow
        Dock runners

1 Ship working ways
(a) *Hanging deck—Canary service—Bad plates*   Complaint that the Plates on *MS Black Watch* hanging deck are in need of repair and could be dangerous. This matter will be investigated on vessel's return. It was pointed out that this matter should have been brought to the notice of a Supervisor at the time so that investigations could have been made then and there.
(b) *Variation of winch drivers*   Complaint that certain men are constantly being allocated to this job—noted.
(c) *Munck Crane—Maintenance*   Complaint that forks of this equip-

ment are out of alignment. It was stated that complete overhaul has been arranged in Oslo. An audible safety alarm which operates when crane is moving up or down is being fitted. New motors are being fitted to make the operation smoother and to stop the crane jerking at the start of its movement.

To obviate men working underneath this crane it must pick up or deposit the pallets at right angles to the side port. The deck will therefore be painted to show loading areas and area where working is restricted will be marked in yellow.

(*d*) *Floormen No. 1 Shed* Complaint that due to regular floormen leaving under severance, men are being given this job at irregular intervals and are therefore not fully familiarised with the requirements. Position of both floormen and lock-up men on a regular basis for all sheds is being reviewed.

(*e*) *22 December* All men will work on the first shift on this day. Any men not required will be given day off on the normal rota. Men at work who have been allocated to vessels that are sailing are expected to co-operate and work until cargo has been completed but other than this custom and practice of men finishing at 1100 hours will be recognised.

2   Communications

Channel Flow   Although this is at present a small operation if successful it could produce an offer to load an average of 15 lorries outwards each week.

1200 hours standing orders suspended.

FFOL   Management stated that they had been informed that the FFOL Line is to cease operations as it has not been a financially viable operation. The main reasons for this being lack of east bound cargo and the long voyage times, for although a round trip time of 56 days was required average times have turned out to be 61 days.

Dock runners   As there are no other canteen facilities at week-ends and evenings for dock runners, request had been made for these men to use the Company canteen. This matter is in the hands of the Amenity Committee and the Manager.

Shrink wrapping   Request that Terminal Force be given day off on New Year's Day. Management stated that this could not be agreed to because of work commitments already made.

There being no further business the Chairman declared the meeting closed at 1310 hours.

GLC HOUSING DEPARTMENT MAINTENANCE STANDARD

Building Maintenance is work undertaken in order to keep, restore or improve every facility, i.e. every part of a building, its services and surrounds to a currently accepted standard and to sustain the utility and value of the facility (definition recommended in R. and D. Bulletin BUILDING MAINTENANCE D. of E.).

Excluding improvements which are the responsibility of Development Branch, there are two main divisions of Maintenance standards: (*i*) Quality Standards and (*ii*) Service Standards.

(*i*) *Quality Standards* An acceptable quality of maintenance work is controlled by supervisory or technical staff. Faults of workmanship can be the cause of complaint and tenant frustration. The production of good quality work gives operatives job satisfaction. The R. and D. Bulletin states that Maintenance Operatives deal with a wider variety of work than those in new construction, they should receive training and cover the skills of more than one craft so that the Maintenance Operative might develop as a general-purpose technician.

Quality control is most important to staff in all levels of maintenance management and vigilance at all times is essential to ensure an acceptable standard of work is carried out by Council workmen or Contractors.

(*ii*) *Service Standards* An acceptable standard should not only be to the satisfaction of the Council but must also satisfy tenants as far as housing and estate maintenance is concerned. It is necessary to quantify service standards in time periods in which the activity should be carried out so that programmes of work can be prepared and performance measured to ensure that acceptable standards are being achieved. They must also be reviewed at intervals and appropriate staff are requested to contribute to proposals for improved standards. Tenants should be informed of these standards, especially on day to day repairs.

The current acceptable standards are as follows and these shall be complied with at all times and have formed the basis of the current financial budget.

1 *Painting and Decorating—external*
(*a*) Generally—every five years (including common staircases to flatted blocks with lifts).
(*b*) New property—to be painted in its 3rd or 4th year if found necessary.
(*c*) Short-life property—to be painted if life is two years or more and it has not been painted for four years.
(*d*) Extensive repairs prior to painting—execute one year ahead of painting programme, minor repairs shall be completed three months before painting commences.

(*e*)   Clubrooms—every five years with adjoining properties.

2   *Painting and Decorating—internal*
(*a*)   Generally—every five years and in accordance with 1968 policy revision: in a house or maisonette—the hall, landing and staircase; in a flat or bungalow—the hall and any landing and staircase together with one bedroom. Sashes and frames throughout the building if required to preserve the fabric.
(*b*)   (*i*)   Empties—repair and redecoration as found necessary to be completed within three weeks of receipt of keys from area office.

      (*ii*)   Empties—General Properties
Expenditure up to £750—completion 3 weeks from receipt of keys.
       "   from £750 to £1000—completion 4 weeks from receipt of keys.
       "   "   £1001 to £1500—completion 5 weeks from receipt of keys.
       "   "   £1501 to £2500—completion 6 weeks from receipt of keys.
       "   over £2500—time to be agreed.

(*c*)   Common staircases in the Council's flatted dwellings without lifts and the main entrances to all blocks of flats to be internally redecorated on average every two and a half years.
(*d*)   Laundries—on average every two years.
(*e*)   Clubrooms (Council responsibility first established)—every two years.

3   *Day-to-day Repairs*
Emergencies — make safe or complete within 24 hours of notification.
Bricklaying — within 5 weeks (average programme)
Carpentry — within 4 weeks ("   "   )
Plumbing — within 3 weeks ("   "   )
Glazing — within 2 weeks ("   "   )
Electrical —within 1-2 weeks ("   "   )
Space Heating— within 3 days ("   "   )

4   *Electrical rewiring*—every 25/30 years.

5   *Renewal of Gas Water Heaters*—every 25 years.

6   *Servicing of Gas Appliances*—annually.

7   *Servicing of Electric Water Heater and Incinerators*—annually.

8   *Cleaning of Ventilation Ducts*—annually.

9   *Swing Doors* (floor springs)—annually.

10   *Gulley Cleaning*—once each year.

11 *Refuse*
   (a)   Hoppers on balconies—clean three times each year.
   (b)   Ground Floor Dust Chute Chamber—clean three times each year
         and paint internally as required.

12 *Garden Work*
   (a)   Grass cutting—generally every 9 working days, reduce to 7 work-
         ing days in peak growing periods or increase to 10 working days in
         slow growth periods of drought.
         See Procedural Note No. 18 July 1968.
   (b)   Hedge cutting—twice each year—April/May and August/Sept-
         ember.
   (c)   Hedge splitting—1/5 each year October/March.

13 *Inspections*—Job tickets to be programmed immediately
   (a)   Estate inspections externally—every three months (Surveyors).
   (b)   (i)   Laundries and Drying Rooms including appliances—annually
               (Surveyors).
         (ii) Electrical inspection of laundries—annually by electricians.
   (c)   All properties externally and internally parts which are Council
         responsibility every five years (Surveyors) followed by preparation
         of programme of necessary works.
   (d)   Playground equipment—monthly (Chargehands); (exhaustive con-
         dition tests) every five years (Surveyors).

C.J.R. WHITEHOUSE
Director of Housing

CHECKLIST FOR IMPLEMENTATION OF CHANGE

1   Get the people who will implement it to be thoroughly involved at the conception of a change. Try to make it 'their' scheme.

2   Try to identify the key people who can make your scheme work and also those most likely to make it fail.

3   Explain the proposals to everyone directly involved, and also to those who, although not directly involved, may be affected or may feel they have the right to know. Personal contact and explanation are infinitely better than written memos.

4   Spend a disproportionately large amount of your time with key individuals instead of treating everyone equally.

5   Wherever possible get a pilot scheme working. Demonstration is the best way to sell an idea.

6   Do not overlook that some people genuinely need detailed explanation of trivial particulars and reassurance on minor points.

7   Provide prompt feedback to tell people how they are doing (control and action meetings). This is particularly important at the early stages of implementation.

8   When the inevitable hitches occur fix them promptly if you possibly can. If they cannot be fixed quickly tell people what is being done.

9   Insist that people give the scheme a proper go and deter short cuts, or reversions to old habits. Be ready to investigate difficulties and rectify them where practical experience has shown this to be desirable.

10   Remember that any change has to overcome the inertia of present habits. To produce management change you need authority. If your own authority is unlikely to be adequate, the obvious support of higher authority is essential.

The last point (10) is very important and therefore authority and subsequent accountability is worth discussing further, and in more detail (see Appendix I).

ACCOUNTABILITY AND AUTHORITY

What is accountability?

The Biblical parable of the Ten Talents tells a moral tale of three serv-
ants, each of whom had to 'account' for the stewardship of his master's
property. The same arrangement holds today. We delegate to a manager
the use of a company's facilities (its staff, money, machines, buildings
and so on) and expect him to 'account' for their wise use. ('Wailing and
gnashing of teeth' can still accompany being called to account.)

Accountability is a familiar concept but its simplicity can be decept-
ive. It is easy to understand the logic of a superior sharing responsibility
with his subordinates, but the implications of the arrangement are far
from simple.

Accountability for what?

Take, say, a professional engineer, who has been given the job of designing a bridge. His boss charges the engineer with responsibility for producing drawings and specifications for a structure to meet function,
cost and completion date. But what has the engineer accepted in his
heart as his responsibility? What does he feel accountable for? Possibly
only to practice his professional skills conscientiously for as long as the
job may take to do—and he may be vague about this.

The job runs late because the drawings are late, the boss jumps up
and down with frustration but the engineer remains unmoved. He
regards his boss's behaviour as an eccentricity of a man who does not
realise that 'you cannot be creative to a timetable'. The engineer feels
deeply upset if any of his calculations are proved wrong but he never
really accepted being held accountable for time.

If this company wants their engineer to meet deadlines of his own
accord, they must first get him to accept that it is in fact possible to
design to a timetable, and that it is his responsibility to do so. Just putting in a system for programming design-office work will not get to the
root of the problem, and will therefore be of limited and transitory
value.

Another example is the foreman who has been promoted from the
shop-floor because he is knowledgeable about the job. This man may
feel fully accountable for technical matters but less so for staff discipline. He accepts his Job Specification but with reservations in his heart
about censuring former mates.

What managements employ people to do, and what the people themselves feel they are being paid to do, can be quite different.

Accountability poses two sorts of puzzle: What makes people willing
to be accountable? (Motivation). How should they account? (Control).

For a person to be accountable requires that:
1   He knows what is expected of him.
2   He knows what he is achieving.
3   He has the knowledge, the authority and the means to sufficiently influence the operations he is responsible for.

These are also the conditions for *control*. To be held accountable a person must be in a position to control what he is accountable for.

Many managers are not in a position to control what they are held accountable for. Or they do not think they are, which amounts to the same thing.

If we want a man to feel accountable, an obvious first step is to make sure that his authority matches his responsibility and to be certain that the man knows what he is expected to do. Often clarification of these things is all that is required to transform his attitude to being held accountable. But more often, unfortunately, the problem goes a lot deeper.

What we are up against is a person's self-esteem. If people are to feel truly accountable for something, we mean they cannot look themselves in the face until they have achieved the things they committed themselves to do; or until they have made an attempt they can be proud of.

When we make a plan and then control the work of putting the plan into practice by measuring actual results, we are 'Managing by Objectives'. This procedure, when applied to people who are not used to having their results measured, can be very disturbing. Disturbing in ways that are not apparent on the surface.

For example, there is a wealth of difference between a man agreeing to a target being possible, and to his feeling deeply committed to achieving it. Because his pride will suffer if he fails, he may secretly reject commitment for results. He says to himself that he will do the things he knows he can do but does not necessarily feel responsible for the end results of his activity. He is willing to 'go through the motions' but not necessarily to 'achieve'.

For this man to be prepared to accept accountability for results, he must feel confident that he can achieve the results. He needs the opportunity to demonstrate to himself that he can be successful. He needs guidance and nursing in his job until he has few failures and mostly successes.

Ideal line-management material—the tough 'self-starters'—present few problems in their attitudes to being held accountable. But these men are only a small proportion of those actually doing line managers jobs. The question is therefore: How do we give the less-confident individuals greater confidence?

Improving confidence

Joe Mitchell was the Bottling Department foreman in a food factory. Technically competent, good with staff and easy to deal with, Joe was in many ways an excellent supervisor. But he never succeeded in running his department efficiently and poor results did not seem to worry him. It was not all Joe's fault. His boss was not demanding and furthermore the organisation structure made his job difficult. For example, Joe was required to deal with central services for materials, handling, the hiring and firing of staff and plant maintenance.

After about three years as a foreman in this environment, Joe got a new boss. The new man, more demanding than his predecessor, was immediately concerned about poor bottling department performance. Recognising both Joe's strengths and weaknesses he did three things:

1   He first demonstrated to Joe that the Bottling Department was in fact capable of doing far more than was required. This was done by carrying out a simple Work Study investigation to measure machine output and to locate the chief causes of lost production.

2   He discussed the Work Study findings with Joe and together they developed a simple control statement to record the reasons for lost output.

3   During the next six months he regularly discussed the control results with Joe and gradually taught him how to decide what had to be done and built up his confidence in getting it done until finally Joe required very little help.

Joe's new boss improved Joe's attitude towards accountability for results by:

1   Helping him to get a new insight into the working of his department.

2   By smoothing his path.

3   By building up his confidence through achieving successes.

4   And above all, by forcing Joe to stretch himself.

Joe's boss used control as a tool for not only teaching Joe but developing Joe's confidence in himself as well.

'Authority' versus 'Evocation'

In the example given above Joe's boss took a lot of trouble to build up Joe's confidence in himself. This leads to the subject of management 'style' (the way a boss deals with his subordinates).

At one extreme there is the manager who 'tells people what to do' at the other extreme there is his colleague who 'leads people to see for themselves what they should do'.

The former tells people they will be accountable, the latter makes them, within themselves, feel accountable. In practice, both managers will use a mixture of both methods but one or other is bound to predominate according to the temperament of the boss, the capability of the subordinate and the nature of the situation.

The *authoritarian* (telling people) approach is entirely appropriate in emergencies, whereas *evocation* (leading people to see for themselves) is the best way of teaching. Authority yields quick, but frustratingly transitory results for the boss who knows evocation encourages people to think for themselves and so yield lasting benefits in building up potential managers.

Supposing we want a branch manager to increase his profits. There are two quite opposite ways to go about it.

1   We could begin by overhauling his information system to give a
     clearer 'figure' picture of his work. Through interpreting figures
     he can see the action he should take and by looking at the figures
     ourselves we can keep a watchful eye on progress.

         The method generally yields quick positive results because the
     manager becomes better informed and we are in a position to
     direct him by remote control. So long as we do! For unless we
     also succeed in developing the man to be a better manager him-
     self, his results will depend too much on us. As soon as our atten-
     tion goes elsewhere results will decline. At root, it is our authority
     that makes this system work.

2   A quite different way is not to start with systems and data but
     with the man himself. Look at his job through his eyes and lead
     him to see more clearly his job through our eyes. Lead him to
     decide what is important and what is trivial, and to decide how to
     measure his own performance and what data would help him.
     Guide him to understand and gain confidence in using simple data
     before bothering about refinements.

         By degrees and with technical help requested by the manager
     himself, a system will evolve bearing remarkable similarity to the
     one we would have imposed authoritatively in the first place.

         But there are some important differences. For one thing it is
     his system. He knows it inside out. He really understands what it
     can do for him. He knows his own capabilities. He has gained con-
     fidence as a manager and new pride in his work.

To be evocative we must sincerely believe that people are reasonable,
and willing, within reason, to do a good job. But we must also recognise
they will need help and above all will need to be given genuine encouragement.

The 'lucky' manager

We have all met the 'lucky' manager; very often a charming, rather
casual individual who drifts along with all the time in the world, while
his staff do the work because 'he is a good man to work for'. It is unfair
that a man, with so little effort, should be so consistently successful.

But to what extent is this man lucky? Or, to what extent has he hit
on a very good way of doing his work? Is it luck for example, to be
acutely aware of the strengths and weaknesses of the individuals on his
staff and to take a great deal of trouble to give them jobs that draw the
best out of them? Is it luck to keep personal touch with the customers
to discover at first hand how they feel they are being treated? Is it luck
that makes the boss attend himself to what is vital while leaving the
detail to others?

Surely a manager who does these things is not so much lucky as
sensible. Competently aware of what has to be done, he recognises an
easier life follows from not flaunting his competence to make people
feel smaller, but using it to make them feel bigger through their own
achievements.

To this 'evocative manager', people really do come first. He vividly knows his success depends on his subordinates and that if he himself is to be successful, he must first make success of them. He gives his staff guidance and encouragement to succeed in themselves. He believes the social environment of people to be as important as their physical environment. He recognises that the aims of the individual must be geared with the aims of the organisation; he has the realism to recognise that given half a chance, individual aims will take precedence anyway.

The 'evocative manager' taps what people already have themselves; he makes it easy for them to give what they want to give. He uses his head in appealing to people's hearts.

'Attitude' versus 'manner'

The 'authoritarian manager' says
> I have decided!
> I know I am right!
> Do it my way!

It implies 'telling' or 'imposing' one's views. The manner of this imposition can be dictatorial and brusque, or charming, polite and patient. The manner depends on the personality of the manager. It frequently obscures the underlying relationship between the man and his subordinate.

'Evocative' means evoking or drawing out a conclusion from within the subordinate. With the 'authoritarian' approach, the manner can obscure the process.

An 'evocative manager' appears to be dictatorial when he says impatiently: 'You know the situation, work it out for yourself!'. He gives a superficial impression of being authoritarian when he roughly throws his subordinate back on his own resources.

The 'authoritarian manager' gives a false impression of evocation when he persuades a subordinate to his own viewpoint. After all, it is he who really makes the decision and his patient explanations may not teach his subordinate to be more self-reliant.

The acid test distinguishing the 'authoritarian' from the 'evocative' approach is the effect on the subordinate. Does he become more effective in thinking, deciding and taking action which results in higher performance?

Evocative management is a way of applying Management by Objectives, i.e. attending to 'ends' rather than 'means'. Management by Objectives emphasises essentials, i.e. results, dwells less on the minutiae of 'how' and therefore affords latitude for individual initiative. It is a systematic way of delegating authority and of encouraging people to think and decide for themselves within the overall needs of the business.

Authoritarian management by contrast is very much more concerned with 'means' on the (often false) assumptions that if a man goes through the right motions, the right results follow automatically. This style of management is sometimes essential. There are many types of work (piloting airliners, salary determination in large organisations, complicated or dangerous processes) where staff must work rigidly to rules.

It is seldom a question of: *either* Authority *or* Evocation, but of degree and a blend of the two. More importantly it is a question of attitude. Whether the boss believes staff are paid to do as they are told and their interests are quite secondary to the interests of the organisation, or whether he believes that the very best results will flow when people's own interests are in line with the interests of the organisation. And most important of all, whether he recognises that at root his people do not in fact work for his organisation, they work for him—it is up to him to inspire them.

The following compares the two approaches and are meant the way they are written, i.e. the words express genuine feeling behind thoughts:

Attitude

Authoritarian	*Evocative*
That is what I want!	Let us agree on the objectives.
Do it my way!	How do you suggest they be reached?
Keep me informed!	What can I do to help?
I will tell you what to do next!	Keep me in touch.
Here are the rules—I expect you to stick to them.	Use your initiative but observe this and that because......
I don't care what you think—you are paid to do the job.	How do you feel about it?
Give me the facts and I will decide.	You have the facts, work it out for yourself—but check with me before you do anything.
As from Monday you will do...	We are thinking of doing... it's not settled yet and it may not happen....
We have worked out a new Budgetary Control System.	This is our problem, got any views?
How do you make them (the idiots!) understand.	What prevents them understanding?
Do what I want.	What do you want?

Advantages

Quick essential in emergencies.	Builds more managers.
Direct satisfaction for the boss of power and in being busy.	Less planning required.
Boss prevents anyone becoming too good and threatening his own job.	Allows boss more time to think.

Boss overworked.	Takes more patience.
Never has any good staff.	More risk of somebody taking your job.
Limits organisation growth.	Maybe misunderstood (by an authoritarian boss) as being soft and lazy.

Regardless of whether our approach is authoritarian or evocative, the objectives to be striven for must have the backing of authority. *For unless subordinates accept that it is right to strive for improvement effective control is doomed.*

DEVELOPMENT OF COLOURED SUPERVISORS AT LEYLAND'S CAPE TOWN PLANT

Introduction

The programme to develop coloured supervision began in August 1972 and by January 1974 over 60 coloured supervisors had completed training courses. Delegates to attend the courses are selected by the Production Management.

What the training covers

The supervisors are given 2 courses:
1   Leadership (job relations).
2   Training and developing employees (job instruction).

1   The Leadership Course

By the end of the course delegates should be able to:
    Identify the main duties of a production foreman.
    Understand the main aspects of motivating people.
    Understand how to handle problems on the job.
    Practice problem solving using typical day to day problems (role-
        playing).

2   Training and developing employees

Delegates learn to:
    Break down a typical job into stages.
    Present or teach a learner how to do the job.
    Develop a training plan for their own area.
    Apply this plan.

Appointment of assistant foremen

Arising from the training programme thirteen persons were given more intensive training and eventually promoted to assistant foreman. This training covered:
1   Job rotation where needed.
2   Monthly performance reviews conducted by a supervisor and
        agreed to by the trainee.
3   Monthly meetings with the training department to iron out day-
        to-day problems on job coaching wherever necessary.

Three assistant foremen have been promoted to senior Foremen at the plant at Elsies River and their wages are comparable to whites doing the same job. Coloured persons are also being trained in work study and toolsetting. Leyland South Africa has discovered a great deal of latent talent within its plants which is responding well to the opportunity being given to grow and learn.

TRAINING SCHEME FOR SUPERVISORS

Job Relations Programme

A SUPERVISOR GETS
RESULTS THROUGH PEOPLE

Foundations for Good Relations

Let each employee know how he stands with you.
  Decide what you expect of him.
  Point out ways to improve.

Give credit when due.
  Look for *extra* or *unusual* performance.
  Tell him right away.

Tell people in advance about changes that will affect them.
  Tell them *why* if possible.
  Get them to accept the change.

Make best use of each person's ability.
  Look for ability not being used.
  Never stand in a man's way.

PEOPLE MUST
BE TREATED AS INDIVIDUALS

Determine Objective

Step 1   Get the Facts
Review the record.
Find out what rules and customs apply.
Talk with individuals concerned.
Get opinions and feelings.
Be sure you have the whole story and the right objective.

Step 2   Weigh and Decide
Fit the facts together.
Consider their bearing on each other.
What possible actions are there?
Check practices and policies.
Consider the effect on the individual—group—production.
Remember your objective.
Don't jump to conclusions.

Step 3   Take Action
Are you going to take the action yourself?
Do you need help in taking your action?
Should you inform your supervisor of your action?
Watch the timing of your action.
Don't pass the buck.

Step 4   Check Results
How soon will you follow up?
How often will you need to check?
Watch for changes in output, attitudes and relationships.
Did your action achieve your objective?

Appendix L

MAIN DUTIES OF A PRODUCTION FOREMAN

Summary of main duties

The following are the main duties of a Foreman. Foremen are expected to carry out these duties and will be judged accordingly for future promotions.

1   The foreman plans, organises, leads and controls to make best use of men, materials, machines and time available.
2   He is therefore a Foreman and *not* an Operator.
3   In supervising he should pay particular attention to:
   (*a*)   Quality
   (*b*)   Quantity
   (*c*)   Cost Saving
   (*d*)   Training employees
   (*e*)   Care of equipment
   (*f*)   Housekeeping
   (*g*)   Safety
4   The following departments exist to help him to achieve his objectives:
   (*a*)   Manufacture and Plant Engineering Department. These services consist of: (*i*) Processing—supply build manuals; (*ii*) Maintenance—machine tools, premises; (*iii*) Work Study —time, labour and methods.
   (*b*)   Personnel. The main services are (*i*) Recruitment and Selection; (*ii*) Training, Clinic and Security.
   (*c*)   Quality Control—defines quality levels.
   (*d*)   Supply and Product Planning—supplies materials and build schedules.
   (*e*)   Finance—regulates back flow in order to make profits.
   (*f*)   Controller—supplies budgets and records performance against budgets.

The Production Foreman's job in detail

1   Purpose of the job   To produce a product at the right time, at the lowest cost, to the required quality standard.

2   The 'tools' available to do the job   The 'tools' or resources to do the job are: Men, Materials, Machines and Time. Of these tools you have most control over men and time. You should therefore concentrate on them.
   Your job is to use these tools to the best advantage to produce the required product. This involves supervising or managing the job. You are therefore employed as a *Foreman* and not as an *Operator*.
   In order to supervise the job you must do the following: Plan, Organise, Lead and Control.

3 *What you must plan* Planning must be done in the following manner:

(a) Find out what you are expected to build, study the programme and produce: (*i*) number of units, (*ii*) correct standard and quality, (*iii*) on time.

(b) Check that your 'tools' are in order, i.e. men, materials, machines.

(c) You have now established your target and you have checked your tools. The next step is to organise to meet the target.

4 *What to organise* To organise you must:

(a) Make sure that your operator is supplied with the correct tools and equipment.

(b) Assign duties or workloads to each operator and define each operator's responsibility.

(c) Be alert to modify the workloads per operator to increase their effectiveness, or adjust to changing conditions in line with scheduled requirements.

(d) Ensure that safety and housekeeping requirements are met and maintained.

5 *How to lead effectively* Leading is the work the Foreman does to get his chargehands and operators to do the job. To lead he must:

(a) Motivate or inspire people to work, he can do this by
  (*i*) Telling the operator what the job is.
  (*ii*) Telling him it is important to do the job well, because a badly built vehicle could mean loss of sales, ultimately affecting his employment, and other employees also.
  (*iii*) Their families would ultimately suffer.
  (*iv*) A bad job could pose a hazard on the road.
  (*v*) By working well he will share the Company's success.
  (*vi*) If he works well he could be given more interesting work.

(b) If none of these approaches work tougher action is needed such as warning the operator that poor workmanship will not be tolerated, and action taken in the following order:
  (*i*) Place a warning on his card.
  (*ii*) Take disciplinary action.
  (*iii*) Discharge him.

(c) In instructing operators always ensure
  (*i*) That the operator is prepared for instruction.
  (*ii*) That instruction is clearly presented.
  (*iii*) That the operator understands and can do the job.
  (*iv*) That he is put to work and the job is checked periodically.

(d) Make sure that your operators are fully trained.

(e) Develop a training programme for your operators. The steps in doing this are:
  (*i*) Get to know the job.
  (*ii*) Get to know each operator's strengths and weaknesses.
  (*iii*) Decide who should be trained by when.
  (*iv*) Keep the programme up to date.

6 *Controlling the job involves:*

(a) Checking expenses and reducing costs.

(b) Checking that operators are complying with Process requirements.

(c) Process Quality Standards.

(d) Quality Company Rules, Safety, Housekeeping, etc.

(e) Keeping your boss informed of progress by accurate production unit lists and accurate manhour recording for performance purposes, and above all, communicating with him.

Appendix M

PERFORMANCE REVIEW–1

CAR DIVISION — PERFORMANCE REVIEW	
(Non-Managerial Salaried Personnel)	
NAME: C. O'CALLAGHAN	POSITION: Prod". Foreman — PERIOD IN THIS POSITION: 2 years
PERIOD OF REVIEW: 1 year	DATE OF REVIEW: 4/10/73

FACTORS UNDER REVIEW:	ACTUAL PERFORMANCE.
List briefly the main duties and responsibilities as well as the objectives which have previously been agreed upon between the supervisor and the employee.	Indicate the employee's actual performance on each factor under review and suggest how he can improve his performance.
1) ATTAINMENT OF PRODUCTION PROGRAMMES WITH ACCEPTABLE UNITS	VOLUMES ARE AT TIMES ATTAINED WITH DIFFICULTY, BETTER ORGANISATION OF OPERATORS UNDER HIS CONTROL WOULD IMPROVE THIS.
2) MAINTENANCE OF QUALITY STANDARDS BY CHECKING ON OPERATORS WORK	QUALITY STD. IS GENERALLY WELL MAINTAINED + OPERATORS WORK IS CHECKED FREQUENTLY.
3) IMPROVEMENT OF QUALITY STANDARD BY FOLLOW UP AND ELIMINATION OF PROBLEMS HIGHLIGHTED BY QUALITY CONTROL	IMMEDIATE EFFORT IS MADE TO ELIMINATE HIGHLIGHTED PROBLEMS.
4) HOUSEKEEPING :- FLOOR CLEANLINESS + TIDY STOCK LAYOUT	THIS AREA IS KEPT IN A NEAT + TIDY CONDITION HOWEVER THERE IS ALWAYS ROOM FOR IMPROVEMENT.
5) OBSERVANCE + CONTROL OF SAFETY REGULATIONS	MORE ATTENTION TO BE PAID + STRICTER DISCIPLINE ENFORCED ON OPERATORS NOT WEARING SAFETY GLASSES
6) COST CONTROL :- (a) MATERIAL COST	REASONABLY WELL CONTROLLED BUT GREATER SAVINGS CAN BE MADE.
(b) OPERATING COST (N° OF MEN VS UNITS PRODUCED)	FAIRLY GOOD, BUT STRICTER CONTROL WOULD INCREASE OUTPUT PER MAN.
7) HUMAN RELATIONS IN HANDLING PROBLEMS	GOOD, HE HAS THE ABILITY TO GET ON WELL AT ALL LEVELS.
8) OPERATOR TRAINING.	FAIRLY GOOD. NEW OPERATORS ARE SHOWN HOW, WHEN + WHERE + ARE ABLE TO PERFORM OPERATIONS ON THEIR OWN AFTER A REASONABLE PERIOD.

PERSONAL PROBLEMS which may be impairing the employee's performance.

NIL

EVALUATION OF PERFORMANCE
(This section is applicable to all employees)

	Unsat.	Sat. Minus	Sat.	Sat. Plus	Excell.	Outst
JOB KNOWLEDGE: How well does the employee know the requirements of his job?	☐	☐	☑	☐	☐	☐
QUANTITY OF WORK: What volume of acceptable work does the employee produce in relation to the normal expectation for this job?	☐	☐	☑	☐	☐	☐
QUALITY OF WORK: Does he consistently produce accurate, neat and thorough work?	☐	☐	☐	☑	☐	☐
CO-OPERATION: How well does he co-operate with his colleagues, his supervisor and personnel from other departments?	☐	☐	☐	☑	☐	☐

ATTENDANCE:
Is he punctual, diligent and consistent in his attendance? If not, please explain.

YES ☑
NO ☐

EVALUATION OF MANAGERIAL POTENTIAL
(This section may be omitted in cases where not applicable)

	Unsat.	Sat. Minus	Sat.	Sat. Plus	Excell.	Outst.
LEADERSHIP: Does he show the ability or the potential to take charge of a situation and to direct and control group activities in a satisfactory manner?	☐	☑	☐	☐	☐	☐
ANALYTICAL ABILITY: Does he analyse problems into manageable pieces for logical sequence of attack?	☐	☐	☑	☐	☐	☐
JUDGMENT: Does he show foresight, usually arriving at clear, well-balanced conclusions?	☐	☐	☑	☐	☐	☐
INITIATIVE: Does he anticipate needs, start action, assume responsibility?	☐	☑	☐	☐	☐	☐
CREATIVITY: Does he conceive new ideas and then put them into practice?	☐	☑	☐	☐	☐	☐
PRESENTATION OF IDEAS: Does he present his ideas clearly and forcefully, either verbally or in writing?	☐	☑	☐	☐	☐	☐

INDICATE POSITIONS YOU BELIEVE EMPLOYEE IS PROMOTABLE TO: (You may use your discretion as to whether or not this section should be discussed with the employee in the interview.)

	Ready Now	Ready 1 Year	Ready later
1.	☐	☐	☐
2.	☐	☐	☐
3.	☐	☐	☐

	Unsat.	Sat. Minus	Sat.	Sat. Plus	Excell.	Outst.
OVERALL PERFORMANCE How well does the employee meet the standards normally expected on this job, as well as the objectives which have been set for him? (Give an explanation if necessary.) GENERAL COMMENT:	☐	☐	☑	☐	☐	☐

ACTION TO IMPROVE PERFORMANCE (Indicate also specific training necessary to help employee improve performance.) HE TENDS TO BECOME TOO INVOLVED IN SPECIFIC OPERATIONS AT THE COST OF OTHER OPERATIONS + SHOULD DISCIPLINE HIMSELF TO LEAVE THE TOOLS + LET HIS MEN DO THE JOB UNDER HIS SUPERVISION.

PREPARED BY: (Supervisor)	*[signature]*	REVIEWED BY: (Manager)	*[signature]*

POSITION: GEN. SUPERINTENDENT DATE: 1/10/73 | POSITION: | DATE: 4/10/73

EMPLOYEE'S COMMENTS: (Freely express your view on the completeness and accuracy of the review.)

NIL

EMPLOYEE'S SIGNATURE: *C O'Callaghan* | DATE: 4 - 10 - 73.

Appendix N

PERFORMANCE REVIEW-2

<table>
<tr><td colspan="2">CAR DIVISION — PERFORMANCE REVIEW
(Non-Managerial Salaried Personnel)</td></tr>
<tr>
<td>NAME: J. LISTER. (6.12.72)

PERIOD OF REVIEW: 6 MONTHS.</td>
<td>POSITION: SUPERVISOR   PERIOD IN THIS POSITION: 1 MONTH.

DATE OF REVIEW: 12 OCT. 1973.</td>
</tr>
<tr>
<td>FACTORS UNDER REVIEW:
List briefly the main duties and responsibilities as well as the objectives which have previously been agreed upon between the supervisor and the employee.</td>
<td>ACTUAL PERFORMANCE.
Indicate the employee's actual performance on each factor under review and suggest how he can improve his performance.</td>
</tr>
<tr>
<td>1. SUPERVISE THE WORK ASSIGNMENTS OF INDUSTRIAL ENGINEERS AND PROVIDE GUIDANCE TO IMPROVE PERSONNEL PERFORMANCE.</td>
<td>1. SATISFACTORY. MUST GIVE PRIORITY TO DEVELOPING HIS TEAM INTO AN EFFECTIVE UNIT. MUST CONCENTRATE ON THE TRAINING ASPECT.</td>
</tr>
<tr>
<td>2. SUPERVISE THE ESTABLISHMENT OF LOCAL DIRECT LABOUR STANDARDS WITH DUE REGARD TO OBJECTIVES.</td>
<td>2. SAT. PLUS. HAS PERSEVERED WITH THIS ASSIGNMENT IN DIFFICULT CIRCUMSTANCES. HOWEVER, MUST KEEP HIS OBJECTIVES IN SIGHT.</td>
</tr>
<tr>
<td>3. MAINTAIN STRICT CONTROL OF MANPOWER TO STANDARD AUTHORISATION IN ALL AREAS OF RESPONSIBILITY.</td>
<td>3. SAT. PLUS. HAS IMPLEMENTED THE WORK STANDARD SUCCESSFULLY. MUST ACHIEVE GREATER INVOLVEMENT WITH PRODUCTION PROBLEMS.</td>
</tr>
<tr>
<td>4. PLANNING OF SPECIAL WORK ASSIGNMENTS AND NEGOTIATING WITH PLANT SUPERVISION.</td>
<td>4. SAT. PLUS. HAS THE ABILITY TO ORGANISE HIS WORK WELL. HE NEGOTIATES SHREWDLY.</td>
</tr>
<tr>
<td>5. ESTABLISHING DOCUMENTATION AND MAINTAINING ACCURATE, EFFICIENT RECORDS.</td>
<td>5. SAT. PLUS. IS ALWAYS NEAT, METHODICAL, ACCURATE AND EFFICIENT.</td>
</tr>
<tr>
<td>6. MAINTAINING GOOD HUMAN RELATIONS WITH PRODUCTION PERSONNEL.</td>
<td>6. SAT. PLUS. HAS GAINED THE RESPECT OF PRODUCTION PERSONNEL THROUGH HIS SINCERITY & GOOD SENSE.</td>
</tr>
<tr>
<td>7. INTERPRETTING PRODUCTION SCHEDULES IN TERMS OF MANPOWER AND CAPACITY LIMITATIONS.</td>
<td>7. SAT. PLUS. HIS JUDGEMENT IS SOUND. MUST GIVE THIS ISSUE THE IMPORTANCE IT DESERVES.</td>
</tr>
<tr>
<td>8. ACHIEVING DEADLINES GENERALLY FOR ALL ASSIGNMENTS.</td>
<td>8. EXCELLENT. ALWAYS EXHIBITS A SINCERE SENSE OF RESPONSIBILITY AND SUBMITS WORK ASSIGNMENTS IN GOOD TIME.</td>
</tr>
<tr>
<td>9. RECOGNISING PRODUCTION PROBLEMS AND RECOMMENDING PRACTICAL SOLUTIONS.</td>
<td>9. SATISFACTORY. MUST GIVE THIS IMPORTANT FACTOR PRIORITY.</td>
</tr>
<tr>
<td colspan="2">PERSONAL PROBLEMS which may be impairing the employee's performance.

NIL</td>
</tr>
</table>

THE DEPARTMENT HAS PASSED THROUGH THE DEVELOPMENT STAGE IN THE LAST 6 MONTHS AND THEREFORE ACTIVITIES SUCH AS METHODS IMPROVEMENT, INDIRECT LABOUR STANDARDS AND MATERIALS STANDARDS HAVE BEEN SECONDARY TO THE SETTING OF WORK STANDARDS FOR DIRECT LABOUR. HOWEVER, THESE ACTIVITIES WILL BECOME PRIORITIES OVER THE NEXT 6 MONTHS

Form 224

EVALUATION OF PERFORMANCE
(This section is applicable to all employees)

	Unsat.	Sat. Minus	Sat.	Sat. Plus	Excell.	Outst.
JOB KNOWLEDGE: How well does the employee know the requirements of his job?	☐	☐	☐	☒	☐	☐
QUANTITY OF WORK: What volume of acceptable work does the employee produce in relation to the normal expectation for this job?	☐	☐	☐	☒	☐	☐
QUALITY OF WORK: Does he consistently produce accurate, neat and thorough work?	☐	☐	☐	☒	☐	☐
CO-OPERATION: How well does he co-operate with his colleagues, his supervisor and personnel from other departments?	☐	☐	☐	☐	☒	☐
ATTENDANCE: Is he punctual, diligent and consistent in his attendance? If not, please explain.	YES ☒ NO ☐					

EVALUATION OF MANAGERIAL POTENTIAL
(This section may be omitted in cases where not applicable)

	Unsat.	Sat. Minus	Sat.	Sat. Plus	Excell.	Outst.
LEADERSHIP: Does he show the ability or the potential to take charge of a situation and to direct and control group activities in a satisfactory manner?	☐	☐	☐	☐	☐	☐
ANALYTICAL ABILITY: Does he analyse problems into manageable pieces for logical sequence of attack?	☐	☐	☐	☐	☐	☐
JUDGMENT: Does he show foresight, usually arriving at clear, well-balanced conclusions?	☐	☐	☐	☐	☐	☐
INITIATIVE: Does he anticipate needs, start action, assume responsibility?	☐	☐	☐	☐	☐	☐
CREATIVITY: Does he conceive new ideas and then put them into practice?	☐	☐	☐	☐	☐	☐
PRESENTATION OF IDEAS: Does he present his ideas clearly and forcefully, either verbally or in writing?	☐	☐	☐	☐	☐	☐

INDICATE POSITIONS YOU BELIEVE EMPLOYEE IS PROMOTABLE TO: (You may use your discretion as to whether or not this section should be discussed with the employee in the interview.)

	Ready Now	Ready 1 Year	Ready later
1. (PROMOTED TO SUPERVISOR, EFFECTIVE 1OCT.A73)	☐	☐	☐
2.	☐	☐	☐
3.	☐	☐	☐

	Unsat.	Sat. Minus	Sat.	Sat. Plus	Excell.	Outst.
OVERALL PERFORMANCE How well does the employee meet the standards normally expected on this job, as well as the objectives which have been set for him? (Give an explanation if necessary.)	☐	☐	☐	☒	☐	☐

GENERAL COMMENT: HAS THE POTENTIAL TO IMPROVE ON THIS PERFORMANCE. HE IS RELIABLE AND CONSCIENTIOUS AT ALL TIMES

ACTION TO IMPROVE PERFORMANCE (Indicate also specific training necessary to help employee improve performance. MUST BRUSH UP ON WORK STUDY THEORY AND TAKE ADVANTAGE OF ALL SUITABLE COURSES WITHIN THE COMPANY IN ORDER TO DEVELOPE FURTHER THOSE SKILLS WHICH WILL HELP HIM MAINTAIN HIS POSITION OF LEADERSHIP.

PREPARED BY: (Supervisor) E. MORGAN (E.Morgan)

REVIEWED BY: (Manager)

POSITION: IND.ENG.MANAGER   DATE: 12.10.73

POSITION: DATE:

EMPLOYEE'S COMMENTS: (Freely express your view on the completeness and accuracy of the review.)

EMPLOYEE'S SIGNATURE: DATE:

GUIDE TO EMPLOYEE PERFORMANCE

Performance factors	Far exceeds job requirements	Exceeds job requirements	Meets job requirements	Needs some improvement	Does not meet minimum requirements
QUALITY	Leaps tall buildings in a single bound	Must take a running start to leap over tall buildings	Can only leap over a short building or one medium with no spires	Crashes into building when attempting to jump	Cannot recognise building at all, much less jump
TIMELINESS	Is faster than a speeding bullet	Is as fast as a speeding bullet	Not quite as fast as a speeding bullet	Would you believe a slow bullet	Wounds self with bullets when attempting to shoot gun
INITIATIVE	Is stronger than a locomotive	Is stronger than a bull elephant	Is stronger than a bull	Shoots the bull	Smells like bull
ADAPTABILITY	Walks on water occasionally	Walks on water in emergency	Washes with water	Drinks water	Passes water in emergencies
COMMUNICATION	Talks with God	Talks with the Angels	Talks to himself	Argues with himself	Loses these arguments

MINUTES OF HELLERMANN DEUTSCH DIVISIONAL COUNCIL MEETING, 20 JANUARY 1976

Those present:

Mr C.E. Addison—*Chairman*	Miss J. Mayo
Mr J.F. Skipper—*Secretary*	Miss B. Baker
Mr J. Harmer—*Elected Secretary*	Mrs M. Suckling
Mr G. Cobb	Mr J. Hall
Mr M. Hitchen	Mr N. Goodall
Mr B. Saunders	Mrs B. Richardson
Mrs I. Easterbrook	

Miss S. Hargreaves was absent due to sickness.

1 MINUTES OF PREVIOUS MEETING

The Minutes were accepted as an accurate record of the previous meeting.

2 MATTERS ARISING

(a) Dismissal Procedure
The Council had considered the draft procedure and felt it quite satisfactory and an improvement on the existing procedure. The Chairman said that the procedure should refer also to procedure DJB/PER/12, which covered serious inefficiency in job function or conduct.

Reference was made to the recent Employment Protection Act and the Secretary informed the Meeting that Seminars were planned for supervisors and Managers bringing them up-to-date with this and other recent legislation.

The Council asked if an extract of these Acts could be prepared for circulation to Divisional Council members.

3 SAFETY

No points for discussion.

4 CANTEEN

A request was made for fruit to be on sale in the Factory No.2 cafeteria. The Secretary replied that fruit would be available if there was sufficient demand.

5 WELFARE

It was generally felt undesirable to discuss cases of personal welfare, and this was best dealt with through Departmental Heads and the Personnel Department.

Items of general welfare could be raised on the Agenda in the normal way.

The Christmas holidays for 1976 would be common to all Southern Divisions within the Group and would be as follows:

Friday 24 December 1976	—Close 1.00 pm. Time lost to be made up during preceding week.
Monday 27 December 1976	—Boxing Day.
Tuesday 28 December 1976	—Exgratia holiday granted by the Company in lieu of 25 December falling on Saturday.
Wednesday 29 December 1976	—Two days from employees' annual
Thursday 30 December 1976	—holiday entitlement.
Friday 31 December 1976	—One day exgratia holiday granted in lieu of New Year's Day falling on a Saturday.

In view of this Board decision a ballot would not be held but the Meeting generally accepted that this weeks shutdown at a cost of two days from the annual holiday entitlement was generous.

7   JOB EVALUATION

The Category III evaluation panel was currently considering eleven appeals and six new job descriptions in respect of East Grinstead jobs.

This relatively small number of appeals indicated that the job evaluation exercise had been completed satisfactorily and it was anticipated that the appellants would be advised of the results of their appeal within the next few days.

The works job evaluation panel would be considering on 21 January 1976, six appeals and five new jobs.

Many other appeals were raised but were outside the scope of the job evaluation panel and these had been dealt with directly by the Managers concerned. In undertaking a job evaluation exercise for the first time and adopting a method by which jobs would be evaluated by a representative panel, some problems were inevitable and anticipated.

The small number of genuine appeals indicates that the exercise had in general terms been most successful and it was now the responsibility of all concerned to tackle the problems that had arisen in an honest and open manner. Solutions to these problems would obviously be found and those concerned were asked to be patient whilst this very important work was being carried out.

Revised salary scales for Category III were circulated which ensured that the formula for converting the 37¼ hour week salary to 42¼ hour salary had been correctly applied.

The staff salary scales gave both job rate and salary maximum figures, whereas the Category I scales gave job rate only. It was suggested that a scale maximum should be applied to the Category I scales to show that payments above job rate were possible.

The Secretary agreed to publish wage scales with maximum merit figures, but stressed that at present there was no review procedure for establishing any merit payments, and that the presence of a maximum merit figure should not create expectation in the minds of job holders that a review could be carried out.

8 FEBRUARY WAGE AND SALARY REVIEW

The Meeting requested that the balance of the Government limit £6.00 be awarded in the February review.

The Chairman replied that Management were currently giving this review urgent consideration, particularly in the light of the continuing increase in operating costs. The considerable cost of equal pay and job evaluation had to be financed and this could not be totally recovered by price increases. Any increases approved by the Price Commission would apply to current orders and the increased income not felt for many months.

Any further increase in payroll cost, which constituted a major part of our operating expenses would have further adverse effects on the Company's position.

It was stressed that the stringent budgetary and financial control operated by the Company had indicated the corrective action to be taken, thus enabling the current level of employment to continue.

9 COMPANY TRADING

	Bookings	YTD	Billings	YTD
HD	110%	99%	98%	87%
HECD	96%	95%	112%	77%

The 87% YTD Billings figure was most significant as the money budgeted in 1975 for the purchase of goods and services was based on achieving 100% Billings figure. This short fall in Billings meant that the Company was not producing the income for the purchase of goods and services, which had already been subject to an unprecedented level of inflation and it was imperative therefore that the budget targets for 1976 are fully realised.

10 ANY OTHER BUSINESS

(a) Tannoy System
The volume of the tannoy system in Goods Inwards Inspection was creating annoyance, and a report from the Maintenance Manager on his investigation would be given at the next meeting.

(b) Car Stickers
It was agreed to adopt the suggestion that car stickers be provided for display in the windows of vehicles giving the owners name and internal telephone number. This would avoid the necessity for frequent tannoy messages requesting the re-parking of vehicles.

(c) Public Telephones
The efficiency of the sound proofing canopies over the telephones was considered inadequate, as cases had already arisen where private telephone conversations were overheard.

It was suggested that improved canopies, similar to those used in record shops should be investigated.

(d)   Payroll
The Secretary reminded the Meeting that the payroll co-ordination function previously carried out in the Personnel Department had been transferred to Finance and that holiday slips, medical certificates, clock cards, etc., should be addressed to Mrs Catlett on the second floor, administration building.

(e)   Canteen
The Secretary agreed to discuss the quality of cheese with the Catering Manager.

(f)   Part-time Employees
In reply to a question the Chairman advised the Meeting that it was policy not to encourage any extension onto part-time hours, and that any current vacancies required full-time applicants.

(g)   Bowthorpe Electric
The Meeting was advised of the decision recently published that the administration departments of Bowthorpe Electric would be transferred to the Company's premises in Brighton during 1976.

11 DATE OF THE NEXT MEETING

The next Meeting will be held on 17 February 1976, in the conference room commencing at 10.00 am.

27.1.76

BIBLIOGRAPHY

BIBLIOGRAPHY

Many, many *Not for Bread Alone* readers informed me that they considered a detailed bibliography was an invaluable addition to any book. The literature suggested in this bibliography is not comprehensive, but it does cover the basic reading in the area of job enrichment and its related fields—also material I have found of value. I hope this assists training managers, students, course participants and all those who requested such an appendix.

A guide to organisational behaviour and development

Books and pamphlets

Michael Argyle, *The Social Psychology of Work*, Penguin (1972).

Chris Argyris, *Understanding Organisational Behaviour*, Tavistock Publications (1960).

Chris Argyris, *The Applicability of Organizational Sociology*, Cambridge Press (1972).

E. Wight Bakke, *Bonds of Organisation: an appraisal of corporate human relations*, Archen Books, USA (1966).

Richard Beckhard, *Organizational Development, Strategies and Models*, Addison Wesley, London (1969).

Gerald D. Bell (Editor), *Organizations and Human Behaviour: a book of readings*, Prentice-Hall (1967).

Warren G. Bennis, *Organizational Development, Its Nature, Origin and Prospect*, Addison Wesley, London (1969).

R. Blake and J.S. Mouton, *Building a Dynamic Corporation through GRID Organisational Development*, Addison Wesley, London (1969).

Martin M. Bruce, *Human Relations in Small Business*, Small Business Administration, Washington DC (Third edition, 1969).

Burns & Stalker, *The Management of Innovation*, Tavistock Publications.

Fred J. Carvell, *Human Relations in Business*, Collier-Macmillan (1970).

Keith Davis *et al.*, *Human Relations and Organizational Behavior: Readings and Comments*, McGraw-Hill (Third edition, 1969).

John Munro Fraser, *Human Relations in a Fully Employed Democracy*, Pitman (1960).

Don Fuller, *Human Relations and Human Engineering in a Nutshell, or Motivating Subordinates and Superiors*, Council on Management Development (1971).

Saul W. Gellerman, *The Management of Human Relations*, Holt, Rinehart and Winston (1966).

R.H. Guest, *Organisational Change*, Tavistock Publications (1962).

Richard Hacon (Editor), *Personal and Organizational Effectiveness*, McGraw-Hill (1972).

Earle S. Hannaford, *Supervisors Guide to Human Relations*, National Safety Council, Chicago (1967).

A.C. Hazel and A.S. Reid, *Enjoying a Profitable Business*, Business Books (Second edition 1976).

192 Gordon Heald (Editor), *Approaches to the Study of Organizational Behaviour: Operational Research and the Behaviour Sciences*, Tavistock Publications (1970).

Paul Hersey *et al.*, *Management of Organizational Behavior: Utilizing Human Resources*, Prentice-Hall (1969).

P. Hill, *Towards a New Philosophy of Management—A Study of the Company Development Programme at Shell UK*, Gower Press (1971).

E.W. Hughes, *Human Relations in Management*, Pergamon Press (1970).

Industrial Co-partnership Association, *Human Relations in Industry in the Seventies*, a Report of the 40th Annual Summer Conference held at Churchill College, Cambridge (10-12 July 1970).

A.S. Irvine, *Improving Industrial Communication (Basic guide for line-managers)*, Industrial Society, Gower Press (1971).

M.W. Ivens *et al.*, *Case Studies in Human Relations, Productivity and Organization*, Business Publications (1966).

R. Kahn *et al.*, *Organisational Stress; Studies in Role, Conflict and Ambiguity*, John Wiley (1964).

H.R. Knudson, *Organizational Behavior: Cases for Developing Nations*, Addison-Wesley (1967).

D.A. Kolb *et al.*, *Organizational Psychology: an Experiential Approach*, Prentice-Hall (1971).

D.A. Laird *et al.*, *Psychology: Human Relations and Motivation*, McGraw-Hill (Fourth edition, 1967).

P.R. Lawrence and J.W. Lorsch, *Developing Organizations*, Addison Wesley (1969).

F. Luthans, *Contemporary Readings in Organizational Behavior*, McGraw-Hill (1972).

D. McGregor, *The Human Side of Enterprise*, McGraw-Hill (1960).

E.J. Miller and A.K. Rice, *Systems of Organisation*, Tavistock Publications (1970).

Human Relations Case Studies; Catalogue of cases and supporting material, Newman Neame (Training) Limited (1966).

K.V. Porter, *Case Studies in Human Relations*, Macmillan (1971).

D.E. Porter *et al.*, *Studies in Organizational Behavior and Management*, Intext Educational Publishers, London (1971).

Rackham, Honey and Colbert, *Developing Interactive Skills*, Wellens Publishing (1972).

W.J. Reddin, *Managerial Effectiveness*, McGraw-Hill.

E. Rhenman *et al.*, *Conflict and Co-operation in Business Organizations*, Wiley-Interscience (1970).

D. Sadler and B. Barry, *Organisational Development*, Longmans (1970).

L.R. Sayles *et al.*, *Human Behavior in Organizatons*, Prentice-Hall (1966).

E.H. Schein, *Process Consultation: Its Role in Organizational Development*, Addison Wesley (1969).

E.H. Schein and W.G. Bennis, *Personal and Organizational Change through Group Methods*, John Wiley (1965).

Swedish Employers' Confederation Technical Department and J. Edgren, *With Varying Success—a Swedish Experiment in Wage Systems and Shopfloor Organisation*, Stockholm (1974).

J.M. Thomas (Editor), *Management of Change and Conflict, Selected Readings*, Penguin Modern Management readings, Penguin Books (1972).

D. Torrington, *Face to Face: Techniques for Handling the Personal Encounter at Work*, Gower Press (1972).

R.F. Tredgold, *Human Relations in Modern Industry*, University Paperbacks, Methuen and Company (1965).

L.S. Trowbridge, *Human Relations*, National Foremen's Institute, Bureau of Business Practice, Waterford, Conn. (1963).

R.E.C. Wegner *et al.*, *Cases in Organizational and Administrative Behavior*, Prentice-Hall (1972).

J. Wellens, *Training in Physical Skills*, Business Books (1974).

M.R. Williams, *Human Relations... A National Extension College Course Prepared in Collaboration with the Institute of Supervisory Management*, Longmans, Green (1967).

D. Willings, *The Human Element in Management*, Batsford (1968).

N.R. Wills *et al.*, *Case Studies in Organisational Behavior*, John Wiley, Sydney (1972).

R. Winsbury, *Modern Japanese Management*, BIM (1970).

J. Woodward, *Behaviour in Organizations*, Imperial College of Science and Technology, London (1970).

Related articles

Business Horizons (August 1972): 'Worker measurement and worker morale: need for changed managerial behavior', by D. Sirota and A.D. Wolfson.

Harvard Business Review (March-April 1972), pp 59-68: 'Conflict at the summit: a deadly game', by A. McDonald.

Ibid. (May-June 1972), pp 119-128: 'Understanding your organization's character', by R. Harrison.

Human Relations (July 1972), pp 215-237: 'The effects of subordinates' behaviour on managerial style', by B.J. Crowe *et al.*

Ibid. (July 1972), pp 252-263: 'The strain towards irrelevance', by D. Harshburger.

Industrial & Commercial Training, Managing Change Series—1973-74, by Lynda King Taylor.

International Management (May 1972), pp 31-34: 'How to avoid favouritism', by A. Uris.

Ibid. (June 1972): 'Marxist approach to staff relations', by E. Mackenzie.

Management in Action (February 1973), pp 6-7 and p 10: 'Face to Face', by A. Jarrett.

Occupational Psychology (1972), 46(1), pp 1-6: 'Minding our own business—current conflicts in the practice of occupational psychology', by K.C.F. Lathrope.

Purchasing Journal (March 1972), pp 36-40: 'Human relations in purchasing', by H. Fearon.

The Business Quarterly (Autumn 1972), pp 22-29: 'Managing in other cultures: some do's and some don'ts', by J.J. Distefano.

Supervisory Management (Autumn 1972), pp 103-106: 'The organization of communication', by H. Compton.

A guide to the selection and training of office staff and supervisors

Books and pamphlets

J.R. Armstrong, *Supervisory Training*, Institute of Personnel Management (1961).

W.E. Baer, *Grievance Handling: 101 Guides for Supervisors*, American Management Association (1970).

C.M. Bowen, *Developing and Training the Supervisor*, Business Books (1971).

British Association for Commercial and Industrial Education, *Three Case Studies in Management and Supervisory Training*, BACIE (1969).

J. Brown, *Training Your Supervisors*, Industrial Society (Revised edition 1970).

Carborundum Company, *Selecting Supervisors* (Seventh edition 1970).

Carpet Industry Training Board, *Training Recommendations: Clerical and Commercial Occupations* (1968).

————, *Training Recommendations: Managers and Supervisors* (1968).

H.L. Carrard, *Practical Office Training*, Cassell (Tenth edition 1965).

Ceramics and Mineral Products Industry Training Board, *Recommendations for Training Office Staff* (1969).

————, *Recommendations for Training Supervisors* (1969).

Chemical and Allied Products Industry Training Board, *Training Recommendations for Clerical and Associated Personnel* (1972).

————, *Recommendations for Management and Supervisory Training and Development of Supervisors* (1972).

Chemical and Allied Products Industry, *Recommendations for Induction Training for Clerical and Associated Personnel* (1969).

V.E. Collinge, *Office Routine*, Pitman (Second edition 1968).

Cornmarket Press, *Supervisory Training Skills: An Introductory Programmed Course* (1970).

Cotton and Allied Textiles Industry Training Board, *Recommendations for the Training of Administrative, Commercial and Clerical Staff* (September 1968).

————, *Effective Supervision: Recommendations for the Training and Development of Supervisors* (1972).

————, *Recommendations for Management and Supervisory Training and Development* (June 1968).

F.A.J. Couldery, *Manual of Business Training: A Complete Guide to Office Routine and Modern Methods of Business*, Pitman (15th edition 1967).

Council of Europe, *Selection and Training of Supervisors, Especially in Small and Medium-sized Firms*, Strasbourg (1970).

J. Cox, *Clerical Duties and Office Practice*, Nelson (1969).

Department of Employment and Productivity, *Training within Industry for Supervisors* (1968).

——, *The Training of Women Returning to Office Work After a Break and Other Adults Entering this Field of Work for the First Time,* Central Training Council, Commercial and Clerical Training Committee (1970).

A.F. Donovan, *Management of Supervisors,* Macmillan (1971).

Electricity Supply Industry Training Board, *Recommendations for the General Training of Clerical Staff* (1967).

——, *Recommendations on the Training of Supervisors* (1968).

Engineering Industry Training Board, *The Training of Clerks* (1967).

——, *The Training of Supervisors* (1966).

——, *The Selection and Preparation of Supervisors for First Appointment.*

Ford Motor Company, *The Professional Supervisor: Training Courses for Supervisors of Staff in Ford of Britain.*

S. Friedman and J. Grossman, *Modern Clerical Practice,* Pitman, New York (1968).

K. Gosling, *The Clerical Training Office: A Basic Course in Office Skills and Procedures,* Pitman, London (1971).

J. Harrison, *Practical Office Exercises,* Pitman (1966).

Iron and Steel Industry Training Board, *Recommendations on Commercial and Clerical Training (1967).*

Joint Committee for Training in the Foundry Industry, *Recommendations on Supervisory and Management Training* (September 1966).

H.W. Johnson, *Selecting, Training and Supervising Office Personnel,* Addison-Wesley (1969).

D. Jenkins, *Supervisory Selection and Training in the Manufacturing Industry,* Staples Press (1968).

D. King, *Training Within the Organisation: a study of company policy and procedures for the systematic training of operators and supervisors,* Tavistock Publications in association with Social Science Paperbacks (1968).

Knitting, Lace and Net Industry Training Board, *Office Personnel, Nonprofessional,* Nottingham (1969).

Local Government Training Board, *Administrative and Clerical Staff; Supplement on Clerical Training,* London (1970).

M. Lund, *A Guide to the Training of Office Supervisors,* British Association for Commercial and Industrial Education (1967).

Man-made Fibres Producing Board, *Recommendations for the Training of Office Staff, Professional and Administrative Trainees, Clerks, Secretaries and Typists, Machine Operators,* London (1970).

J.P. de C. Meade and F.W. Greig, *Supervisory Training: A New Appro Approach for Management—A Study by the Industrial Training Service,* HMSO for Ministry of Labour Training Council (1966).

G. Mills *et al., Office Administration,* Pitman for Institute of Office Management (1966). (See Chapter 12—The Training of Clerks.)

Ministry of Labour and Central Office of Information, *Supervisory Training Pays,* HMSO (Revised edition 1966).

Ministry of Labour: Central Training Council, Training for Office Supervision, *A Report by the Commercial and Clerical Training*

196   *Committee of the Central Training Council*, HMSO (1968).

———, *A Report by the Commercial and Clerical Training Committee*, HMSO (1966).

V. Mortensen, *Training Your Supervisors*, Industrial Society (Second revised edition 1965).

K. Oakley and W. Richmond, *A Systematic Approach to Commercial and Clerical Training*, Pergamon Press (1970).

N. Rackham, *Development and Evaluation of Supervisory Training*, Air Transport and Travel Industry Board (1971).

Rubber and Plastics Processing Industry Training Board, *Training for Profit: Recommendations for Supervisor Training* (1971).

Stanton and Staveley Limited, *Selection and Training of Supervisors: An Operational Guide*, Stanton and Staveley (1966).

F.C. Thurling, *Office Practice Today*, Pitman (Third edition 1968).

K.E. Thurley and A.C. Hamblin, *The Basis of Supervisory Training Policy*, Pergamon Press (1967).

P.B. Warr and M.W. Bird, *Identifying Supervisory Training Needs*, HMSO (1968).

R. Warson, *Grebby's Modern Business Training*, Macdonald & Evans (19th edition 1967).

J.J. Weger, *Motivating Supervisors*, American Management Association (1971).

Wool, Jute and Flax Industry Training Board, *Recommendations for Managerial and Supervisory Training* (1968).

Related articles

Industrial and Commercial Training (October 1970), 2(10): pp 467-471 — 'The training of office workers' by J. Wellens; pp 458-466 — 'The training of clerical workers' by M. Walker.

Ibid. (July 1970), 2(7), pp 314-319: 'An adaption of the group training concept for commercial and clerical workers' by A.C. Wise.

Industrial Training International (July 1971), pp 198-201: 'Evaluation of external supervisory courses', By M. Cordery.

Ibid. (April 1972), pp 117-118: 'Supervisor training—group learning', by D. Biddle.

Management Education and Development (January 1972), pp 142-148: 'An evaluation of supervisory training and organisational change' by P. Jackson *et al.*

Office Management (Spring 1971), 25(1), pp 32-35: 'In-company office training' by Diana Orton.

Personnel Journal (July 1972), pp 489-494, 529: 'The production foreman today: his needs and his difficulties' by R.H. Schappe.

Supervisory Management (Autumn 1972), pp 132-133: 'Thoughts on the training of operators and managers' by M.J. Machin.

Training and Development Journal (September 1971), pp 6-11: 'A critical incident evaluation of supervisory training' by P.D. Couch *et al.*

Ibid. (June 1971), pp 12-14: 'Supervisory training can be measured objectively on the job' by G.L. Morrissey.

Ibid. (July 1970), pp 36-39: 'Training clerical help' by E. Krag *et al.*

Books and pamphlets

M. Argyle, *The Social Psychology of Work*, Penguin Press (1972).
American Management Association, *Motivation and Job Performance*,
  Reprints from AMA periodicals (1969).
C. Bacon, *Selecting, Appraising and Motivating Employees*, Industrial
  Education International (1969).
J.D. Batten, *Beyond Management by Objectives*, American Management
  Association (1966).
M. Beer, *Leadership, Employee Needs and Motivation*, College of Com-
  merce and Administration, Ohio State University (1966).
W.G. Bennis *et al.*, *Leadership and Motivation: Essays of Douglas
  McGregor*, edited with the collaboration of C. McGregor, Massachus-
  etts Institute of Technology.
W.J. Bowles, *The Management of Motivation: a Company-wide Pro-
  gram*, American Management Association (1966).
G.A. Bradt, *The Secrets of Getting Results Through People*, Parker
  Publishing, West Nyack, NY (1967).
British Institute of Management, *A Behavioural Science Approach to
  Sales Training* (A one-day forum held in London on 14 September
  1970), London (1970).
————, *What is Behavioural Science?*, London (1971).
M. Brown, *The Manager's Guide to the Behavioural Sciences*, Industrial
  Society (1969).
P.C. Buchanan, *The Leader Looks at Individual Motivation*, Leadership
  Resources, Washington (Revised edition 1966).
Bureau of Business Practice, *Action Guide to Human Maintenance: A
  New Concept of Motivation*, Waterford, Connecticut (1969).
E.C. Caplan, *Management Accounting and Behavioural Science*,
  Addison—Wesley (1971).
R.M. Cyert *et al.*, *A Behavioural Theory of the Firm*, Prentice-Hall
  (1963).
R.I. Drake and P.J. Smith, *Behavioural Science in Industry*, McGraw-
  Hill (1973).
P. Elliott, *The Sociology of the Professions*, Macmillan (1972).
R.N. Ford, *Motivation through the Work Itself*, American Management
  Association (1968).
S.W. Gellerman, *Management by Motivation*, American Management
  Association (1968).
————, *Motivation and Productivity*, American Management Associa-
  tion (1963).
C.W. Golby and G. Johns, *Attitude and Motivation*, HMSO (1971).
J. Goldthorpe *et al.*, *The Affluent Worker: Industrial Attitudes and
  Behaviour*, Cambridge University Press (1968).
J.S. Guildford and D.E. Gray, *Motivation and Modern Management*,
  Addison-Wesley (1969).
R.C. Hackman, *The Motivated Working Adult*, American Management
  Association (1969).

198 G. Heald, *Approaches to the Study of Organizational Behaviour: Operational Research and the Behaviour Sciences,* Tavistock (1970).

P. Hersey *et al.*, *Management of Organizational Behaviour Utilizing Human Resources,* Prentice-Hall (1972).

F. Herzberg *et al.*, *The Motivation to Work,* John Wiley (Second edition 1959).

G.H. Hofstede, *The Game of Budget Control:* 'How to live with budgetary standards and yet be motivated by them', Van Gorcum, Esse (1967).

G. Holroyde, *Managing People: How to Get the Best from Your Staff,* Mantec Pubs, Rugby (1969).

Imperial Chemicals Industries, Plastics Division, Personnel Department, *Management, People and Change,* ICI (Third edition 1969).

B.P. Indik, *The Motivation to Work,* Rutgers University, Institute of Management and Labor Relations (1966).

D. Katz and R.L. Kahn, *The Social Psychology of Organizations,* John Wiley (1966).

Lynda King Taylor, *Not for Bread Alone,* Business Books (1973).

J.R. Lawrence, *Operational Research and the Social Sciences,* Tavistock Publications (1966).

C. Lilleker and R.L. Smith, *Job Satisfaction and Women in the Pottery Industry,* Keele Department of Economics, Keele University (1971).

R. Likert, *New Patterns of Management,* McGraw-Hill (1961).

G.H. Litwin *et al.*, *Achievement, Motivation and Risk-taking in a Business Setting,* Technical Report of a Research Study Conducted in the Small Aircraft Engine Department at Lynn, Mass, NY, Behavioral Research Service, Relations Services, General Electric Co (1961).

F. Luthans, *Contemporary Readings in Organizational Behavior,* McGraw-Hill (1972).

A.H. Maslow, *Motivation and Personality,* Harper and Row (1954).

T.R. Masterson and T.G. Mara, *Motivating the Underperformer,* American Management Association (1969).

D.C. McClelland and D.G. Winter, *Motivating Economic Achievement,* Collier?Macmillan (1969).

National Training Laboratories, Institute for Applied Behavioral Science, *Behavioral Science and the Manager's Role,* edited by W.B. Eddy *et al.*, Washington (1969).

N. Ni Bhroin, *The Motivation and Productivity of Young Women Workers,* Irish National Productivity Committee (1970).

Ohio State University, College of Commerce and Administration, Bureau of Business Research, *Team Achievement Under High Motivation* by R.M. Stodgill, Columbus (Ohio) (1963).

C. Perrow, *Organizational Analysis: A Sociological View,* Tavistock (1970).

D.E. Porter *et al.*, *Studies in Organizational Behavior and Management,* Intext Educational Publishers, London (Second edition 1971).

H.M.F. Rush, *Behavioral Science Concepts and Management Application,* National Industrial Conference Board, New York (1969).

E.H. Schein, *Organizational Psychology,* Prentice-Hall (1965).

W.G. Scott, *Organization Theory: a Behavioral Analysis for Management,* Irwin (1967).

Social Organisation Limited, *Work, Remuneration and Motivation of*
Directors, London (1970).

S. Srivastva (Editor), *Behavioural Sciences in Management,* Asia Publishing House, London (1967).
R.E. Tannehill, *Motivation and Management Development,* Butterworths (1970).
Sir Geoffrey Vickers, *Towards a Sociology of Management,* Chapman and Hall (1967).
V.H. Vroom *et al., Management and Motivation: Selected Reading,* Penguin (1970).
————, *Motivation in Management,* American Foundation for Management Research (1965).
————, *Work and Motivation,* John Wiley (1964).
M.S. Wadia, *Management and the Behavioral Sciences: Text and Readings,* Allyn & Bacon, Boston (1968).
R. Wild and A.B. Hill, *Women in the Factory: a Study of Job Satisfaction and Labour Turnover,* Institute of Personnel Management, London (1970).

Related articles

Business Horizons (June 1972), pp 87-93: 'The executive abroad: minimising behavioral problems' by R.D. Hays.
Conference Board Record (January 1971), pp 52-56: 'Motivation through job design' by H.M.F. Rush.
East African Management Journal (March 1969), 3(2), pp 10-13: 'Motivation' by P.A. Neck.
European Journal of Marketing (Winter 1971/2), 'Theory and nonsense of motivation research' by C. Jameson.
European Marketing Research Review (Winter 1970), pp 23-30: 'The art of asking 'Why' motivational research' by L. Collins.
Export (April 1971), pp 6-7: 'About motivation and communication' by D. Lord.
Graduate Appointments Register (January 1971), pp 25-39: 'A profile of the office temp.: an investigation into the attitudes and motivation of temporary office staff'.
Harvard Business Review (May-June 1970), pp 97-110: 'Motivating people with meaningful work' by W.J. Roche *et al.*
Hydrocarbon Processing (November 1968), pp 252, 266: 'Motivation through job enrichment'.
Industrial and Commercial Training (June 1971), pp 268-280: 'Collecting behavioural data' by M.J. Colbert, M. Morris and S. Tribe.
————, (Series 73-74): 'On organisational change through behavioural sciences' by Lynda King Taylor.
————, (April 1973), pp 190-194: 'Measuring group behaviour' by R. Bennett.
————, (July 1970), 2(7), pp 333-337: 'Professor Frederick Herzberg on management of motivation' by J. Wellens.
Industrial Relations Journal (Spring 1973), pp 43-49: 'The behavioural side of management by objectives: a measurement problem' by S. Fineman and R. Payne.

200   *Industrial Society* (December 1970), pp 13-14: 'Motivating managers'
by F. Patten.

Internal Auditor (May-June 1970), pp 12-20: 'Approaches to motivation—yesterday, today and tomorrow' by A.J. Ledingham.

International Management (April 1973), pp 54-58: 'Ways to change managerial behaviour' by D. Oates.

————, (July 1970), pp 46-48: 'Making the job motivate the man' by I. Carson.

Journal of Applied Behavioural Science (1971), 7(2), pp 215-229: 'Achievement motivation training and executive advancement' by J. Aronoff *et al.*

Journal of Applied Psychology (October 1970), pp 452-461: 'Motivation—hygiene theory of job attitudes: an empirical investigation and and attempt to reconcile both the one- and two-factor theories of job attitudes' by H.M. Soliman.

Journal of Contemporary Business (Summer 1972), pp 9-22: 'Behavioural science theories underlying organisation development' by J. Mouton *et al.*

Journal of Systems Management (February 1973), pp 32-35: 'Accounting and behavioural science' by M.F. Usty and M. Nix.

Management by Objectives (October 1971), pp 52-54: 'Attitude surveys and motivation' by H. Marlow.

Management International Review (1973), 13(2/3), pp 51-64: 'What behavioural science implies for cost accounting' by G.F. Haepfner.

Management Today (May 1972), pp 35, 38, 42, 48: 'Making managers: the new executive trauma' by D. Hoare.

————, (Annual Review 1970), pp 27-28, 30, 31: 'The mechanics of motivation', by W.J. Paul.

————, (January 1971), pp 63-65, 126: 'Motivating Europe's manpower' by A. Wilkinson.

Management Decision (Winter 1968), pp 215-217: 'Measuring morale and motivation' by T.G.P. Rogers.

Marketing (January 1969), pp 38-39: 'What motivates your sales force?' by D.W. Smallbone.

OMEGA—The International Journal of Management Science (June 1973), pp 297-303: 'A behavioural classification of managerial jobs' by R. Stewart.

Organizational Dynamics (Winter 1973), pp 51-67: 'Can behavioural scientists help managers improve their organizations?' by A.B. Chems.

————, (Summer 1972), p 73: 'The impact of behavioural science on business and industry' by R. Lennon and G.P. Hollenbeck.

Personnel Administration (July-August 1968), pp 8-23: 'Motivation and job performance' by M. Sorcher *et al.*

Personnel Journal (November 1970), pp 900-906: 'The relevance of motivational concepts to individual and corporate objectives' by C.J. Nouri and J.J. Fridl.

Personnel Management (February 1973), pp 32-35: 'Industrial relations and the behavioural scientist' by A. Gottschalk.

————, (December 1971), pp 33-34: 'Motivating your juniors' by G. Bevan.

Personnel Psychology (Summer 1970), 23(2), pp 223-237: 'Job attitudes
and employee motivation: theory, research and practice' by
E.E. Lawler.
——, (Winter 1969), pp 426-435: 'Job design and employee motiva-
tion' by E.E. Lawler.
——, (Summer 1971), pp 155-189: 'The Herzberg controversy' by
V.M. Bockman.
Purchasing (6 August 1970), pp 57-58: 'Does money really motivate?'
by F. Herzberg.
Research Management (January 1972), pp 19-32: 'What motives
researchers in times of economic undertainty' by G.C. Bucher *et al.*
——, (January 1969), xii(1), pp 5-24: 'Employees of technical
organizations can be motivated' by H. Bogaty.
Retail Business (January 1969), No. 131, pp 28-35: 'Motivational
research'.
Sales Management (10 September 1968), pp 30-34: 'New ways to moti-
vate your salesmen'.
The Accountant (1 July 1971), pp 9-11: 'Changing thinking about
motivation in industry' by A.F. Earle.
The Quality Engineer (May/June 1970), 34(3), pp 12-15: 'Motivation
for quality' by B.W. Jenney.
Work Study and Management Services (March 1972), pp 131-134:
'Situational sensitivity' by W.J. Reddin.
——, (September 1970), 14(9), pp 714-720: 'People, participation
and motivation' by I.S. McDavid.
——, (August 1970), pp 645-649: 'One way to measure motivation'
by D. Wilson.

A guide to job enrichment and work restructuring

Books

C. Argyris, *Integrating the Individual and the Organisation,* John Wiley
(1964).
M. Brown, *The Manager's Guide to the Behavioural Sciences,* Industrial
Society (1970).
Conference Board, *Job Design for Motivation: Experiments in Job
Enlargement and Job Enrichment,* by H.M.F. Rush, New York (1971).
P.C. Brown, *Smallcreep's Day,* Pan (1973).
S. Cotgrove *et al., The Nylon Spinners: A Case Study in Productivity
Bargaining and Job Enlargement,* Allen & Unwin (1971).
R.H. Cyert *et al., A Behavioural Theory of the Firm,* Prentice-Hall
(1963).
P. Drucker, *The New Society,* Heinemann (1951).
O.G. Edholm, *The Biology of Work,* Weidenfeld & Nicolson, London
(1967).
R. Ford, *Motivation through the Work Itself,* American Management
Association (1970).
S.W. Gellerman, *Management by Motivation,* American Management
Association (1968).

202   ———, *Motivation and Productivity*, American Management Association (1963).

M. Haire, *Psychology in Management*, McGraw-Hill (1964).

F. Herzberg *et al.*, *The Motivation to Work*, Wiley (1959).

———, *Work and Nature of Man*, Staples Press (1968).

P. Hill, *Towards a New Philosophy of Management—A Study of the Company Development Programme at Shell UK*, Gower Press (1972).

Institute of Work Study Practitioners, *A Survey of Some Western European Experiments in Motivation* (1971).

Lynda King Taylor, *Not for Bread Alone—An Appreciation of Job Enrichment*, Business Books (1973).

H.J. Leavitt, *Managerial Psychology. An Introduction to Individuals and Groups in an Organisation*, Chicago University Press (1964).

R. Likert, *New Patterns of Management*, McGraw-Hill (1961).

R. Likert, *The Human Organization: Its Management and Value*, McGraw-Hill (1967).

T. Lupton, *Management and the Social Sciences*, Hutchison (1966).

J.R. Maher, *New Perspectives in Job Enrichment*, Van Nostrand Reinhold, NY (1971).

A. Maslow, *Motivation and Personality*, Harper & Row (1954).

E. Mayo, *The Human Problems of an Industrial Civilization*, Macmillan (1933).

D. McGregor, *Leadership and Motivation*, MIT Press, USA (1968).

———, *The Human Side of Enterprise*, McGraw-Hill (1960).

———, *The Professional Manager*, McGraw-Hill (1960).

E.J. Miller *et al.*, *Systems of Organization*, Tavistock Publications (1967).

M.S. Myers, *Every Employee a Manager: More Meaningful Work through Job Enrichment*, McGraw-Hill, NY (1970).

W.J. Paul *et al.*, *Job Enrichment and Employee Motivation*, Gower Press, London (1970).

Philips, Gloeilampenfabriken, NV, *Work Structuring: A Summary of Experiments at Philips—1963 to 1968*, Personnel and Industrial Relations Division, and Technical Efficiency and Organisation Department, Eindhoven (1969).

Rackham *et al.*, *Developing Interactive Skills*, Wellens Publishing (1971).

G.R. Taylor, *Rethink—A Paraprimative Solution*, Secker & Varburg (1972).

E. Schein, *Organisational Psychology, Foundation of Modern Psychology Series*, Prentice-Hall (1965).

P.P. Schoderbek *et al.*, *Job Enlargement: Key to Improved Performance*, Ann Arbor, Bureau of Industrial Relations, Graduate School of Business Administration, University of Michigan (1969).

Sheppard *et al.*, *Where Have All the Robots Gone? Worker Dissatisfaction in the 70s*, Collier-Macmillan (1972).

P.A. Stewart, *Job Enlargement—In the Shop—In the Management Function*, Iowa, University of Iowa, College of Business Administration, Center for Labor and Management (1967).

R. Tannehill, *Job Enrichment*, Dartnell Corporation (1974).

V.H. Vroom, *Work and Motivation*, John Wiley (1964).

M.S. Wadia, *Management and the Behavioural Sciences (Text and*

R. Winsbury, *Modern Japanese Management*, BIM (1970).

Appendix

A Survey of Job Enrichment Projects prepared by Vincent Maculuso *et al.*, the Division of Planning, Office of Program Development, Employment Standards Administration, US Department of Labor and Lynda King Taylor, Work Research Unit, 11 Tothill St, London SW1.
A series of articles by Lynda King Taylor on the above subject has appeared in *Education & Training* and in *Industrial and Commercial Training* from 1973 to date.

Related articles

A three-week series by Stephen Aris on the techniques now sweeping UK Boardrooms! *The Game Managers Play* including UK companies' experiences with the Management Grid, the theories of Frederick Herzberg, and the work of Reddin, Coverdale, *et al. Sunday Times*, 24 and 31 January and 7 February 1971.

Administrative Science Quarterly (March 1967), pp 601-628: 'Attitude change during management education' by E.H. Schein.

British Institute of Management (28 November 1967): 'Motivation through effective management' by R. Beckhard, Paper read to the British Institute of Management Conference, London (1967).

Business Management (September 1969), pp 46-48: 'Making work fit' by A. Leigh.

Employee Relations Bulletin (25 March 1970), Report No.1186, pp 1-6: 'Enriched jobs turn on bored employees'.

Harvard Business Review (March-April 1969), 47(2), pp 61-78: 'Job enrichment pays off' by F. Herzberg *et al.*

Ibid. (November/December 1969): 'Management's new role' by P.F. Drucker.

Ibid. (August 1966): 'Breakthrough in on-the-job-training' by E.G. Gomersall *et al.*

Ibid. (January/February 1968): 'One more time—how do you motivate employees?' by F. Herzberg.

Ibid. (January/February 1966): 'Who are your motivated workers?' by M.S. Myers.

Ibid. (January/February 1968): 'What job attitudes tell about motivation' by L.W. Porter *et al.*

Hydrocarbon Processing (November 1968), pp 252, 266: 'Motivation through job enrichment' by S. Gellerman.

Industrial Engineering (November 1969), pp 23-26: 'Enriched jobs mean better inspection performance' by J. Maher *et al.*

Industrial and Commercial Training (1973-1974 series): 'Worker participation in Sweden' (and associated articles) by Lynda King Taylor.

204 *Journal of Business* (October 1960), **33**, pp 357-362: 'Reduced costs through job enlargement: a case' by M.D. Kilbridge.

Journal of the Institute of Personnel Management (March 1967): 'A 3-D development in management style theory' by W.J. Reddin.

Management in Action (February 1970), London: 'The manager's introduction to behavioural science' by Lynda King Taylor.

Management Today (November 1968), pp 106-110: 'Jobs fit for men' by D.R. Francis.

Marketing (May 1967), pp 249-251: 'What motivates your salesman?' by H. Goldman.

New Society 16 February 1967), pp 227-229: 'The urge to achieve. Psychological research suggests that the will to get on can be isolated as a motive and taught' by D.C. McLelland.

Newsweek (March 1973): 'Who wants to work?'

Personnel Psychology (Winter 1967), pp 369-389: 'Herzberg's dual-factor theory of job satisfaction and motivation: a review of the evidence and a criticism' by R.J. House *et al.*

Ibid. (Autumn 1967), pp 231-257: 'Work psychology and business values: a triad theory of work motivation' by T.V. Purcell.

Philips Report (1969): 'Work structuring: a summary of experiments at N.V. Philips, Eindhoven, 1963-68'.

Research Management (January 1966), pp 45-60: 'Social structures and motivation for reducing research costs' by J.W. Forrester.

Sunday Times (31 January 1971), p 47: 'The games managers play 2: the sweet enriched life of Professor Herzberg' by Stephen Aris.

Training and Development Journal (June 1970), pp 7-9: 'Job enrichment: challenge of the 70's' by R. Janson.

Ibid. (August 1971), pp 2-6: 'Organisational change through jobe enrichment' by W.W. Dettleback *et al.*

Works Management (September 1970), pp 12-13: 'Job enrichment' by C.B. Troughton.

Work Study and Management (December 1964), pp 543-549: 'Methods of wage payment, organisational change and motivation' by T. Lupton.

A guide to management by objectives and performance appraisal

Books and pamphlets

American Management Association *Make Performance Appraisals Work for You*, selected reprints from AMA periodicals, edited by N. Percival, NY (1969).

E. Anstey, *Staff Reporting and Staff Development*, Allen & Unwin, for the Royal Institute of Public Administration, London (1969).

J.D. Batten, *Beyond Management by Objectives*, American Management Association, NY (1966).

A.C. Beck *et al.*, *A Practical Approach to Organization Development Through MBO—selected readings*, Addison-Wesley, Reading, Mass., (1972).

British Institute of Management, *Management by Objectives—A Critical*

Review of Progress, Third International Conference held 15 March
1972 in London (1972).

————, *MBO and the Computer—Making the Computer an Effective Part of the Business,* A one-day seminar held 18 January 1972 in London (1972).

————, *Management by Objectives in Barclays Bank DCO,* a one-day forum held in London on 26 February 1970, London (1970).

————, *Management by Objectives in Marketing and Selling,* Seminar held 9 July 1968, London, BIM (1968).

————, *Management Appraisal Practices,* BIM, London (March 1967).

————, *Performance Appraisals: What Managers Think, A Detailed Survey of Management Appraisal Systems and Procedures in Four Large UK Organisations,* by F.H. Haeri, BIM, London (1969).

Bureau of Business Practice, *Action Guide: How to Set and Achieve Goals,* Waterford, Conn. (1969).

Chemical and Allied Products Industry Training Board, *The Management Appraisal Interview: as abridged for smaller companies,* Staines Middx. (1971).

P. Drucker, *The Practice of Management,* Chapter 11 'Management by Objectives and Self-Control', Mercury Books (Heinemann) (1961).

J. Doulton *et al., Managerial and Professional Staff Grading,* Allen & Unwin, for the Royal Institute of Public Administration, London (1969).

A. Forrest, *The Manager's Guide to Setting Targets,* The Industrial Society (Revised edition 1973).

J. Garrett *et al., Management by Objectives in the Civil Service,* HMSO, London, for the Civil Services Dept. (1969).

S. Gellerman, *The Management of Human Relations,* Chapter 7 'Performance Appraisal and Employee Counselling', Holt, Rinehart & Winston (1966).

J.W. Glenlinning and R.F.H. Bullock, *Management by Objectives in Local Government,* Charles Knight & Co. Ltd. (1973).

Harvard Business Review, *Performance Appraisal Series,* Reprints from Harvard Business Review, Boston, Mass, Graduate School of Business Administration, Harvard University (1970).

R. Hoppock, *Ground Rules for Appraisal Interviewers,* American Management Association, NY (1961).

J. Humble, *Improving Business Results,* McGraw-Hill (1971).

————, *Improving Management Performance: A Dynamic Approach to Management by Objectives,* Management Publications, London (New revised edition and enlarged edition 1969).

————, *Management by Objectives,* Management Publications, London, for the British Institute of Management (1972).

————, *Management by Objectives in Action,* McGraw-Hill (1970).

Imperial Chemical Industries, Plastics Division, *A Management Guide to Management by Objectives,* Training and Personnel Development Department, Welwyn Garden City (1970).

Industrial Society, *Management by Objectives and Target Setting: A Survey of Company Practice,* the Society, London (1968).

Institute of Bankers, *Management by Objectives in Banking: Two Lectures on MBO and its Application to Banking,* London (1970).

206   W.L.T. Isbister, *Performance and Progress in Working Life: A Study,* Pergamon Press (1968).

C.L. Jaffe, *Effective Management Selection: The Analysis of Behavior Simulation Techniques,* Addison-Wesley, Reading, Mass. (1971).

M.S. Kellogg, *Closing the Performance Gap: Results-Centred Employee Development,* American Management Association, NY (1967).

———, *What to Do about Performance Appraisal,* American Management Association, NY (1965).

H. Koontz, *Appraising Managers as Managers,* McGraw-Hill (1971).

M.W.B. Knight, *Management by Objectives,* * (Smith's Industries-Electronics, etc.), Smiths Industries Limited (1966).

D.D. McConkey, *How to Manage by Results,* American Management Association, NY (1965).

D. McGregor, *The Human Side of Enterprise,* McGraw-Hill (1960).

E.C. Miller, *Objectives and Standards of Performance in Production Management.* Also in *Marketing Management,* American Management Association (1967).

Ministry of Agriculture, Fisheries and Food, *Management by Objectives,* Report of the Working Party, Chairman J.H. Perrin, HMSO (1972).

National Industrial Conference Board, *Measuring Salesmen's Performance,* New York (1965).

R.L. Noland, *How to Conduct Better Performance Appraisal Interviews,* Motivation Incorporated, Springdale, Conn. (1968).

J. O'Hea, *Questions and Answers on MBO,* Management Publications, London (1971).

G.S. Odiorne, *Management by Objectives: A System of Managerial Leadership,* Pitman (1965).

B.J. Pascoe, *Case History of Management by Objectives in the Royal Naval Supply and Transport Service in the Ministry of Defence (Navy) London,* British Institute of Management (1969).

W.J. Reddin, *Effective MBO,* * Management Publications, London (1971).

V.K. Rowland, *Evaluating and Improving Managerial Performance,* McGraw-Hill, NY (1970).

S. Sloan *et al., Hospital Management ... An Evaluation,* Bureau of Business Research and Service, University of Wisconsin, Maidson (1971).

Standard Oil Company (NJ), *Summary Report of the Early Identification of Management Potential Research Project in Standard Oil Company (New Jersey) and Affiliated Companies,* Employee Relations Department, Social Science Research Division of Standard Oil Company (1961).

W. Steffy *et al., Performance Evaluation Systems,* Industrial Development Division of the Institute of Science and Technology, University of Michigan, Ann Arbor (1969).

M. Williams, *Appraising Performance,* Institute of Supervisory Management, London (1968).

———, *Performance Appraisal in Management,* Heinemann (1972).

———, *Training in Performance Appraisal,* The Association of Teachers of Supervisory Studies, Lichfield, Staffs. (1969).

Colt Heating and Ventilation Limited, *Case History on Management by Objectives*, Surbiton, Surrey (Revised edition).
John Player & Sons, *Management by Objectives: the John Player Case Study* (1970).
Powell Duffryn Group, *Management by Objectives. Explanatory Notes + forms.*
A. Reid, *Introduction of Management by Objectives at Tennent Caledonian Breweries Limited*, Glasgow (1970).
Simon Engineering Dudley Limited, *Management by Objectives into Simon-Barron Limited*, London (1970).
Warburtons Limited, *Management by Objectives Documentation*, Bolton, Lancs.

Periodical articles

Business Management (December 1967): 'Fine Fare – the management revival',* (Fine Fare: Supermarkets), by M. Wade.
Business Management (July 1967): 'The only way to manage–far reaching effects of managment by objectives'* (GKN: Engineering, Smith's Industries: Electronics) by M. Wade.
Canadian Chartered Accountant (May 1972), pp 30-33: 'Performance appraisals: the tip of the iceberg' by F.D. Hollingworth.
Chartered Mechanical Engineer (September 1966): 'Setting objectives' by D.E.P. Owen.
Computer Management (March 1971), pp 23-26: 'Management by objectives in the computer room' by K. Grindley.
European Business (Autumn 1971), pp 70-79: 'The day our President and MBO collided' by D. Froissart.
Financial Times (4 May 1967): 'What kind of bonuses for management success?' by G. Cyriax.
Financial Times (January 1968): 'Making biscuits with science'* (McVitie and Price food), by E. Ganguin.
Guardian (16 November 1967): 'An object lesson in business planning'* (Pilington's Glass), by M. Dixon.
Guardian (20 February 1968): 'Management by objectives sets the targets'* (Carborundum: Abrasives and Pottery), by M. Dixon.
Harvard Business Review (November-December 1971), pp 64-69: 'Make you MBO pragmatic' by J.B. Lasagna.
Hosiery Trade Journal (February 1967): 'Management by objectives (hosiery industry)' by A.M. Dowson.
Human Resource Management (Spring 1972), pp 18-22: 'A new look at performance appraisal: the specimen check-list' by B.M. Cohen.
Industrial Training International (March 1971), pp 74-76: 'Appraisal and its place in management development' by K. MacCallum.
Ibid. (November 1971), pp 330-331: 'The ABC of MBO. Definitions' by W.J. Reddin.
*Those articles and books marked thus relate to MBO in specific industries and companies.

Journal of Business (July 1971), pp 299-305: 'The relationship of characteristics of the review process to the success of the "management by objectives" approach' by S.J. Carroll *et al.*
Journal of Management Studies (March 1964): 'An appraisal of appraisals' by K. Rowe.
Management by Objectives (January 1972), pp 6-12: 'Shortcomings and pitfalls in managing by objectives' by H. Koontz.
Ibid. (January 1972), pp 17-24: 'Updating the practice of management' by P.F. Drucker.
Ibid. (January 1972), pp 13-16: 'Improving public sector management performance' by S.D. Walker.
Ibid. (January 1972), pp 25-28: 'A guide to the introduction of MBO' by G. Humphreys.
Ibid. (January 1972), pp 35-39: 'How KLM improved marketing performance' by J.F.A. de Soet.
Ibid. (January 1972), pp 40-45: 'How to evaluate MBO,' by B. Pascoe.
Management (June 1971), pp 21-24: 'MBO—an integral part of corporate planning and organisation development' by E. Singer.
Management Decision (Spring 1971), pp 51-61: 'Effective MBO' by B. Reddin.
Management in Action (June 1971), pp 39-41: 'Re-appraising appraisal' by P. Honey.
Management by Objectives (October 1971), pp 11-15: 'When necessary —break the rules, MBO' by G. Gilbert.
Management Today (November 1967): 'Clarifying the objectives'* (Viners: cutlery, by A. Lumsden.
Ibid. (October 1970), pp 37-40, 44: 'Why appraisal fails' by G. Salaman and J. Bristow.
Personnel Management (February 1972), p 10: 'Management appraisal and development programme at United Glass'.
Rydge's (October 1971), pp 154-155, 157: 'Understanding the philosophy of MBO' by R. Cullen.
The Journal of Management Studies (February 1970), pp 23-36: 'Increasing the value of management appraisal schemes: an organizational learning approach' by A.P.O. Williams.
Training and Development Journal (December 1970), pp 4-7: Training: key to realistic performance appraisals' by R. Prather.
Work Study and Management Services (October 1971), pp 649-651: Management by objectives: an appraisal of progress' by S.D.H. Mosey.

A guide to creative thinking, brainstorming and decision making

Books and pamphlets

M.L. Johnson Abercrombie, *The Anatomy of Judgement: An Investigation into the Process of Perception and Reasoning*, Hutchinson (1960).
J. Adair, *Training for Leadership*, The Industrial Society (1968).

E.J. Benge, *Ten Top Management Problems—How to Solve Them,*
Swarthmore, Pa, *Personnel Journal* (1967).
R.R. Blake & J.S. Mouton, *Group Dynamics: Key to Decision Making,*
Gulf Publishing Co. (1961).
———, *The Managerial Grid-Key. Management Orientations for Obtaining Production Through People,* University of Texas (1962).
C.R. Bonini, *Simulation of Information and Decision Systems in the Firm,* Prentice-Hall (1963).
British Institute of Management, *Brainstorming and Creative Thinking,* A one-day seminar held in London on 29 September 1970 by J.G. Rawlinson of PA Management Consultants Limited, London, BIM (1970).
Bureau of Business Practice, *Action Guide: Generating Profitable Ideas,* Waterford, Conn. (1969).
R. Buron, *Decision Making in the Development Field,* Organisation for Economic Co-operation and Development, Paris (1966).
A. Crosby, *Creativity and Performance in Industrial Organization,* Tavistock Publications (1968).
E. de Bono, *Five Day Course in Thinking,* Allen Lane, Penguin Press (1968).
———, *Lateral Thinking for Management,* McGraw-Hill (1970).
———, *The Use of Lateral Thinking,* J. Cape (1967).
P.F. Drucker, *The Effective Executive,* Heinemann (1967).
M.B. Folsom, *Executive Decision Making; Observations and Experiences in Business and Government,* McGraw-Hill (1962).
G.S. Fulcher, *Common Sense Decision Making,* Evanston, Northwestern University Press (1965).
H.W. Gabriel, *Technique of Creative Thinking for Management,* Prentice-Hall (1961).
J.R. Greene and R.L. Sisson, *Dynamic Management Decision Games,* Wiley, NY (1959).
C.E. Gregory, *The Management of Intelligence: Scientific Solving and Creativity,* McGraw-Hill (1967).
J.W. Haefele, *Creativity and Innovation,* Reinhold Publishing (Chapman & Hall) (1962).
E. Hodnett, *The Art of Problem Solving: How to Improve Your Methods,* Harper, NY (1955).
E. Jaques, *Work, Creativity and Social Justice,* Heinemann Educational Books (1970).
G.A. Luoma, *Accounting Information In Managerial Decision Making for Small and Medium Manufacturers,* National Association for Accountants, New York (1967).
N.R.F. Maier, *Problem-Solving; Discussions and Conferences: Leadership Methods and Skills,* McGraw-Hill (1963).
S.J. Mantel, *Cases in Managerial Decisions,* Prentice-Hall (1964).
J.S. Morgan, *Improving Your Creativity on the Job,* American Management Association, NY (1968).
National Development and Management Foundation of South Africa, *Change the Problem: Some Illuminating Cases of Reversing or Changing Problems for a Solution,* NDMF Johannesburg (1967).
National Industrial Conference Board, *Problem-Solving Conferences;*

How to Plan Them, How to Lead Them, How to Make Them Work, by G.V. Moser, NICB, New York (1960).

G.M. Prince, *The Practice of Creativity: A Manual for Dynamic Group Problem Solving*, Harper & Rowe (1970).

J.G. Rawlinson, *Creative Thinking and Brainstorming*, British Institute of Management, London (1970).

N. Shankar, *Tapping Management Potentialities: The Brainstorming Technique*, National Development and Management Foundation of South Africa, Johannesburg (1967).

A.L. Simberg, *Creativity at Work; The Practical Application of a Complete Program*, Industrial Education Institute, Boston, Mass. (1964).

H.A. Simon, *Administrative Behaviour: A Study of Decision Making Processes in Administrative Organization*, Macmillan, New York (1957).

E. Smith, *The Manager as an Action-Centred Leader*, The Industrial Society, London (1970).

P. Smith, *Think Tanks and Problem Solving*, Business Books (1971).

C.S. Whiting, *Creative Thinking*, Reinhold, NY (1958).

R. Winsbury, *Modern Japanese Management*, BIM (1970).

Periodical articles

Business Administration (September 1971), pp 91-93: 'Whatever's happening to think tanks' by D. Cohen.

Business Management (January 1970), pp 28-31: 'Put a thinker in your tank' by B. Pitts.

Cost and Management (January-February 1971), pp 29-36: 'Creative and logical thinking in problem-solving' by M. Clay.

International Management (March 1970), pp 61-63: 'De Bono—Apostle of sideways thinking'.

Personnel (May-June 1971), pp 8-18: 'Creativity and the role of lateral thinking' by E. de Bono.

Personnel Journal (July 1970), pp 552-558, 562: 'Using mini-surveys to start problem solving processes' by G.F. Turell.

Work Study (August 1970), pp 15-19: 'The use of creative thinking in management' by R. Jack.

Training programme

Creative Thinking and Brainstorming, UK Management Training Limited, in association with the British Institute of Management. A two-hour programme consisting of a sound tape, slides and leader's guide. J.G. Rawlinson, PA Management Consultants Limited. Available from Guild Sound and Vision Limited.

Books and pamphlets

J.R. Appleyard, *Workers' Participation in Western Europe*, Institute of Personnel Management, London (1971).

P. Blumberg, *Industrial Democracy: The Sociology of Participation*, Constable, London (1968).

J. Brekic, *Organization of Work in the Self-Managing Relationships, (Summary)*, Ekonmski Institute, Zagreb, Yugoslavia (1970).

F. Broadway, *Power on the Shop Floor: Co-operation, Control or Chaos?*, Aims of Industry, London (1972).

Lord Wilfred Brown, *Participation*, MCB (Management Decision) Limited, Bradford, Yorkshire (1972).

M. Butteriss, *Job Enrichment and Employee Participation—A Study*, London Institute of Personnel Management (1971).

R.O. Clarke *et al.*, *Workers' Participation in Management in Britain*, Heinemann Education (1972).

I. Clegg, *Industrial Democracy*, Shead & Ward, London (1969).

K. Coates (Editor), *Can the Workers Run Industry?*, Sphere Books (1968).

K. Coates *et al.*, *Industrial Democracy in Great Britain: A Book of Readings and Witnesses for Workers' Control*, McGibbon & Kee, London (1968).

———, *Workers' Control: A Book of Readings and Witnesses for Workers' Control*, Panther, London (1970).

R. Davis, *Theories of Workers' Control*, IMG Publishing, London (1971).

Department of Employment and Productivity, *Appointment of Workers' Representatives to the Boards of Public and Private Undertakings*, London (1970).

F.E. Emery *et al.*, *Form and Content in Industrial Democracy: Some Experiences from Norway and Other European Countries*, Tavistock Publications, London (1969).

Gallup Poll, *Awareness and Attitudes to Workers' Participation*, London (1969).

Sir Reay Geddes, *Industry and Worker Participation*, Industrial Educational and Research Foundation, London (1969).

German Trade Union Federation, *Co-determination Rights of the Workers in German*, Dusseldorf (1967).

G. Goodman, *Industrial Democracy*, Pergamon Press, Oxford (1968).

I. Gordon-Brown, *Participation in Industry: An Introductory Guide*, Industrial Co-partnership Association, London (1972).

W.F. Hay *et al.*, *Industrial Democracy for Miners*, Institute for Workers' Control, Nottingham (1968).

Industrial Educational and Research Foundation, *Worker Representation on Company Boards*, London (1969).

Institute of Personnel Management, *New Works Council Law in West Germany and Absenteeism*, London (1972).

International Labour Office, *The Role of Employers' and Workers' Organisations in Programming and PLanning in the Iron and Steel Industry*, Geneva (1970).

212   International Labour Office, *Workers' Management in Yugoslavia,* Geneva (1962).

International Labour Organisation, *The Role of Employers' and Workers' Organisations in Programming and PLanning in the Metal Trades,* International Labour Office, Geneva (1967).

E. Jaques, *Employee Participation and Managerial Authority: One Practical Basis for Resolving the Growing Crisis in Industrial Relations,* School of Social Sciences, Brunel University, London (1968).

Lynda King Taylor, *Not for Bread Alone—An Appreciation of Job Enrichment and Participation,* Business Books (1973).

Labour Party, National Executive Committee, *Industrial Democracy: A Statement by the NEC,* Labour Party Press and Publicity Department, London (1968).

V.G. Mhetras, *Labour Participation in Management: An Experiment in Industrial Democracy in India,* Manaktalas, Bombay, Edinburgh, W. & R. Chambers (1966).

R. Moore, *Self Management in Yugoslavia,* Fabian Society, London (1970).

H. Nightingale, *Report on Workers' Participation in Management,* British Institute of Management (1967).

Professor E. Rhenman, *Industrial Democracy and Industrial Management: A Critical Essay on the Possible Meanings and Implications of Industrial Democracy,* Assen Van Gorcum, Tavistock Publications, London (1968).

E. Roberts, *Workers' Control,* Allen & Unwin (1973).

R. Sawtell, *Sharing our Industrial Future? A Study of Employee Participation Sponsored by William Temple College, Rugby,* Industrial Society, London (1968).

W.C. Scaife *et al., Communications in Industry Between Management and the Shop Floor,* Irish National Productivity Committee, Development Division, Dublin (1970).

H. Scanlon, *The Way Forward for Workers' Control,* Nottingham Institute for Workers' Control (1968).

F. Singleton *et al., Workers' Control in Yugoslavia,* Fabian Society, London (1963).

Swedish Council for Personnel Administration, Research Department, *Experiments with a Participation Process for the Development of the Supervisory Function in a Company,* Project Outline by Hans Wirdenius, Stockholm (1970).

Swedish Employers Confederation, *The Development of Industrial Democracy in Denmark, Norway and Sweden,* Stockholm (1972).

J.Y. Tabb *et al., Workers' Participation in Management: Expectations and Experience,* Pergamon Press, Oxford (1970).

G.F. Thomason, *Experience in Participation,* Institute of Personnel Management, London (1970).

K.F. Walker, *Industrial Democracy: Fantasy, Fiction or Fact?,* Times Newspapers, London (1970).

P.H. Van Gorkum *et al., Industrial Democracy in the Netherlands: A Seminar,* J.A. Boom en Zoom, Mappel (1969).

J. Vanek, *The Economics of Workers' Management: A Yugoslav Case Study,* Allen & Unwin (1972).

B.F.R. (November 1966): 'Managerial ideology and labour relations' by A. Fox.

British Institute of Management : 'Industrial democracy: some implications for management' [Occasional Papers (New Series) OPN 1] (1968).

Business Administration (April 1972), pp 26-28: 'Shop-floor franchise: workers' buck-sharing vote' by D. Harvey.

Ibid. (May 1972), pp 88-89: 'Blue collars in the boardroom' by E. Bacot.

Business Horizons (February 1972), pp 31-39: 'Worker Management in Yugoslavia' by W.F. Glueck *et al.*

Business Quarterly (Winter 1971), pp 73-79: 'Participative management: the CIL experience' by W.J. Mandry.

The Engineer (18 January 1973), pp 44-46: 'More power to the workers: all change in our boardrooms' by D. Millichamp.

Ibid. 15 February 1973), pp 34-35: 'Some people fear having workers in the boardroom' by B. Hammond.

European Business (Winter 1973), pp 30-36: 'Industrial democracy at Norst Hydro' by N. Foy.

Financial Times (September 20, 1972), p 19: 'A workers' charter at GKN' by P. Cartwright.

Ibid. (6 October 1972), p 1: 'EEC plan for worker participation' by H. Olslager.

Fortune (May 1967), pp 166-170, 197, 198, 200: 'Participative management: time for a second look' by R.C. Albrook.

Guardian (20 March 1973), p 16: 'Workers across the board' by A. Campbell.

Harvard Business Review (November-December 1972), pp 70-81: 'How to counter alienation in the plant' by R.E. Walton.

HMSO: 'Industrial sociology and industrial relations' by A. Fox, Research Paper No.3: Royal Commission on Trade Unions and Employers Associations (1966).

Human Relations (1948), pp 512-32: 'Overcoming resistance to change' by L. Coch *et al.*

Industrial and Commercial Training (January 1973): 'Worker participation in Sweden' by Lynda King Taylor.

Ibid. (1973/74)—numerous: 'Managing Change Series' by Lynda King Taylor.

Industrial Participation (Spring 1972), pp 19-23: 'Joint consultation in Danish industry and recent thinking on participation'.

Ibid. (Summer 1972), pp 5-8: 'European trends in personnel and participation' by H. Freidrichs *et al.*

Ibid. (Summer 1972), pp 9-12: 'Participation in German industry' by E.-G. Erdmann *et al.*

Ibid. (Autumn 1972), pp 24-25: 'The employee director experiment—A research view' by P. Brannen *et al.*

Industrial Relations Review and Report (March 1972), pp 14-16: 'The role of a worker—director: the Report to the British Steel Corporation'.

214 *Industrial Society* (September 1972), pp 17-20: 'Participation pays' by L. Peacock.

Institute of Industrial Relations, University of California (Berkeley), 'Symposium on workers' participation in management': *Industrial Relations* (February 1970), 9(2), pp 148-60: 'Influence structure on Yugoslav enterprise' by V. Rus.

Institute of Labour Relations (January 1970): 'Developments in labour-management relations in the undertaking' by J. de Givry.

International Institute for Labour Studies Bulletin (1972), pp 173-207: 'Workers' participation in management in Great Britain (No. 10).'

Investors' Chronicle (January 1974): 'What about the workers'—Survey on Europe and the City of London.

The Labour Party, 'Industrial democracy—Working Party Report' (1967).

Local Government Chronicle (7 July 1972), pp 1146: 'Worker participation in local government' by H. Keast.

Management Today (April 1970), pp 90-93, 162: 'The road to joint control' by T. Fletcher.

Management International Review (1972), 12(1), pp 17-22: 'Participative management in the United States: a corporative experience' by S.M. Klein *et al.*

New Society (16 June 1966), pp 14-15: 'Joint consultation revived? Trends in Personnel Management'.

Personnel (November-December 1972), pp 8-19: 'Participative management—a practical experience' by F.B. Chaney *et al.*

Personnel Management (September 1972), pp 39-42: 'Patterns of European industrial relations' by R.O. Clarke.

Personnel Review (Autumn 1971), pp 22-28: 'Organisational change: 'tip-down' or 'bottom-up' management?' by T. Lupton.

Sunday Times (5 March 1972), p 55: 'Worker directors win a reprieve'.

Times 9 October 1972), p 17: 'What worker participation would mean to Britain's boardrooms' by I. McBeath.

Ibid. (6 November 1972), p 20: 'Reaping the rewards of worker participation' by A. Hamilton.

Ibid. (June 1973); 'Scope for industrial training—South African survey' by Lynda King Taylor.

Ibid. (July 1973): 'Proposals for workers' profit sharing and participation into international context' by I. Macbeath.

Trade Union News (Winter 1972), pp 8-15: 'Worker participation in the European community', from the European Community No.10.

Vision (February 1972), pp 30-36: 'Workers demand their say in management' by S. Hugh-Jones.

A series of articles by Lynda King Taylor on this topic has appeared in *Education & Training* from November 1974 through 1975.

Books and pamphlets

Sir William Armstrong, *Personell Management in the Civil Service*, A speech given to the Institute of Personnel Management, 13 October 1971, HMSO, London (1971).

D. Barber, *The Practice of Personnel Management*, Institute of Personnel Management, London (1970).

M.L. Berger *et al.*, *Group Training Techniques*, Gower Press, Epping (1972).

E.O.T. Blanford, *Management Education: Training in Scotland*, paper read to British Institute of Management and confederation of British Industry Scottish Management Conference, Gleneagles Hotel on 20 April 1968, BIM, London (1968).

J. Brandis, *Manpower: Personnel Management*, Educational Explorers, Reading (1972).

British Institute of Management, *Business Schools and Companies: The Scope for Co-operation*, A checklist for business schools, London (1972).

————, *Business Schools and Companies: The Scope for Co-operation*, A checklist for companies, London (1972).

————, *Business School Programmes: The Requirement of British Manufacturing Industry*, London (1971).

————, *Facts on Management: Education Courses in 1969-70*, London (1970).

————, *Management Development and Training: A Survey of the Schemes Used by 178 companies*, London (1969).

British Institute of Management and Confederation of British Industry, *Report of Working Party on Management Education in Scotland*, BIM and CBI, Glasgow (November 1968).

British Leyland Motor Corporation, *Background Data on Personnel Policies in Spain* (1972).

Business Graduates Association Limited, *British Industry's Attitudes to Business Graduates and Business Schools*, A Business Graduates Association Survey, 29 June 1971, London (1971).

H.J. Chruden *et al.*, *Personnel Practices of American Companies in Europe*, American Management Association, New York (1972).

J. Collingridge *et al.*, *Personnel Management: Problems of the Smaller Firm*, Institute of Personnel Management, London (1970).

Consultative Council of Professional Management Organisations, *Professional Management Education and Training*, CCPMO, London (1968).

Corrosion and Welding Engineering Limited, *Company Personnel Policy*, Redhill, Surrey (1970).

M.W. Cuming, *Hospital Staff Management*, Heinemann, London (1971).

W.W. Daniel *et al.*, *The Right to Manage? A Study of Leadership and Reform in Employee Relations*, Macdonald, London, for the Political and Economic Planning (1972).

W.W. Daniel, *Business Education at 18+, A Survey of HND Business Studies*, Political and Economic Planning, London (1971).

E. Denny, *The Merchant Apprentices: A Guide to the Training and*

216   *Administration of Staff in the Distributive Trades*, Collins, London
(1970).
————, *Signposts to Staff Management: A Brief Guide for Managers of
Small Businesses*, Institute of Personnel Management, London (1970).
Department of Employment, *Training for the Management of Human
Resources*, Report by the Personnel Management/Training Sub-Com-
mittee of the Joint Industrial Training Boards Committee for Com-
mercial and Administrative Training, HMSO (1972).
————, *Survey on Management Training and Development*, Report to
The Central Training Council by its Training Survey Unit under the
Chairmanship of A.C. Mumford, HMSO (1971).
R.L. Desatnick, *Innovative Human Resource Management*, American
Management Association, New York (1972).
D. Douglas, *Management Training—A Critical Assessment*, Sydney Uni-
versity Extension Board, Department of Adult Education (1968).
Economic Development Committee For the Distributive Trades, *Man-
agement Training in the Distributive Trades*, HMSO (1969).
Engineering Industry Training Board, *The Training of Managers*, London
(1968).
J.M. Fraser, *Introduction to Personnel Management*, Nelson, London
(1970).
Gas Industry Training Board, *Training Recommendations, Development
and Training of Managers*, London (1970).
Independent Assessment and Research Centre and Association of
Teachers of Management, *Managers in the Making* by T.W. Harrell *et
al.*, Independent Assessment and Research Centre Limited, London
(1971).
Institute of Personnel Management, *Flexible Working Hours*, IPM Infor-
Mation Department, London (1972).
Irish Management Institute, *Education and Training for Management*,
Report of the Consultative Board, Dublin (1971).
K.C. Lawrence, *Personnel Management*, Hutchinson (1972).
Lockyer & Partners Limited, *Report on Field Management Training and
Development*, London Oil & Chemical Plant Constructors' Associat-
ion (1970).
T. Lupton, *Industrial Behaviour and Personnel Management*, Institute
of Personnel Management (1964).
T.P. Lyons, *The Personnel Function in a Changing Environment*,
Pitman (1971).
Management Centre Europe, *Attitudes of European Managers Towards
Their Job and Towards Management Training*, Brussels (1972).
A. Mant, *The Experienced Manager: A Major Resource*, British Institute
of Management, London (1969).
G. Millard, *Personnel Management in Hospitals*, Institute of Personnel
Management, London (1972).
E. Mitchell, *The Employer's Lawyer*, Business Books, London (1971).
National Development and Management Foundation of South Africa,
Information Bulletins relating to Personnel Management, Johannes-
burg (1972).
National Economic Development Office, Management Education Train-
ing and Development Committee, *Education for Management: A*

Study of Resources, A report by D. Jones *et al.,* HMSO (1972).
———, Management Training and Development Committee, *Marketing Education in the UK,* London (1971).
———, *The Training of British Managers: A Study of Need and Demand,* A Report written by T.W. Leggatt for the Institute of Manpower Studies, University of Sussex, HMSO (1972).
G.S. Odiorne, *Training by Objectives: An Economic Approach to Management Training,* NY, Macmillan, London, Collier-Macmillan (1970).
J. Partridge, *Education for Management in the 1970's,* Scottish Academic Press, Edinburgh (1971).
P. Pocock (Editor), *Personnel Management Handbook,* Business Books, London (5th edition 1971).
W. Rodgers, *Practical Statistics for Personnel Management,* Industrial and Commercial Techniques Limited, London (1968).
H.B. Rose, *Management Education in the 1970's: A Preliminary Inquiry,* in conjunction with D.G. Clark and E. Newbigging, London (1970).
Scottish Education Department, *Management Education in Scotland,* HMSO, London (1972).
E.J. Singer *et al., Human Resources; Obtaining Results from People at Work,* McGraw-Hill (1971).
H.C. Spear, *Training for Management: Today's Top Priority,* Institute of Personnel Management, London (1971).
B.T. Turner, *Management Training for Engineers,* Business Books, London (1969).
Unigate Limited, *Management Development and Training Manual,* London (1972).
R.C. Veness, *Management Training in Retailing,* Longmans (1969).
R. Ward, *A Survey of the Effectiveness of the Course in, and Qualification of, Diploma in Management Studies in the Resettlement of ex-regular Forces Personnel into Civilian Life,* School of Management Studies, Portsmouth Polytechnic (1971).
P. Warr *et al., Evaluation of Management Training: A Practical Framework, with Cases, for Evaluating Training Needs and Results,* Gower Press, London (1970).
M. Wheatcroft, *The Revolution in British Management Education,* Pitman (1970).
M. Whitelaw, *The Evaluation of Management Training—A Review,* Institute of Personnel Management, London (1972).

NB *The Personnel and Training Management Year Book,* available annually from Kogan Page, London, is also of value.

Periodical articles

Business Week (10 June 1972), pp 82-84: 'Training MBA's for the public sector'.
Ibid. (2 September 1972), pp 42-43: 'Small business goes to Harvard'.
Dun's Review (March 1971), pp 40-43: 'It's hell in personnel' by T.J. Murray.

218 *Education* (25 August 1972), pp 154-155: 'Key issues in teaching about management' by W. Davey.

Education Training (July 1972), pp 234-235: 'The right man for the wrong job' by T.M. Husband.

European Training (Spring 1972), pp 55-64: 'Evaluating the effectiveness of management courses' by D.W. Cowell.

Ibid. (Spring 1972), pp 89-111: 'Current problems of educational technology and training' by I.K. Davies.

Financial Times (22 September 1972), p 17: 'Why Shell's man resigned' by M. Dixon.

Human Resource Management (Summer 1972), pp 35-40: 'Learning times; a key factor in managerial personnel decisions' by M.L. Moore.

Industrial and Commercial Training September 1972), pp 438-442: 'A face lift for the executive development' by D.J. Page.

Ibid. (July 1972), pp 325-330: 'Management training and the smaller company: SWOT analysis' by N.H. Strait.

Ibid. (July 1972), pp 344-348: 'How managers learn' by E. Belbin and M. Toye.

Industrial Marketing Management (January 1973), 1(2), pp 247-253: 'The industrial marketing manager and the changing pattern of management education' by K. Ball.

Industrial Society (June 1972), pp 12-13: 'The will to manage' by K.W. Browning.

Industrial Training International (June 1972), pp 168-169: 'Forging links between education and training' by J. Green.

Ibid. (May 1972), pp 158-160: 'The training factory' by J. Gregory.

Ibid. (May 1972), pp 152-153: 'Training international OD consultants in industry' by R. Harrison.

International Labour Review (December 1972), pp 527-542: 'Personnel management in Soviet undertakings under the economic reform' by V. Poliakov *et al.*

International Management (April 1972), pp 30-32, 34: 'The battle of business graduates' by E. Mackenzie.

Local Government Chronicle (1 September 1972), pp 1479-1480: 'The future of personnel management' by M. Keast.

Management (July-August 1972), pp 67-68: 'Does training managers improve results?' by J. McConnell.

Management by Objectives (May 1972), pp 46-50: 'Developing the experienced manager' by K. Lathrope.

Management Education and Development (January 1972), pp 128-138: 'Management training needs—a typology' by D. Garbutt.

Ibid. (May 1972), 3, Part 1, pp 63-73: 'Project management—a relevant option in business schools' by J.K. Lawrence.

Management of Personnel Quarterly (Fall 1971), pp 15-20: 'The care and feeding of MBA's' by W.H. Gruber and J.S. Niles.

O & M Bulletin (November 1972), pp 175-182: 'Personnel management —what can you expect?' by J.E.B. Drake.

Personnel Journal (September 1972), pp 648-654: 'Selecting personnel without tests' by L. Lipsett.

Personnel Management (February 1973), pp 22-25: 'Personnel Management in the public service' by R. Womack *et al.*

by L. Peach.
Personnel Review (Autumn 1972), pp 15-27: 'Selecting, training and rewarding the expatriate' by J. Carney and A. Wilbraham.
Rydge's (September 1972), pp 18-22: 'A wasteland of potential managerial talent' by H. Wallace.
Training and Development Journal January 1973), pp 48-52: 'An organisation development design for personnel management' by E.R. Mazze *et al.*
Ibid. (May 1972), pp 12-15: 'Organization development and training?' by D. Coffee.
Ibid. (May 1972), pp 26-29: 'Involvement techniques for manager training' by D.P. Crane.
Ibid. (April 1972), pp 24-27: 'Evaluation of an in-company management training program' by J.J. Holder.
Training Officer (May 1972), pp 140-141: 'The real management training needs' by J.W. Rogers.

A guide to leadership

Books and pamphlets

J. Adair, *Training for Leadership*, MacDonald, London (1968).
A. Adamson, *The Effective Leader*, Pitman (1970).
M. Beer, *Leadership, Employee Needs and Motivation*, Bureau of Business Research College of Commerce and Administration, Ohio State University, Columbus (1966).
W.G. Bennis *et al.*, *Leadership and Motivation; Essays of Douglas McGregor*, Edited with the collaboration of C. McGregor, MIT, Cambridge, Mass. (1966).
C. Hawley, *The Quality of Leadership*, American Management Association, New York (1960).
Industrial Society, *The Action-Centred Leader: A Two Day Course, Tutor's Manual*, by Edwin P. Smith, Industrial Society, London (1969).
———, *Leadership Training: A Report on the Application of Action-Centred Leadership*, London (1970).
H. Levinson, *The Exceptional Executive; A Psychological Conception*, Harvard University, Cambridge, Mass. (1968).
D. McGregor, *The Professional Manager*, edited by C. McGregor and W.G. Bennis, McGraw-Hill (1967).
S.W. Roskill, *The Art of Leadership*, Collins (1964).
Royal Military College of Science, *Theory z: A Concept of Leadership, Command and Management for 1975-85*, by C.G. Kitchen, Swindon, Wiltshire (1971).
S.J. Schreiner, *An Introduction to the Art of Leadership of Community Service Organizations*, Vantage Press, New York (1970).
E.P. Smith, *The Manager as an Action-Centred Leader*, Industrial Society, London (1969).
B.P. Smith, *Leadership in Management: the Elusive Element*, Based on

the E.W. Hancock paper presented to the Institution of Production
Engineers, 19 September 1968, PA Management Consultants
Limited, London (1968).

Periodical articles

Business Horizons (December 1971), pp 33-43: 'Six propositions for
managerial leadership' by N. George *et al.*
Business Management (November 1969), pp 32-35: 'The action-centred
leaders'.
California Journal of World Business (July-August 1969), IV(9), pp 67-
73: 'Learning and leadership' by L.F. Urwick.
Industrial Society (July 1969), pp 139-141: 'Management in 3D' by
W.J. Reddin.
International Management (July 1971), pp 18-21: 'Effect on Leadership
changes on a work group' by R.C. Grote.
Management Australia (May 1969), 9(2), pp 7-9, 20: 'What's wrong
with 'Style' theories?' by W.J. Reddin.
Management of Personnel Quarterly (Fall 1971), pp 21-25: 'Leadership:
the effective use of power' by R.E. Boyatzis.
Management Today (May 1972), pp 105-106, 108: 'Setting manage-
ment's style' by B.P. Smith, PA Management Consultants Limited.
Personnel (March-April 1972), pp 8-15: 'The Protean managerial leader'
by J.C. Cribbin.
Personnel Journal (October 1970), 49(10), pp 832-833, 846: 'A management audit in 3-D' by T.L. Wood.
The Production Engineer (January 1969), 48(1), pp 26-33: 'Leadership
in management—the elusive element' by B.P. Smith, PA Management
Consultants Limited.
Ibid. (December 1968), 47(12), pp 579-591: 'Leadership in management—the elusive element' by B.P. Smith, PA Management Consultants Limited.
Training and Development Journal (July 1971), pp 18-21: 'Effect of
leadership changes on a work group' by R.C. Grote.

A guide to industrial democracy

C. Balfour *et al.*, *Participation in Industry*, Croom Helm, London (1974).
Business International European Research Report, *Industrial Democracy
in Europe*, Business International (1974).
F.H. Blum, *Towards a Democratic Work Process*, Harper, New York
(1953).
W.M. Blumenthal, *Co determination in the German Steel Industry*,
Princeton University Press, Princeton (1956).
J.A.C. Brown, *The Social Psychology of Industry*, Penguin Books,
Harmondsworth (1954).
Lord W.B.D. Brown, *Exploration in Management*, Heinemann (1962).
K. Coates, *Essays on Industrial Democracy*, Spokesman Books (1971).

G. Copeman, *Employee Share Ownership and Industrial Stability*, Institute of Personnel Management (1975).

N.H. Cuthbert, *Communication and Participation*, Conference paper 9, HRH Duke of Edinburgh's Study Conference (1974).

P. Derrick *et al.*, *Co-ownership, Co-operation and Control: An Industrial Objective*, Longmans (1969).

A. Etzioni, *A Comparative Analysis of Complex Organisations*, Free Press, Gelncoe (1961).

A. Flanders, *Collective Bargaining*, Penguin Books, Harmondsworth (1969).

A. Flanders *et al.*, *Experiment in Industrial Democracy: A Study of the John Lewis Partnership (Society Today and Tomorrow)*, Faber & Faber (1968).

F.K. Foulkes, *Creating More Meaningful Work*, American Management Association, New York (1969) and Bailey Bros & Swinfen (1969).

J.H. Goldthorpe *et al.*, *The Affluent Worker: Industrial Attitudes and Behaviour*, Cambridge University Press, Cambridge (1968).

F. de P. Hanika, *New Thinking in Management*, Hutchison, London (1965).

P.G. Harvey, *Communication and Participation, Putting Theory into Practice*, Lessons drawn from the experience of ICI over the past ten years. HRH Duke of Edinburgh's Study Conference, Conference Paper 10 (1974).

P. Hill, *Towards a New Philosophy of Management—A Study of the Company Development Programme at Shell UK*, Gower Press (1971).

J. Henderson, *Effective Joint Consultation and Examples of Joint Consultation*, Industrial Society (1970).

Industrial Society, *Practical Policies for Participation, A Guide to Action by Management, Unions and Government* (1974).

Institute for Workers' Control, *Democracy in the Motor Industry. Bertrand Russell and Industrial Democracy. Democracy on the Docks.* (All published 1970).

E. Jaques, *The Changing Culture of a Factory: A Study of Authority and Participation in an Industrial Setting*, Tavistock (1951).

J. Kelly, *Is Scientific Management Possible? A Critical Examination of Glacier's Theory of Organisation*, Faber & Faber (1968).

J. Kolaja, *Workers' Councils: The Yugoslav Experience*, Tavistock London (1965).

K.H. Lawson, *Universities and Workers' Education in Britain*, ILR (January 1970).

A.J. Marrow *et al.*, *Management by Participation*, Harper & Row (1967).

D. Pym, *Industrial Society: Social Sciences in Management*, Penguin, Harmondsworth (1968).

R. Sawtell, *Sharing our Industrial Future*, Industrial Society (1970).

W.H. Scott, *Industrial Leadership and Joint Consultation*, University of Liverpool Press (1952).

J.Y. Tabb *et al.*, *Workers' Participation in Management*, Pergamon, Oxford (1970).

R.H. Tawney, *Religion and the Rise of Capitalism*, John Murray (1926).

Archbishop William Temple, *Nature and Man and God*, Macmillan (1934).

D. Weir, *Men and Work in Modern Britain*, Fontana.

Books and pamphlets

British Institute of Management, *Attitudes Towards Industry*, BIM, London (1970).

Economic Development Committee for Food Manufacturing, *A Study of Labour Turnover*, National Economic Development Office, London (1968).

Economic Development Committee for Hosiery and Knitwear, *Increasing Profitability Through the Reduction of Labour Turnover*, National Economic Office, London (1971).

Economic Development Committee for Hotels and Catering, *Staff Turnover*, HMSO (1969).

Economic Development Committee for the Clothing Industry, *Labour Turnover*, National Economic Development Office, London (1967).

Economic Development Committee for Rubber, *Costing Your Labour Turnover*, National Economic Development Office, London (1967).

J.W. House *et al.*, *Mobility of the Northern Business Manager*, Report to the Department of Employment and Productivity, Newcastle-upon-Tyne, the University, Department of Geography (1968).

L.C. Hunter and G.L. Reid, *Urban Worker Mobility*, Organisation and Development, Paris (1968).

International Labour Office, *International Differences in Factors Affecting Labour Mobility*, Report Prepared for the Manpower Administration, Office of Manpower Policy, Evaluation and Research, United States Department of Labor, Geneva, ILO (1966).

E.M. Knight, *Men Leaving Mining, West Cumberland, 1966-67*, Report to the Department of Employment and Productivity, Newcastle-upon-Tyne, the University, Department of Geography (January 1968).

National Economic Development Office, *Labour Turnover: A Manager's Guide to Action*, NEDO, London (1969).

D.B. Newsham, *The Challenge of Change to the Adult Trainee: A Study of Labour Turnover During and Following Training of Middle-Aged Men and Women for New Skills*, HMSO, London, for the Department of Employment and Productivity, (1969).

Lynda King Taylor, *Not for Bread Alone, An Appreciation of Job Enrichment*, Case studies illustrate decreases in labour turnover, Business Books (1975).

Organisation for Economic Co-operation and Development, *Bibliography: International Migration of Manpower*, OECD, Paris (1969).

P.J. Samuel, *Labour Turnover? Towards a Solution*, Institute of Personnel Management (1969).

United States, Bureau of National Affairs, *Turnover and Job Satisfaction*, Washington (1970).

R. Wild and A.B. Hill, *Women in the Factory: A Study of Job Satisfaction and Labour Turnover*, Institute of Personnel Management, London (1970).

Financial Times (20 October 1970), p 10: 'Reducing Office Staff
Turnover' by E. Ganguin.
The Journal of Management Studies (February 1970), pp 78-86: 'Job
satisfaction and labour turnover amongst women workers' by R.
Wild *et al.*
The Hospital (November 1970), pp 380-382: 'Labour turnover' by
M.W. Cuming.
Administrative Management (March 1971), pp 64-65: 'How to cut
absenteeism and turnover' by W. Clark.
Personnel Practice Bulletin (September 1971), pp 227-235: 'Labour
turnover and absence in a medium sized firm' by K. Hutchison.

A guide to effective report and letter writing

Books and pamphlets

R. Beasley, *The Art of Successful Report Writing*, National Develop-
ment and Management Foundation of South Africa, Johannesburg
(1967).
C.J. Beattie, *The New Report Style for Communication to Industry
Management, and How to Write A Report for Management*, British
Iron and Steel Research Association, London (1970).
―――, *How to Write a Report for Management*, Bisra, London (1970).
M. Bosticco, *Instant Business Letters*, Business Books, London (1968).
―――, *Personal Letters for Businessmen*, Business Publications,
London (1966).
British Institute of Management, *Report Writing*, BIM, London (1968).
Bureau of Business Practice, *Guide: How to Write Effective Reports*,
Waterford, Conn. (1969).
E.A. Buckley, *How to Write Better Business Letters*, McGraw-Hill, NY
(1957).
Carborundum Company Limited, *Letter Writing*, Manchester (1958).
M.H. Cobbald, *From the Top of your Head to the Tip of your Pen*,
Newman Neame, London (1966).
P.P. Colbourne, *Composing Reports and their Presentation to Manage-
ment*, National Development and Management Foundation of South
Africa, Johannesburg (1967).
H. Compton, *Composing the Project Report*, Institute of Supervisory
Management, Lichfield (1973).
B.M. Cooper, *Writing Technical Reports*, Penguin Books (1964).
A.E. Darbyshire, *Report Writing: the Form and Style of Communica-
tion*, Edward Arnold, London (1970).
R.H. Dodds, *Writing for Technical and Business Magazines*, John Wiley
(1969).
D. Fuller, *How to Present Your Case Effectively*, Council on Management
Development (1971).
R. Ironman, *Writing the Executive Report; A Guide for Those Engaged
in Science and Management*, Heinemann (1966).

224   E. Mitchell, *The Businessman's Guide to Letter Writing and to the Law on Letters*, Business Books, London (1970).

National Development and Management Foundation of South Africa, *Eleven Hints for Letters to Employees*, Johannesburg (1968).

A. Roberts, *Retraining Older Men in the Art of Writing*, Institute of Personnel Management (1966).

H.A. Shearing *et al.*, *Reports and How to Write Them*, Allen and Unwin (1965).

E. Sidney, *Business Report Writing; The Written Word in Industry and Commerce*, Business Publications (1965).

W.D. Smith, *Business Letters and Reports*, Collins (1968).

F.A. Symonds, *Commercial Correspondence*, Teach Yourself Books, London (New edition 1970).

B. Trott, *Report Writing*, Heinemann Educational Books, London (1966).

G.C. Yorke, *Working With Words*, Blackie (1965).

The medical field

Articles

Australian Health Advisory Digest (December 1969): 'Curbing hospital costs', Crawford.

Australian Nurses' Journal (February 1972): 'Nurses are learning to 'manage' in large hospitals' by Davenport.

Hospital & Health Care (September/October 1971): 'Major achievements in nursing management' by Beer.

The Lancet (29 April 1972): 'Sharing authority'—Editorial.

Medical Journal of Australia (4 October 1969): 'The socio-technical balance in hospital management' by Crawford, Ritchie and Whyte.

Medical Journal of Australia (1969a), p 1098: 'Replanning Sydney hospital: 1 the functional brief' by Crawford *et al.*

Medical Journal of Australia (1969b), 2, p 700: 'Replanning Sydney Hospital: 2 the socio-technical balance in hospital management'.

National Hospital (November 1971): 'Changing traditional attitudes and establishing new values' by Crawford.

Index